Assessment
and Accountability
in Reference Work

Forthcoming topics in *The Reference Librarian* series:

• Modern Library Technology and Reference Services, Number 39

Published:

Access Services: The Convergence of Reference and Technical
    Services, Number 34
In the Spirit of 1992: Access to Western European Libraries
    and Literature, Number 35
Library Services for Career Planning, Job Searching,
    and Employment Opportunities, Number 36
The Reference Librarian and Implications of Mediation, Number 37
Assessment and Accountability in Reference Work, Number 38

Assessment and Accountability in Reference Work has also been published as *The Reference Librarian*, Number 38 (Volume 17) 1992.

The Haworth Press, Inc., 10 Alice Street, Binghamton, NY 13904-1580 USA.

Library of Congress Cataloging-in-Publication Data

Assessment and accountability in reference work / Susan Griswold Blandy, Lynne M. Martin, Mary L. Strife, editors.
    p. cm.
Also published as v. 38 (1992) of the Reference librarian.
Includes bibliographical references.
ISBN 1-56024-358-9 (alk. paper)
    1. Reference services (Libraries)-Evaluation. 2. Reference librarians-Rating of. I. Blandy, Susan Griswold 1938- II. Martin, Lynne M. III. Strife, Mary L.

Z711.A8 19
025.5'2-dc20   92-26676
                                             CIP

Assessment and Accountability in Reference Work

Susan Griswold Blandy
Lynne M. Martin
Mary L. Strife
Editors

The Haworth Press, Inc.
New York • London • Norwood (Australia)

Assessment and Accountability in Reference Work

CONTENTS

PART III: PATTERNS OF ASSESSMENT

PART IV: TAKING HUMAN BEINGS INTO ACCOUNT

ABOUT THE EDITORS

Susan Griswold Blandy is Professor, Assistant Librarian at Hudson Valley Community College in Troy, New York. She is currently Periodicals Librarian and Liberal Arts Liaison but has held every position in the Library except Director. She has published articles on library instruction and co-authored with Anne Roberts *Public Relations for Librarians* and the second edition of *Library Instruction for Librarians*. She teaches American Architecture and the (credit) research course as an adjunct professor.

Lynne M. Martin is Monographic Cataloguer at the University Libraries, The University at Albany (SUNY) Albany, New York. She has worked in college, medical and public libraries including a time as Library Director of the Hudson, New York Public Library. She is currently editor of the ENY/ACRL newsletter, chair of the 1992 SUNYLA Conference programming and co-editor of the NYLA:ASLS newsletter. She has published and given presentations on cataloguing and automation as well as tenure.

Mary L. Strife is Public Services Coordinator at the S.U.N.Y. Institute of Technology Library, Utica, New York and former Laser Lab and Geology/Map Librarian for the University of Rochester (NY). She has held several board positions in the New York Library Association Academic and Special Libraries Section and is currently co-editor of its newsletter.

The editors are co-chairs of the New York Library Association Academic and Special Libraries Section Publications and Communications Committee.

Introduction

This volume was tackled in response to three recent events: the publication in the *Federal Register* of regulations on educational effectiveness, the nation-wide recession affecting library services at all types of libraries and the publication of both Sharon Baker's and F. Wilfrid Lancaster's *Measurement and Evaluation of Library Services* (2d ed.) and ACRL's *Measuring Academic Library Performance* by Nancy Van House, Beth Weil and Charles McClure.

A carefully balanced outline was developed and librarians from academic, school, public and special libraries across the U.S. were invited to contribute. Real life crises immediately began to claim the attention of the contributors. When a library loses a bond issue or a tax district vote, the staff must respond immediately without taking time to consider philosophically the options and their repercussions. In many cases the libraries did not have procedures in place and had not already gathered the data needed to make decisions. In other cases the data turned out to be counts of what was easily countable rather than assessments of what mattered. The more heroically libraries had been struggling to maintain services, the less likely they were to have articulated an emergency contingency plan. There was an element of disbelief: how much worse can it get?

Academic libraries are now faced with justifying their role on campus. Various testing companies have stated that information acquisitions skills cannot be tested and therefore are not part of the standardized college student assessment package so frequently asked for by state legislators and

---

Susan Griswold Blandy is Professor and Assistant Librarian at Hudson Valley Community College, Troy, NY 12180.

Lynne Martin is Monographic Cataloguer and Assistant Librarian at University at Albany, Albany, NY 12222.

Mary Strife is Public Services Coordinator at the SUNY Institute of Technology Library, Utica, NY 13504-3051.

The editors gratefully acknowledge the support of the board of the New York Library Association's Academic and Special Libraries Section, of our co-workers, and of Maureen Pastine, Director, Central University Libraries, Southern Methodist University.

accrediting agencies. Colleges and universities have seen the importance of independent library use downgraded in the accreditation review making the library collections thereby less significant to budget planners.

Accountability–justifying to some governing agency your allocation of finite resources–is a form of linear thinking that assumes clear cause and effect, that claims foresight and control over identifiable causes and/or contributions to the library's performance. Librarians have tried to clear a playing field for discussing accountability by establishing standards, usually quantitative standards but more recently qualitative standards. These standards are used to measure both the library and its governing agency which should support it. There has been much debate over the usefulness of these standards, especially when they are not met. Basically the question, beyond that of the standards' legitimacy, is whether meeting the quantitative standards equals adequate delivery of services.

It is poor management to spend time measuring without a plan for what to do with the results and a timetable for evaluating the impact(s) of (re)allocation of resources. It is poor science to measure without understanding something of the statistical process and the way variables and assumptions contaminate any conclusions you may draw. The process of strategic planning becomes one of strategic response. In adversity the need for evaluation and good public relations for building bridges, for couching our vision in other people's lingo, becomes ever more critical.

As the ACRL committee worked on the output measures manual they had to repeatedly stress that the manual would show how to measure what a library does, not what librarians do, that measures are not standards, and that the data collected had to be useful. There is a real concern that if librarians do not actively adopt performance measures and manipulate the results, the work will be done by those who neither understand nor value libraries.

Reference librarians will find that, whether they are academic, public, school or special librarians, they will need to clarify the "educational objectives" of their service. The reference service can be assessed either as a collaborator (with the library as a variable) or independently (with library service as a value added). The choice depends upon the requirements of the governing agency, one's public, and the problems that need to be solved. And so our articles range from New England town meetings to OPAC's to open vs. closed stacks. They acknowledge the tension caused by shifting resources to technologies, they look at the stress of turning evaluation techniques on staff.

As our authors struggled with their crises–and the stories we heard made us yearn for the simple life of Marian the Librarian in the *Music*

Man–we became convinced that the question of accountability will dominate the 1990's, not just for libraries but for all social services, environmental impacts, corporate decisions, and our political and educational processes. The authors of these articles, who have put so much effort into them, will be happy to respond to any of your questions or comments.

Susan Griswold Blandy

I. REQUIREMENTS
AND METHODOLOGIES

Federal Register:
Rules and Regulations 1988:
602.17 and 602.18:
Focus on Educational Effectiveness

FEDERAL REGISTER, VOLUME 53, NO. 127,
FRIDAY, JULY 1, 1988,
RULES AND REGULATIONS

§ 602.17 Focus on educational effectiveness.

The Secretary determines whether an accrediting agency, in making its accrediting decisions, systematically obtains and considers substantial and accurate information on the educational effectiveness of postsecondary educational institutions or programs, especially as measured by student achievement, by–

a. Determining whether an educational institution or program maintains clearly specified educational objectives consistent with its mission and appropriate in light of the degrees or certificates it awards;

b. Verifying that satisfaction of certificate and degree requirements by all students, including students admitted on the basis of ability to benefit, is reasonably documented, and conforms with commonly accepted standards for the particular certificates and degrees involved, and that institutions or programs confer degrees only on those students who have demonstrated educational achievement as assessed and documented through appropriate measures;

c. Determining that institutions or programs document the educational achievements of their students including students admitted on the basis of ability to benefit, in verifiable and consistent ways, such as evaluation of senior theses, reviews of student portfolios, general educational assessments (e.g., standardized test results, graduate or professional school test results or graduate or professional school placements), job placement rates, licensing examination results, employer evaluations, and other recognized measures;

d. Determining that institutions or programs admitting students on the basis of ability to benefit employ appropriate methods, such as preadmissions testing or evaluations, for determining that such students are in fact capable of benefiting from the training or education offered;

e. Determining the extent to which institutions or programs broadly and accurately publicize, particularly in representations directed to prospective students, the objectives described in paragraph (a) of this section, the assessment measure described in paragraph (c) of this section, the information obtained through those measures, and the methods described in paragraph (d) of this section, and;

f. Determining the extent to which institutions or programs systematically apply the information obtained through the measures described in paragraph (c) of this section toward steps to foster enhanced student achievement with respect to the degrees or certificates offered by the institution or program.

(Authority: 20 U.S.C. 1058 et al.)
[FR Doc. 88-14912 Filed 6-29-88; 9:14 am]

§ 602.18 Regard for adequate and accurate public disclosure.

The Secretary determines whether an accrediting agency, in making its accrediting decisions, reviews elements of institutional or program integrity as demonstrated by the adequacy and accuracy of disclosures of information that do not mislead the public (and especially prospective students) as to–

a. The institution's or program's resources, admission policies and standards, academic offerings, policies with respect to satisfactory academic progress, fees and other charges, refund policies, and graduation rates and requirements;

b. The institution's or program's educational effectiveness as described in § 602.17;

c. Employment of recent alumni related to the education or training offered, in the case of an institution or program offering training to prepare students for gainful employment in a recognized occupation, or where the institution or program makes claims about the rate or type of employment of graduates; and

d. Data supporting any quantitative claims made by the institution with respect to any matters described in paragraphs (a), (b) and (c) of this section.

(Authority: 20 U.S.C. 1058 et al.)
[FR Doc. 88-14912 Filed 6-29-88; 9:14 am]

Reference Services:
Research Methodologies
for Assessment and Accountability

Jo Bell Whitlatch

SUMMARY. Research on reference service is still in the beginning stage. Librarians must select appropriate methodologies and carefully analyze the data collected in order to evaluate and improve reference service. Good measures are valid, reliable, practical and useful; standards must also be carefully chosen because so much assessment of effectiveness depends upon subjective values. Data collection strategies include quantitative measures derived from the experimental sciences and qualitative measures derived from the social sciences, including familiar methods such as surveys, questionnaires, interviews and case studies. These measures are discussed in terms of their appropriateness for reference service evaluation with citations to published studies.

The purpose of this essay is to present research methodologies which are valuable to the practicing reference librarian in evaluating reference services. Here reference service is defined as the personal assistance given by library staff to users at reference desks. This includes answering questions, performing quick literature searches, instructing in use of the library and bibliographic indexes, and providing advisory services. Methodologies for assessing bibliographic instruction and online searches typically scheduled by appointment are not covered.

The first section of the paper focuses on the preconditions for successful assessment of effectiveness. The next section reviews the characteris-

Jo Bell Whitlatch is Associate Library Director for Access & Bibliographic Services Division, San Jose State University, San Jose, CA 95192-0028 and frequent author/editor on the topic of reference statistics and evaluation.

9

tics of good measurement. The final section provides an introduction to strengths and weaknesses of various data gathering strategies. Examples of reference service evaluation are provided in order to enable the practicing reference librarian to locate quickly an actual reference research study using each methodology.

ASSESSMENT OF EFFECTIVENESS: STANDARDS

Reference service quality or reference effectiveness may mean many different things. There is no right way to measure effectiveness of reference service because assessments of effectiveness depend upon values and are essentially subjective. Determining the effectiveness of an organizational service, such as reference service, requires assessing performance against a standard. One of the fundamental questions which must be answered before designing data collection methods is: what standard or standards should be used to measure reference effectiveness?

Some of the common standards used in assessing the effectiveness of organizational services are: (1) economic assessments such as productivity (e.g., how many questions can a reference librarian answer in an hour?) and efficiency (e.g., how much does it cost the library to answer each question? or, from the user view: how long was the wait for service?); (2) assessments of the service process such as participant satisfaction (e.g., are users satisfied with reference service?) and effort of service providers (e.g., time spent with the user or number of sources consulted); (3) assessments of ability to acquire valued resources (e.g., how many new CD ROMs were purchased this year?); and (4) assessments of quality of outcomes (e.g., accuracy of answers). Different groups of people, such as managers, reference librarians, users, government agencies, and the general public will tend to use different standards for assessing service effectiveness. Managers tend to prefer structural measures focusing on capacity to deliver service (e.g., how many reference librarians are available to deliver service?), while librarians tend to prefer process measures focusing on the effort involved in delivering service (e.g., how much intellectual effort did the librarian expend answering the question?). Users, on the other hand, prefer outcome measures (e.g., did the user get what he/she wanted?) unless outcomes are difficult to judge. Because users often have difficulty judging the quality of outcomes, they may rely on measures of process such as general satisfaction with the courtesy of the staff (e.g., did the reference librarian appear interested in helping me with my question?). Other important groups, such as government agencies and taxpayers, will tend to rely on secondary characteristics (e.g., visibility in the community) because outsiders have difficulty evaluating service quality.[1]

Once the question of whose standards to use has been carefully considered and resolved, standards must be clearly and explicitly stated before the evaluator can address the question of how to measure the attainment of standards. Standards or goals must be stated in very specific terms. "Providing high quality reference service to library users" is an example of a statement which is too general and thus not useful for developing measures. Measures and data collection strategies could be designed around specific standards such as: (1) Providing correct and complete answers to 80 per cent of all factual questions; (2) Providing all information wanted to 80 per cent of user inquiries; and (3) Providing courteous service and positive non-verbal communication to 90 per cent of users.

CHARACTERISTICS OF GOOD MEASURES

Good measures are valid, reliable, practical and useful.[2] Valid measures are those which accurately reflect the concept being studied. In other words, validity refers to the meaning of a measure. Valid measures should reflect common agreements and mental images associated with a particular concept. A way to assess the validity of a measure is to ask if the variable measures what the evaluator intended to measure. For example, if the evaluator intended to measure people's success in finding needed information in the library, asking users how satisfied they are with library service is probably not a valid measure of user success in locating needed material. Users may be satisfied because they received friendly, courteous service even though they did not find what was wanted.

Reliable measures are those that are stable and dependable. Measurements which are reliable can be depended upon to secure consistent results with each repeated use. Pretesting instruments, adequate sample size, and good sampling selection procedures are important to insure reliability of measures. As an example, in unobtrusive studies, test questions must be carefully selected or the questions may not be representative of the population of questions typically asked at library reference desks.

A practical measure involves ease of data collection. Useful measures provide information for library decision making. Could the research be used to provide information useful in improving services, identifying service alternatives, or opportunities for innovation? Research should provide the library with information to shape library service priorities and policies. Reference research useful for decision making is usually related to one of the following assessments: (1) monitoring effectiveness of present reference services and seeking information on reasons for service success and failure; (2) assessing effectiveness of reference service innovations; or (3) assessing effectiveness of reference service priorities/policies and generating data useful in improving reference systems and services.

Providing information useful for library decision making requires that the purpose of the research be carefully defined. What are the problems to be studied and how will the information be useful in planning and managing reference services? Once the issues involved with the goals of the research have been carefully considered and resolved, the evaluator should begin to outline the specific objectives to be accomplished in the study. These specific objectives should be used to identify the information to be collected in the research study. At this point, the evaluator is ready to consider selection of the most appropriate data collection strategies.

DATA COLLECTION STRATEGIES: QUANTITATIVE

Quantitative and qualitative measures are both important in designing an effective data collection strategy. Each type of measure has certain weaknesses and strengths. Using a combination of quantitative and qualitative measures will result in a more effective assessment of reference service.

Quantitative methods were developed in laboratory settings using experiments and are most commonly used in scientific disciplines. Experimental research determines the effect of a change in one variable on another variable. Change is made in only one variable at a time in a highly controlled environment. Strengths of experimental methods are related to the high degree of control of the environment. Because only one variable gets changed in the experiment, cause and effect can be determined. Weaknesses of experimental and quantitative methods are that generally the world is oversimplified in the laboratory or any very highly controlled social experiment. The experiments do not capture the complexity and detailed interactions of real world social settings.

Evaluative studies of reference services have not tended to use laboratory experiments because of the limits of the laboratory setting. Research occurs in the environment of the program application, not in the laboratory. Library researchers have used experimental methods in the field where variables are manipulated in a natural setting.

Childers notes that in the ideal form of evaluative research the state of the program is measured and described, and the old and new states are compared.[3] An experimental design in this ideal form of evaluative research is Hernon and McClure's study of reference effectiveness where reference performance was measured, a treatment (training program) was applied, and performance was again measured.[4] However, most evaluative research is after the fact and quasi-experimental in design. Gothberg's study on the effect of communication upon the reference process is an excellent example of a quasi-experimental design where verbal and non-verbal behaviors were manipulated through role playing in a natural setting.[5]

DATA COLLECTION STRATEGIES: SURVEYS

Qualitative methods, such as surveys, observation, structured or unstructured interviews and case studies, were developed through studies in the field and have been most commonly used in disciplines such as anthropology. Strengths of qualitative methods are that studies capture the detail, depth and complexity of the particular social setting. Weaknesses are that these studies involve small samples and findings often cannot be applied to the society or profession at large. Furthermore, evaluators may not be detached, making bias more difficult to control or account for. Also, results from qualitative research tend to be descriptive with findings which are difficult to categorize and summarize.

Survey questionnaires are best at obtaining present attitudes and opinions about relatively simple phenomena. A difficulty of questionnaires is related to inconsistent associations between questionnaire measures and actual behaviors. Some users may respond to a questionnaire by stating that they seldom find what they are seeking in the library; however, observation of actual user behavior may indicate that on the average they find more than half of the materials they are seeking. Thus, surveys can be used to study attitudes, but not behavior.

Surveys are not very effective in providing information on why a library system is working well or motivations for use; they tend to be designed from the library rather than from the user perspective. Surveys are more likely to focus on library information resources and processes and are less likely to focus on how users view their information needs or how users ultimately use the information they acquire. Surveys assessing reference effectiveness should take into consideration user goals. When evaluating success in locating materials on a topic, one must know whether the user wants: (1) only a single item on a topic; (2) a representative selection of items on a topic; or (3) a comprehensive list of everything available.

Surveys can be mailed or be conducted as personal or telephone interviews. The mail survey is the least expensive to administer, but also the most limited in collecting detailed information from respondents. Low response rate is also a serious problem with mail surveys. Interviews require both more time to administer and careful training of interviewers, but are a source of much richer and more detailed data. Interviews can focus on interviews with experts, individual in-depth interviews, or focus group interviews with groups of 6-10 people.

Interview methods range from the highly structured where researchers tend to get highly reliable answers (the same responses from similar groups of people) to the unstructured which are more effective for collecting valid information (true feelings of people). Unstructured interviews are particularly useful when researchers are first beginning to explore a topic, but these interviews are particularly subject to interview bias and interpretation. The small samples generally associated with unstructured interviews mean that results are less likely to be representative of the population as a whole.

Although surveys are very popular, good survey design requires a sophisticated understanding of survey research methods. Surveys appear deceptively simple to design, but actually involve difficult questions such as : (1) organizing data within mutually exclusive categories; and (2) minimizing errors due to inaccuracy in people's responses because of ignorance, illiteracy, social bias, time pressures, inaccurate recall, and errors in recording of information. Murfin and Gugelchuk's article on designing a reference transaction instrument contains an excellent discussion of the problems associated with designing questions, especially use of the too broad, general satisfaction question and the pitfalls of using single questions to measure complex concepts such as satisfaction.[6]

To overcome the difficulties inherent in designing survey questionnaires, librarians interested in conducting survey research can adopt several strategies. One of the most effective strategies is to work with an experienced librarian or other social science researcher in designing and administering an initial questionnaire. Librarians should also consult the introductory research guides published by Sage.[7] Another excellent strategy for beginning survey research is to use a questionnaire that has already been extensively tested for validity and reliability.[8]

DATA COLLECTION STRATEGIES: OBSERVATION

Observation looks at people's behavior rather than the attitudes or opinions they express. Observation can be an especially valuable complement to a survey questionnaire. Observation may take many forms–direct observation, observers disguised as patrons, self-observation (e.g., keeping diaries), reference interview recording devices, and physical traces (e.g., papers in books which record use if paper is moved). Observation may provide biased results if there are sampling problems or observer bias. In direct participant observation, the researcher must gain the confidence of people being studied and not interrupt or otherwise influence the regular activities of research subjects.

Systematic structured observation, which requires using standardized categories for collecting data, has been used effectively by Kantor to measure the availability of reference service.[9] Use studies of the reference collection generally involve collection of observational data.[10] Cost studies of reference service have also involved the collection and analysis of observational data.[11]

The most extensive use of observation in assessing reference services has been the unobtrusive studies reference service. In these studies predetermined test questions are administered to reference librarians who are unaware that their responses are being evaluated. Proxies who pose as library users receive training in how to administer test questions to unsuspecting librarians. Hernon and McClure have developed measures of accuracy which have been carefully tested for reliability and validity.[12] Unobtrusive testing studies take considerable time to design and administer. Test questions must be representative of level of difficulty and take substantial time and effort to formulate. Although test questions have been verified as representative of typical questions encountered at reference desks, they may not represent the full range of reference questions in proportions occurring in actual reference desk situations.[13]

Crews has provided an excellent review of the variables influencing reference accuracy and what has been learned from the unobtrusive studies.[14] Reference accuracy can be utilized to look at the influence of collection size, library budget, reference staff size, librarian and user characteristics, demand for reference services, hours open, question characteristics, question negotiation, feedback efforts, time allowed, and librarian verbal and non-verbal behavior. Unobtrusive testing eliminates possible bias because the effect of being tested cannot influence the normal behavior of the librarian. However, Crews lists eight studies in which librarians were aware of being tested and notes that the accuracy rates were only slightly higher when librarians knew they were part of a study.

Direct observation of transactions has been less common because of the potential problems with influencing user and librarian behavior and the difficulty in analyzing extensive descriptive data which is difficult to categorize, summarize, and interpret. Studies by Ingwerson, Kazlauskas, and Lynch provide librarians with models for replication.[15]

Existing data have also been used to study the reference process. In using existing data, one must ask why the data were collected, how valid and reliable the data are based on the data collection method; the adequacy of data may be difficult to determine. However, good studies have been collected using existing data as part of the data collection effort.[16]

DATA COLLECTION STRATEGIES: CASE STUDIES

Case studies usually study a single situation but tend to use a variety of methods, such as interviews, structured and unobtrusive observations, and existing documents and records. Case studies provide much better in depth understanding of the one group or organization and tend to focus on patterns and typical cases within that group. The findings from a case study generally cannot be applied to other situations. Lawson's case study of two academic libraries combined several data collection methods: examination of library records and reports, interviews conducted, questionnaires distributed to library staff, and direct observation of reference services.[17] Von Seggern also used an effective combination of methods (audio-taping interviews, Reference Transaction Assessment Instrument by Murfin and Bunge, and observer notes) to evaluate the reference interview.[18] Unobtrusive testing has also been very effectively combined with interviews, surveys, and daily logs of questions in order to study reasons for low accuracy rates in more depth.[19]

CONCLUSION

Choosing data collection methods involves a series of difficult compromises. The goals of the research must be matched with the strengths and limitations of possible methods. If the major goal of the research is to determine how well the reference service is performing, a short, well designed questionnaire relying primarily on quantitative data may be most appropriate. However, if the goals of the research also involve diagnosing why the system is working well, the quantitative data collection methods must be supplemented by more qualitative data collection methods. Combinations of quantitative and qualitative techniques are especially valuable because each assists in compensating for the limitations inherent in the other methodology. If time and budget permit, the best solution is generally a combination of two or more different methods.

Equally important is the value of collecting data from more than one source. Evaluation of library services frequently focuses primarily on library performance goals and reduction of library costs. User needs and reduction of user costs are much less likely to be the primary focus when evaluating reference service effectiveness. In assessing reference services, collecting data on user assessments of service as well as staff assessments will aid staff in obtaining a more balanced assessment of reference effectiveness.

Four Steps for Effective Studies

Four steps are important in conducting effective reference studies:

1. Defining the purpose of the research and obtaining agreement from library staff involved in the research. An important consideration is the value of the research for library decision making: will the study provide information useful in improving library services?
2. Providing concise statements of study goals and objectives and the information that is needed;
3. Selecting appropriate methodologies related to study objectives; this requires a careful analysis of the strengths and weaknesses of possible methodologies; and
4. Collecting and analyzing the data.

In their review of library research, Jarvelin and Vakkari note that combining data collection methods in one study is rare, qualitative methods are little used and use of experiments is rare. The field is so survey oriented that almost all problems are seen through the survey viewpoint. In research the institutional rather than the end-user's viewpoint tends to be emphasized.[20]

What is true of the field as a whole also tends to be true of evaluation of reference services. However, the revival of case studies with interesting and effective combinations of methodologies holds much promise for the future. The potential for case studies could be much enriched by teams of librarians and library school faculty from several institutions designing rich case study methodologies which could be administered in a number of institutions.

Replication of previous reference evaluation studies within the same institution and in other situations is also badly needed. The Evaluation of Reference and Adult Services Committee of RASD has prepared a manual of recommended reference evaluation instruments. One objective in preparing the manual is to encourage practicing reference librarians to replicate earlier studies by making instruments and notes on the use of each instrument easily available. This manual could assist those interested in evaluating reference services to focus their studies, building on findings of earlier studies, and gaining additional knowledge about the nature of reference service effectiveness.

Research on reference service effectiveness is still in the beginning stage. Relatively few library school faculty are active in research on reference service. Studies by librarians actively practicing the art of reference service are essential if the profession is to successfully assess reference services and improve our understanding of the reference process.

REFERENCES

1. W. Richard Scott, *Organizations: Rational, Natural and Open Systems* (Englewood Cliffs, N.J.: Prentice-Hall, 1981).

2. Nancy A. Van House, Beth T. Weil, and Charles R. McClure, *Measuring Academic Library Performance* (Chicago: American Library Association, 1990).

3. Thomas Childers, "Evaluative Research in the Library and Information Field," *Library Trends* 38 (Fall 1989): 250-267.

4. Peter Hernon and Charles R. McClure, *Unobtrusive Testing and Library Reference Services* (Norwood, N.J. Ablex, 1987).

5. Helen Gothberg, "Immediacy: A Study of Communication Effect Upon the Reference Process," *Journal of Academic Librarianship* 2 (1976): 126-129. Another example of a controlled experiment which studies the effects of gender and communication behaviors on competence at the reference desk is R.M. Harris and B.G. Michell, "The Social Context of Reference Work," *Library and Information Science Research* 8 (January/March 1986): 85-101.

6. Marjorie E. Murfin and Gary M. Gugelchuk, "Development and Testing of a Reference Transaction Assessment Instrument," *College & Research Libraries* 48 (July 1987): 314-338.

7. Sage Publications publishes papers on both quantitative and qualitative research methods. These papers provide an excellent, concise and practical introduction to all common research methods. For example: J.D. Douglas, *Creative Interviewing* (Beverly Hills: Sage, 1985) discusses structured and unstructured interview methods.

8. Two highly recommended questionnaires surveying the quality of reference service are contained in Murfin and Gugelchuk, "Development and Testing..."; and Nancy A. Van House, Beth T. Weil and Charles R. McClure, *Measuring Academic Library Performance* (Chicago: American Library Association, 1990).

9. Paul B. Kantor, "Analyzing the Availability of Reference Services," *Library Effectiveness: A State of the Art* (New York: American Library Association, Library and Management Association, 1980), 131-149.

10. Libraries have conducted studies analyzing the amount and type of use reference materials received based on observations of materials to be reshelved. See Daniel R. Arrigona and Eleanor Mathews, "A Use Study of an Academic Library Reference Collection," *RQ* 28 (Fall 1988): 71-81; and Carolyn M. Moore and Linda Mielke, "Taking the Measure: Applying Reference Outputs to Collection Development," *Public Libraries* 25 (Fall 1986): 108-111.

11. John J. Regazzi and Rodney M. Hersberger, "Queues and Reference Service: Some Implications for Staffing," *College & Research Libraries* 39 (July 1978): 293-298; and Carol C. Spencer, "Random Time Sampling with Self-Observation for Library Cost Studies: Unit Costs of Reference Questions *Bulletin of the Medical Library Association* 68 (January 1980): 53-57.

12. Hernon and McClure, *Unobtrusive Testing.*

13. Jo Bell Whitlatch, "Unobtrusive Studies and the Quality of Academic Library Reference Services," *College & Research Libraries* 50 (March 1989): 181-194.

14. Kenneth D. Crews, "The Accuracy of Reference Service," *Library and Information Science Research* 10 (1988): 331-355.

15. Peter Ingwerson, "Search Procedures in the Library Analyzed from the Cognitive Point of View," *Journal of Documentation* 38 (September 1982): 165-191; Edward Kazlauskas, "An Exploratory Study: A Kinesic Analysis of Academic Library Public Service Points," *Journal of Academic Librarianship* 2 (July 1976): 130-134; and Mary Jo Lynch, "Reference Interviews in Public Libraries," *Library Quarterly* 48 (April 1978): 119-142.

16. Marjorie E. Murfin, "National Reference Measurement: What Can It Tell Us About Staffing?" *College & Research Libraries* 44 (September 1983): 321-333; and Nancy A. Van House and Thomas Childers, "Unobtrusive Evaluation of a Reference Referral Network: The California Experience," *Library and Information Science Research* 6 (July/September 1984): 305-319.

17. Venable Lawson, *Reference Service in University Libraries* (Unpublished doctoral dissertation, Columbia University, 1971).

18. Marilyn Von Seggern, "Evaluating the Interview," *RQ* 29 (Winter 1989): 260-269.

19. Charles R. McClure, Peter Hernon, and Gary R. Purcell, *Linking the US National Technical Information Service with Academic and Public Libraries* (Norwood, N.J.: Ablex, 1986).

20. Kalervo Jarvelin, and Pertti Vakkari, "Content Analysis of Research Articles in Library and Information Science," *Library and Information Science Research* 12 (1990): 395-421.

All the World Is Data
and We But the Ciphers in It....
William Shakespere 1992

Anthony Walsh

SUMMARY. In this age of decisions based on data collection libraries will be expected to gather statistics to describe, evaluate and justify their existence. Whether librarians count people, things, or interactions, even when they use questionnaires, they must understand how assumptions and uncontrolled variables contaminate their work and therefore its implications. Over the past hundred years libraries have been transformed in response to users, politicians, pressure groups and now technologies. How will librarians control and evaluate this resource allocation to preserve mission effectiveness?

While Shakespere did not write the above words, he might share those sentiments were he alive today. Indeed, he might take exception to the self-aggrandizing motif that we live in the *information age*. More correctly we live in the data collection age; that is, data is relentlessly collected on the assumption that if enough is collected by whatever means possible it can somehow be magically transformed into useful information which will inevitably lead to better decision-making. Since all institutions must undergo regular evaluations to justify their existence, data collection has become the sine qua non of institutional life. While this is understandable, it is imperative that those collecting, "massaging," interpreting, and applying this data/information appreciate some of the pitfalls in the process.

Anthony Walsh is Associate Professor in the Social Sciences Department, Hudson Valley Community College, Troy, NY 12180.

21

What follows is only the briefest of overviews of methodology but it is hoped that it will be instructive nonetheless.

COUNTING PEOPLE

All data collection procedures assume at the outset that the process will result in a reasonable representation of the population studied. This may be an appropriate assumption in some enterprises and under highly controlled conditions; however, in a library setting it is very questionable. For example, if the data collection technique chosen were a turnstile counter, the data would fail to distinguish among the various categories of entrants such as casual browsers, one-time users, intensive but sophisticated users who require little attention but extensive resources, those users who require intensive attention but minimal resources, or those "users" who find the library a warm haven with a restroom! The list could go on, but the point remains the inability of the data collection method to generate useful information due to its failure to distinguish among the various categories of user population or those who enter-leave-enter during the time frame chosen. Manual headcounting is only slightly better than the turnstile for many of the same reasons.

A refinement of the foregoing is the use of a register of members as a measure of demand. This assumes at least two things which can be easily questioned. First, it assumes that only members use the facilities or at worst that outsiders are not a significant proportion of the users. Secondly, it further assumes that registered members actually use the library. Even if these two assumptions were largely correct, it would not clarify the nature or extent of the demand since not every member puts the same demand upon the staff or holdings. What the register can show is the "peak demand" potential of the library if all users were to show up at the same time. This is much like the concept of "peak demand" as used by utility companies to plan for capital investment. The utility must be able to meet the absolute maximum demand placed upon the system even if it occurs only once per year. While this is good utility planning for obvious reasons, is it good planning for a library? Should a library plan for its potential maximum demand level, especially in an era of shrinking resources? Add to the foregoing another problem with register-based data. The register only captures those persons formally associated with that particular facility. How is the library to incorporate into its count those populations linked to it via co-operative agreements among communities and educational institutions? In short, the register is not even a record of all the potential users for peak demand purposes!

COUNTING THINGS

Since counting users seems to be fraught with problems, institutions might shift their emphasis to counting "things" in the hope of improving both the quantity and quality of the data. One obvious easy choice would be to count the size of the book collection. What is not clear in this data collection technique is the relationship between the quantity (size) and quality of the collection. Even if it were assumed that they were directly related, the data would still be subject to question since size of holdings and demand for services are at best only tenuously related. To accommodate this discrepancy, it might be decided to include in the count the number of books actually lent. Once again it must be recognized that the data collection technique yields questionable data which is easily distorted by a single heavy user/borrower. Of course, central to these techniques is the obvious emphasis on book lending as the primary purpose of the library. While this may be true on some level of analysis, it again represents a distortion when compared to the full array of services and functions provided by even the smallest of facilities.

Since counting books alone yields only partial data, a library might decide to count other kinds of print and non-print matter such as journals, periodicals, slide collections, etc. This information could be used to enhance the overall completeness of the data, but it too has its limitations. Firstly, the question of quality vs. quantity must be addressed. Unfortunately, this issue quickly becomes entangled in prestige/status-based arguments and leads to an informal ranking system which almost inevitably places local materials below national or international ones even though local materials better serve the needs of the community. At this point, the evaluation of the holdings has shifted from a service to the community basis to a comparison based on some more global definition of function. Secondly, the possession of materials is a poor proxy for demand for those same resources and again yields information of limited value. Of course, if demand/service is not the critical dimension, then counting "things" might be adequate.

In addition to the foregoing, there are many other "things" which might be counted and added to the data set. A modern library might include such things as computers, electronic subscription and network services, software, or any other number of technological assets. Once again, the count yields an abundance of data about some aspect of the library. As always, this data must be viewed critically and its underlying assumptions questioned. The possession of electronic enhancements is something easily quantified; hence, a temptation to count, but in what context is it meaningful?

COUNTING INTERACTIONS

Clearly counting people and things while instructive leaves much to be desired. Perhaps the solution to this dilemma is to count some aspect(s) of interaction among the users, users and staff, or users and the electronic systems. This route usually involves either recording the number of inquiries made in some time frame or observations of perceived user interactions. Like all data collection systems, the recording of inquiries is easily and quickly corrupted if the staff feel threatened by it. It is easy to record a request for the time of day or the directions to the restroom as an inquiry (it is) even though such inquiries are not the kind of data sought. In short, the data may be intentionally distorted regardless of instructions given to staff. Aside from such an obvious problem with the data, counting inquiries treats all inquiries as equal regardless of the time/effort required to service the request. For example, sophisticated users generate few but demanding inquiries while the public in general may generate many but elementary inquiries. This same pattern is true even when the interaction is between the user and a machine. Of course one advantage in counting user/machine interactions is that it eliminates the possibility of including non-essential inquiries in the data. Regardless of the problems cited, at least the count is based upon some truly discrete and measurable phenomenon, namely inquiry units. In sharp contrast is data collection based upon perceived user interaction which is fraught with problems. Without being disruptively intrusive, such collection must of necessity rely upon detached observational techniques; therefore what is counted as a user/user interaction will be contaminated by the observational skills of the staff and the assumption by each observer about what constitutes a viable unit of countable interaction. Testimony to the difficulty of such studies is the fact that research literature is filled with cautionary notes about observational studies and the problem of observer bias. The distilled essence of these cautions is that the observer must be constantly aware of the temptation to impute motive to the behavior observed. In the context of an observational study of user interaction in a library setting, this is advice well taken. As might be expected, assuming that any interaction is task-related (impute motive) is risky as it might be anything from a frivolous encounter to a tryst! Still, if data collection is the life blood of the modern age . . . an interaction is an interaction is an interaction (apologies to Gertrude Stein).

USING QUESTIONNAIRES

One final data collection technique which is widely used by all kinds of institutions is the questionnaire, a simple, straightforward series of closed ended questions highly focussed on very few issues. In a library setting that might be a survey of user preferences about days and hours. The operationalization of a user survey is rather difficult in such an environment. For example, if the survey were to be available at a counter or checkout desk, how could "stacking the deck" by interested parties be prevented; that is, how would the process prevent users from filling out more than one form each? Even if a tighter system of control were developed and the survey were administered only in classrooms, there would still be questions about the accuracy of data collected under duress. On the other hand, if it were strictly voluntary, then the problem with the data would come from the self-selective nature of such a sample. In other words, only those who held strong opinions on the issue(s) would complete the form thus introducing bias into the sample. In addition to such possibilities, there is another vast area of contamination which derives from the nature and structure of the survey itself. Simply put, it means that the manner in which the questions are asked (worded, ordered) greatly impacts upon the way people perceive and respond to them. Beyond problems stemming from the way respondents reply is the way in which those responses are interpreted. For example, if the original question asked if the library should be open more hours/days a response of "yes" should not be assumed to mean that the respondent intends to use the facilities during those added times. The obvious solution to this problem would appear to be to follow that question with one which asks if the respondent intends to use the facility if the hours were expanded. By placing the two questions in close sequence, the questionnaire may compel the respondent to reply "yes" to both in order to lend an air of credibility to the first reply; however, if the second question were located either earlier or later in the questionnaire, the respondent might give quite a different answer. Once again, the data collection technique and its application may be skewing the data itself, not to mention what it might be doing to any future attempts to turn the data into meaningful units of information.

MASTERING DATA COLLECTION

While it should be clear that no technique is perfect, it does not follow that there is no hope. Rather, the "solution" lies in being aware of pitfalls, being careful in method selection, being diligent in the application stage, and being cautious in the interpretation of the data. There is no substitute for good data, good information and good decisions. Good information includes valid data and reliable collection. The results should be replicable or comparable in similar situations, between similar institutions. Therefore the good decision that rests on data collection takes into account the untested assumptions.

As many authors have reminded us, the data persuade best when they reinforce or illuminate seasoned personal experience, and when they suggest a successful direction for action, management being the art of making decisions based on incomplete information. Not only must the appropriate data collection procedure be used, but the library must expect some changes simply as a result of undertaking the project. Known as the "Hawthorne effect" from Roethlisberger's study at Western Electric, and just as well known to quantum physicists, the process of observation works on the situation and on the observer's perception so that one may look back at a year-old study and then see the badly-designed measures, the missed opportunities, the unmeasured strengths. In the interim the situation itself may actually change because it has been targeted for attention, especially if it is people's behavior that is being observed.

LIBRARY TRANSFORMATION:
TOO MANY MASTERS, TOO FEW RESOURCES

The choice of data collection procedures is driven not only by the situation and by the anticipated results but also by the "masters" to whom the librarians are accountable. These are masters to whom the library delivers services as well as the cultural ideas currently governing the climate of the organization.

One of the major transformations in the way in which libraries deliver services was the shift from closed stacks to open stacks. This caused a reallocation of scarce personnel resources away from clerical-like "go and fetch" duties to more professional and highly personalized services to the public. Of course, there was also a loss involved. Control over access to materials was impossible to maintain, which raised fears that young people might be exposed to materials which had previously been off limits via the closed stack system. Further, it increased the possibility that library users could steal from the collection without detection. Still, it was perceived as a desirable change enabling libraries to provide a wider range of services to a more diverse user population without any increase in funding. In short, the resources could be stretched further and any funding increases that might become available could be directed into enriching the holdings rather than into hiring more "professional" clerks.

This very simple change raised many issues for libraries as the various "masters" attempted to exercise their power or at least express their concern for how libraries were now being operated. The moralists in the community were fearful that young impressionable minds would be corrupted by sexually explicit materials, political masters feared the gullible public would fall easy prey to seditious literature, and the public felt it was not being waited upon in the customary manner, librarians feared their control over the enterprise was waning, and boards of directors were uncertain of the fiscal wisdom of letting the public into the stacks. Each fear had some basis in fact; yet, each had a counter point to offset it; young minds found the library filled with all kinds of information and an exciting place to browse, the public enjoyed expanded freedom of access, citizens became better informed, librarians were liberated into professional life, and funds were stretched further. The stage was set for what was soon to transform libraries radically and to alter dramatically the allocation of resources–the electronic master!

Electronic Masters

As the Twentieth Century draws to a close, libraries are being modernized via various electronic enhancements. At the heart of all this modernization is a largely unchallenged belief that the delivery of a service faster is necessarily better. Scarce resources are readily expended upon terminals, printers, data bases, and electronic network services so that users can access more information more quickly. This not only transforms libraries per se, it also transforms the way in which facilities are evaluated; hence a problem. The measure of a library begins to shift away from human resources and personalized services toward a hardware/software axis; thus libraries are required to allocate more and more of their scarce funds on ever more expensive and sophisticated enhancements. At the same time, libraries find that they must cut back on periodicals, new acquisitions, and staffing levels. Ironically, as libraries progress technologically, they run the risk of regressing on other measures of success.

Users as Masters

How does all this relate to the user population and the function(s) of libraries? Quite simply, if the users are *technologically* literate, the result is generally satisfactory. Note, that even the definition of "literate" is now preceded by a qualifier. However, for the bulk of the population, all is a mystery and requires an expenditure of scarce staff time in a trainer-like capacity which is the modern equivalent of the "go and fetch" librarians of old. The users are now able to access extraordinary numbers of citations in minimal time without having to actually physically browse through the shelves to see just what is in the various selections. The loss should be obvious. On the one hand the library and the staff have completed their tasks. On the other hand, they have failed to provide the instructional guidance they might have. The staff is overallocated to menial tasks and underutilized vis á vis professional services to the users. Since the driving allocative force is technology, the library in this instance will be evaluated positively both in terms of technological assets and number of inquiries made. Whether or not the library has fulfilled its functions is another matter. Of course if the user is not technologically literate, then the result is even more problematic. Given that the quality of experiences is highly related to economic class, this emphasis upon electronic enhancements at the expense of human resources can only serve to widen the gap between the haves and the have-nots in society. Does this mean that libraries will become the province of an educated elite rather than a major force for democratization via their information resources and informed staffs? If libraries chose to allocate their funds to on-site holdings and personnel rather than electronics, would they have difficulty in securing increased funding? Would the more affluent, hence more politically active, users object to what they might perceive as archaic practices and so force libraries to cater to their needs at the expense of the larger community of users? Would professional assessment bodies hold such libraries in lower regard? Whichever of the many masters prevails will determine the scope and direction of future resource allocations.

Political Masters

All these electronic systems of information accessing also have a management side–the capacity for enhanced record keeping. Here there are clearly two masters, the library and the authorities. That libraries should keep records is beyond question. What happens to the data collected is the source of problems for the professional staffs as was seen during the Robert Bork Supreme Court confirmation hearings when his opponents wanted to look at his borrowing records! This was not the first time that one of the "masters" attempted to gain access to the borrowing habits of private individuals. In each case they were rebuffed, much to the credit of the staffs. What is significant however is that person(s) or institutions felt free to try to gain access to the records for clearly political reasons. Since most libraries depend upon the public sector for funding and receive their charter from the public sector, they are very vulnerable to outside pressures. What needs be to more clearly understood by the public are the precise information needs of libraries, what will be the system requirements, and who may have access to that data. If powerful external masters are able to dictate the data collection needs, then it can be expected that they will structure them more for their own interests than for libraries' and the potential for conflict of interest and privacy violations will be increased. In short, staff time and system time will be misallocated at the expense of the users and the services.

Community Masters

As if libraries did not have enough problems already, communities themselves must be recognized as demanding masters. Not only may they demand greater involvement in technology, they may also try to dictate the nature of the holdings, by demanding either the removal of certain materials or the purchase of others. The issue for the 1990's appears to be "politically correct" acquisitions which puts enormous pressure upon libraries to allocate their resources in the least offensive manner even if that is not the best path. If communities were at least monolithic it would be bad enough; however, since that is not the case, the problem more closely resembles wrestling with a hydra-headed monster. As special interests pursue their own agendas, they must do so at the expense of others, given finite resources. The burden of determining who wins and who loses is, thus, thrust upon libraries. No matter what choice libraries make they will be wrong and must bear that burden (be held accountable) while the real culprits escape the blame.

LIBRARY MISSION

In spite of the endless competition among the various masters electronic, users, political, community, etc.–for their fair share of the scarce resource pool, libraries function remarkably well. Still, it must be recognized that the trend toward electronic enhancements must inevitably consume a larger and larger share of the resource pool at the expense of both on-site holdings and human resources. Complimentary to this is the change to evaluating libraries by their technological assets. Since the way something is evaluated is a powerful force for either change or continuity, it can be expected that this magnification of technologies and access over ownership will only accelerate in the future while other measures decline in importance. What must not be lost in all this change is recognition of the distinction between "efficiency"–lowest per unit cost–and "effectiveness"–successfully accomplishing a mission. For the moment it would appear that efficiency is in ascendance and the mission is in jeopardy. Rather than being intimidated by "techno-speak" and co-opted by temporary cultural trends, librarians must master the nuances of numerically-based evaluation and its presentation in order to continue to justify the library mission.

II. THE ECOLOGY OF ASSESSMENT: THE ENVIRONMENT OF THE LIBRARY

The Small Town Library: Discovering Relevancy

Ellen L. Hardsog

SUMMARY. In New England's small towns, achieving funding for library services requires an annual presentation at town meeting, where the library's constituency, not elected officials, have the final word on how much support the library will receive and, consequently, how much service the library will be able to provide.

Because many town meeting attendees are non-library users for whom the library may have little relevancy, it is important for the library to demonstrate relevancy in order to gain their support. The very nature of small towns that personalizes the budget process also affords the library a number of opportunities to demonstrate relevancy to the lives of the town's residents. Among those opportunities are greater accessibility, networking with businesses, involvement of the Board of Trustees, individualized information service, and raising community consciousness through fundraising.

Ellen L. Hardsog is Director of the Exeter Public Library, Founders Park, Exeter, NH 03833. She is also a member of the New Hampshire Library Association (Past Treasurer), New England Library Association, and the American Library Association.

Correspondence may be addressed to the author at her business address: Exeter Public Library, Founders Park, Exeter, NH 03833 or her home address: 20 Partridge Lane, Derry, NH 03038.

Many of America's mid-sized and large libraries are facing one of the worst fiscal periods in their history. Every issue of our professional publications brings fresh stories of new atrocities against urban libraries: branches closed, personnel laid off, book budgets frozen, programs suspended, and information sources closed off to those who need them most. There is widespread–and justified–concern that it will take decades of planning and politicking to recover the library service that will be lost before the economy recovers.

To the staff of a small town library, however, the response to this crisis might be "What else is new?" Many town libraries have been hanging on by their teeth for years. Their daily lives consist of trying to please the public with pinched pennies while continually arguing to justify their own existence. They're veterans at survival skills that urban librarians are now, painfully, being forced to learn.

In New England, where most of the libraries serve populations under 50,000 and many serve populations under 10,000, the deep and prolonged recession has had an especially paralyzing effect on public services. Even police and fire departments, those "siren services" that seldom have to explain what they do for the community, are, at best, joining libraries in holding the bottom line. Demands for frugal management and stricter accountability for public funds are cropping up at every town meeting, and no town department is spared.

ON THE FIRING LINE:
WELCOME TO TOWN MEETING

Historians regard the New England town meeting as the very foundation of government by the people. Those whose job is to defend a budget request view town meeting as a direct descendant of the Christian persecutions, with the taxpayers starring as the lions and the town departments as their dinner.

Town meeting is usually held on a Saturday morning or a week night in March. A meeting with many articles on the warrant may continue for several days. When townspeople simply can't get enough of this sport, there may be a pre-town meeting or public hearing, which affords all participants a chance to review the warrant and sharpen their tongues and arguments for the big fight.

The meeting is usually held in a school gym. In very small towns, the town hall auditorium or a church vestry may accommodate the turnout. Refreshments and childcare may be offered. Knitting or some other handwork is de rigueur for the women.

A moderator, often a local attorney with a commanding voice and a large gavel, patiently guides the meeting through the complexities of parliamentary procedure. Many amendments to articles will be proposed and many votes taken before the meeting adjourns.

Attendance at town meeting varies. Generally, the smaller the town, the larger the percentage of voters that will attend. For example, a town of 500 might attract 75 registered voters to town meeting, but a turnout of 500 in a town of 10,000 is a remarkable event. An especially debatable article, such as approval for a recycling facility or a new wing for the library, might bring out more people. A large turnout for a controversy, though, usually means more "no" votes than "ayes."

Town meeting attendees fall into two broad categories: natives and newcomers, newcomers being defined as anyone who isn't a native, even if they've lived in town for 50 years. Natives seem to think of newcomers as being spendthrifts, and newcomers tend to regard natives as being tight-fisted, but the distinction is not that clear. No one is tougher about spending than a Massachusetts tax exile living in New Hampshire who's discovered that the state motto "Live Free or Die" has nothing to do with property taxes.

On some warrants, the entire town budget, including the library's appropriation, is lumped together into one figure that will be approved or disapproved on a voice vote. In other towns, however, the library appropriation may be one of several that are singled out for separate action. This may be due to some special status or provisions stemming from the original establishment of the library, or it may simply be a preference of the town's elected officials. Library Trustees prefer to see the library's request appear as a line in the town budget. A separate vote on the library's budget is an invitation for all members of the public, usually non-users, to challenge library programs and expenditures. That's when the library's annual fight for its life begins.

TODAY, A NEW BUILDING– TOMORROW, BOOKS

When librarians from small towns get together, the stories they tell about town meeting budget battles are so much alike that, in time, they begin to sound like folk tales with global themes. The attitude of non-users, the people that librarians need to win over, is remarkably similar from one town to the next.

One familiar challenge concerns school libraries vs. public libraries.

The argument goes like this: "Why are we spending money on two libraries? Why don't we just open the school library more hours and close the public library?" Sometimes the suggestion is to close the school library, but non-library users often place a little higher status on the schools, since they have more experience with schools than libraries.

Pre-school programs, one of the busiest services in small libraries, might be described as "babysitting services" that should not be supported with tax dollars. Libraries that are popular haunts for school age children, some of whom may be latchkey kids, hear this argument, too. The fact that children are being encouraged to read and use the library for information is overlooked in the heat of the moment.

Salaries are a hot issue, especially if the staff is predominantly female. Most critics stop short of blatant sexism, but phrases like "expensive bodies" and "warm bodies pushing pieces of paper around" were heard recently at one New England town meeting. The need for library education might be questioned. Many non-users feel that the library could be adequately staffed with volunteers.

When a library is up for major expansion or renovation, the opposition's vanguard usually consists of non-users, who feel that (a) the library doesn't need more space because no one uses it, (b) the library doesn't need a parking lot because the few people who do use it walk to it, and (c) if they have a larger building, the next thing you know they'll want money for books. Heaven forbid. Some of the most traumatic and frustrating hours in the lives of small-town librarians have been spent listening to arguments against building programs.

It would be easy to characterize the people who fight library budgets as ignorant and stingy, but this is not necessarily true. If not college-educated themselves, most support the concept of higher education. Many are professionally employed; some are even elected officials of the town. The library is simply not relevant to them, not a town service they use or expect to use. If they have to pay a few more tax dollars, they'd rather send it to the police and fire departments. They believe that their chances of having a robbery or fire are greater than the chance they'll need something from the library. So when the dust settles, the library is lucky to come away with the requested crumbs—one to three percent of the total town budget. But increasingly, the library gets even less than it asked for, as belts are tightened and everyone scrambles for the dwindling crumbs.

WHAT GOOD IS THE LIBRARY, ANYWAY?

Ironically, the same provincialism that challenges small-town library service can afford the greatest opportunities for small-library support. Not all small libraries leave town meeting with subsistence funding. Some libraries achieve budget growth in the teeth of recession, even in the midst of taxpayer revolts. What makes these small libraries so different? They have clearly demonstrated their relevancy and worth to their communities, and its residents, in turn, support the library.

The small public library is more accessible to the public than an urban or mid-sized library. It's easy to find, often in a central downtown area. The building is welcoming, the arrangement of the stacks and furniture is informal, policies may be a little more relaxed than in an urban library.

The staff is smaller and more visible, comprised mainly of local people whom the library patrons may know from other town activities. Contact with patrons is more personal and individual. Their library business concluded, patrons like to stop and chat with the staff about all sorts of things. They come bearing gifts of homemade pastries, boxed chocolates, and vegetables from their summer gardens, accompanied by brief notes of appreciation for kindnesses extended. To a few small-town residents, the library is much more than just a place to borrow books. They would be lost without their weekly library visits. The library does not need to prove its relevancy to them. Proving library relevancy to non-users is the real challenge.

LIBRARY PROMOTION: NEVER ENOUGH!

Small-town librarians talk forever about how to get more people into the library. Maybe we need to be open more hours. Maybe we need more books, videos, programs, what-have-you. Then we run up against reality—there isn't enough money to do more. Does this mean we can't attract more people to the library? No! It means we have to get them in to use the services we already have. But first we have to *tell* them what we have.

Librarians in small towns tend to rely on the local newspaper for all their publicity. The editor may offer a regular spot, complete with the national library symbol, into which all the library news goes. Library users read these notices. Non-users don't, since, by definition, they have (or think they have) no interest in what the library is promoting. So the newspaper article becomes an ineffective way to get the library's message to non-users.

The newspaper can be used in other ways, though. The classifieds can work as well for the library as they do for small businesses. For instance, if the paper has a classified column for car pools, you might run an ad publicizing your books-on-tape for commuters. The used car section might be a good place to remind car shoppers to compare book values at the library. Promote your home improvement collection in the home repair classifieds. Sneak up on your non-users to get their attention. The possibilities are endless.

If you can find or raise a small PR budget, try a newsletter. A bulk mailing permit and a town mailing list can get your message out to every household in your community. Even if you do this only once or twice a year, it will pay off. Focus these newsletters on special services beyond reading such as children's programs, job-hunting materials, public-access computers, and museum passes for loan. Have a little fun. A trivia quiz or "Match the Literary Lovers" game might generate enough curiosity to bring a new user to the library.

An even more effective way to reach non-users is to get library services out of the library and into the places non-users already visit. Connect the library with other services and businesses they patronize:

- Leave a bibliography of car-repair manuals at the auto parts store.
- Make a display of the library's gardening books at a nursery.
- Supply the pediatrician's office with extra copies of child-care books, wearing big stickers that read THIS BOOK MAY BE BORROWED FROM YOUR PUBLIC LIBRARY.
- Give the local kindergartens library card applications and information sheets on how parents can use the library to nurture young readers.

The chances for "connecting" are limited only by your imagination and the cooperation of local businesses.

Cultivate a good relationship with town business people. If your town has a Chamber of Commerce, join it. Get something from the library in the Chamber's monthly mailing. Tell businesses what you can do for them–and what they can do for you. One New Hampshire town library, faced with a one-third cut in subscription funding, raised nearly $1,500 by asking local businesses to sponsor a magazine for a year. One of those businesses now promotes the library by posting the librarian's thank you note where waiting customers can read it. A good relationship with local businesses benefits all parties.

Try to get the library table space at local job and health fairs, business network meetings, and other places where people are looking for information. Remember that most people who don't use the library may simply not be into reading, but they do need information from time to time. You want them to come to the library for that information. Once they begin to use the library when they need it, the library will become relevant and valuable to them, and they will support you when your Board of Trustees presents them with the budget request.

When marketing library relevancy, the Board of Trustees is the small library's greatest asset. Elected by the voters or appointed by the town fathers, this group of select and interested individuals is a direct information pipeline. Close to the activities of the town, they do much of the politicking that translates into a bigger piece of the town budget.

RELEVANCY AT THE REFERENCE DESK

Once you've lured non-users through the door, how will you serve them? The library's reference and public services personnel–often one and the same in the small library–will be most responsible for demonstrating the library's worth to new users. The way in which librarians approach the public and the way they manage materials and services will define new users' perceptions of the library and determine whether they feel the library is worthy of their patronage and support.

In a small public library, the reference staff needs to be skilled in what one librarian calls "dirty" reference. These are the questions that come right out of patrons' daily living needs: toilet training a toddler, communicating with an alcoholic spouse, raising African violets, changing spark plugs, writing a living will, choosing a nursing home. These are the kinds of questions that bring many non-users into the library for the first time.

The non-user with a need for information visits the library accompanied by a plethora of anxieties and misconceptions: everyone here is smarter than I am, my question is dumb, the librarians are too busy or unfriendly to help me, I'll never find what I need. This load of baggage held over from childhood library experiences is often enough to send the patron out the door empty handed before the question is asked. The astute reference librarian learns to recognize and intercept this person before he or she gets away.

Approachability is the key. A sign on the reference desk inviting BOTHER ME WITH QUESTIONS or MAY I ANSWER YOUR QUESTION? is a good start. Even better: get out from behind the desk. A reluctant and confused patron is more likely to approach a free-floating librarian than one firmly entrenched behind a desk with a stack of papers. Beware of people who ask for the card catalog's location. Chances are that (a) this person has not been to the library before, and (b) he or she is looking for something specific and doesn't know where to begin.

Reassure the patron by remarking, "Oh, yes, we've had that question before. I'm sure we can help." or "I'm glad to help. It's the best part of my job." People don't get "warm fuzzies" from the fellows that pave the roads, but they can get them at the library. A warm but professional attitude says that you care as much about the patron's feelings as you do about finding the right information.

Don't leave this patron until the information is in hand. Sent alone to the catalog, with little knowledge of how to translate the hieroglyphics on the catalog card to shelf locations, this patron will soon vanish. Accompany him or her to the catalog and explain how to use it. Interpret the catalog entry; some people do not distinguish titles from subject entries, others think the ISBN is the call number. With call numbers in hand, take this patron right to the shelves to locate the material. Finally, be sure the patron understands what you have given them and how it can be used to answer the question.

Before the new user leaves (hopefully with the requested information and a library card), make sure he or she has the library's brochure and an invitation to return soon for other services. "Now that you've found us, don't be a stranger. Come again, and bring your family. We have something for everyone."

While it's true that this personal approach is labor intensive, the benefits far outweigh the time invested. Though it may be several months before the patron needs the library again, he or she will be back and will remember this experience when town meeting comes around.

RAISING FUNDS, RAISING CONSCIOUSNESS

Fund raising is a fact of life for the small town library. Tax dollars alone cannot cover the cost of small-library services. Many small libraries are blessed with trust funds, but for most, the trusts are small with strictly limited purposes. Grant writing is time-consuming with variable results. Local fund raising, however, can be used effectively by small libraries as both a means for raising money and a vehicle for demonstrating relevancy.

An effective way of creating an ongoing fund to supplement the library's budget is an annual direct mail appeal for contributions from people who already use the library. All you need is a mailing list, a bulk mail permit, and a well-written "begging letter."

Your approach to the appeal letter can make a vast difference in the donor response. One small library attracted more donors by merely changing the focus of its letter. While earlier appeals spoke of the library's "needs," the revised letter sang of pleasures to be found at the library. Tapping the results of a user survey, the letter promised that contributions would be used for specific materials, all of which were in high demand. The result: a 60% increase in donor response, in the midst of a regional recession.

This annual letter goes beyond raising money. It reminds users of the things you do for them and of the library's importance in their lives. If you raise money in this way, be sure to protect your credibility by spending the money on the things you promised. Donors will remember—next year.

SMALL IS BEAUTIFUL

Despite the challenge of delivering quality service on a shoestring, most small-town librarians would not willingly change places with their urban counterparts. Our position close to the heart of the community gives us powerful status that could not be duplicated in a larger library. We have the ability to influence lives, and furthermore, to see the evidence of that influence, daily, without need of formal assessments and measurements.

What we have is relevancy, a personal connection with our communities and their residents. The library that can establish and nurture its relevancy will thrive and, no matter how small, will be rich in community support.

Assessment and Accountability at Toledo-Lucas County Public Library

Jane Pinkston

SUMMARY. Toledo-Lucas County Public Library is, by all accounts, a unique public library. Located in an area of decreasing population and rising unemployment, use of the county-wide system is at an all-time high. In a county with only 462,361 residents, T-LCPL circulated 5,849,356 items in 1991, an average of 12.7 items per capita. This figure puts the library system in the top 10% of the nation. But will the library continue its apparent success story with threatened operating budget cuts and a recently failed bond levy? This article purports to answer that question by examining how the library system monitors itself and its standing in the community, and, perhaps more importantly, how the library system prepares its workforce to provide quality assistance to the general public. The article will discuss citizens surveys of the past ten years, usage statistics now readily available through computer programs, and in-house studies undertaken periodically to determine the quality of reference service. Secondly, the article will discuss the system's emphasis on proper training, continuing education, and recently expanded standards of interpersonal relations for its front-line employees. Finally, a look to the future will focus frankly on what the Toledo-Lucas County Library System is doing to convey the scope of its importance to legislators and taxpayers.

INTRODUCTION

Toledo-Lucas County Public Library is, by all accounts, a unique public library. Located in the "Rust Belt" just south of Detroit, and tradition-

---

Jane Pinkston is Manager in the Social Science Department, Toledo-Lucas County Public Library.

41

ally linked to the fortunes and trials of the big automobile manufacturers, Toledo's immediate economic past has been rocky, to say the least. The latest census shows a serious drop in population in Lucas County–from 471,741 in 1980 to 462,361 in 1990. The unemployment rate now stands at 7.5%, higher than the national average. Yet during the past ten years, Toledo's county-wide library system has shown ever-increasing usage statistics. In 1991, T-LCPL circulated 5,849,356 items, an average of 12.7 items per capita. Thus, the Lucas county system is in the top ten percentile of urban libraries nationwide.

Usage statistics such as these are traditionally touted as proof of a healthy library having the support of the majority of its potential clientele. Yet, administrators at T-LCPL realize the inherent dangers of relying only on use statistics to evaluate present value and future promise. No library in tough economic times can stand on its past laurels and simply hope that its patronage will not take it for granted. It must continue to monitor itself and its standing in the community. It must continue to listen to its patrons and communicate with local government officials. It must continue to train and motivate staff to deal with the concerns of its users and potential users. The purpose of this article is to share some of the ways in which the Toledo-Lucas County Public Library evaluates the level of citizen satisfaction with library service and operations.

USER SURVEYS

The first way in which T-LCPL has attempted to measure public library activity and satisfaction has been through several citizen surveys undertaken in the past ten years. The most comprehensive user survey was done in 1986 under the direction of Jeannine Wilbarger, the library system's circulation coordinator. With input from the library's Public Information Officer and a focus group of twenty-five Friends of the Library board and committee members, the users survey asked both multiple choice and open-ended questions. Five hundred five surveys were completed by users of the Main Library and the eighteen branches, each branch being given a specific number of surveys to correspond to its per cent of total system circulation. The surveys were distributed at random to actual library visitors, and the users were asked to complete the four-page questionnaire before leaving the building.

Besides the normal demographic data usually collected in such surveys–age, sex, education level attained, income, etc.–the 1986 survey purported to find out the major reasons patrons used the public library.

Eighty-five percent of those responding said they used the library for personal leisure reading. The second highest choice was for reference/informational needs, with the majority of respondents saying they needed the information for personal use as opposed to business use. When asked what drew the patrons to a particular branch, 77% said nearness of the agency to their homes and 48% said availability of materials.

However, the majority of all those surveyed cited the downtown Main Library as the library they used the most. In a somewhat surprising outcome, 72% of the respondents said they use the library more as an adult than they did as a child, and once-a-week library visits were the most popular frequency by an over two-to-one ratio.

When asked to rank certain positive statements about the library (from a numerical "1" for "strongly disagree" to "5" for "strongly agree") the respondents gave eight out of the eleven statements a "4" or more. This included such statements as "If I cannot find the information I want, a librarian is always available" and "The library usually has the information I want." The lowest ranked of the statements dealt with programming, e.g., "I would attend book discussions if they were held during lunch or after working hours" or "Library programs for children are important to the community," but even these scored 2.9 or above.

The open-ended question "Please tell us what we are doing that you really like" received numerous comments, among them multiple expressions of appreciation for the library staff, thanks for the video and audio collections, and favorable words about the children's materials and programs. The top three responses for the question "What do you believe we can do even better?" were (1) Expanded hours; (2) More videos; (3) Quiet libraries down. When asked "What is it you would like us to do that we currently are not doing," a number of individual, thoughtful responses were received, many of them similar to remarks made to the previous question . . . improve the air conditioning at Main, help improve reading skills and promote family reading, add more microcomputers, photocopiers, and parking spaces at the Main Library, etc.

The 1986 user survey at Toledo Public Library was undertaken a year and a half previous to a vital operating levy on the ballot in November 1987. Eight months before the election, the library contracted for another citizens' survey, this one done by phone to 270 adults in Lucas County. Unlike the 1986 survey, the citizens contacted were not necessarily public library users, nor were the questions solely about library issues. Again, however, survey results showed that 222 of the people contacted at random had library cards and that the library was well regarded with an average overall grade of 4.34 on a 5 point scale. Prospective voters indicated a 75% favorable vote for the potential levy, with minorities, home renters, 18 to 34 year olds, and those with at least some college education being the most favorable. When asked how any potential new funds should be used, the respondents ranked overall collection development as the number one priority with children's services and multiple copies of best sellers as close seconds. Interest in bricks and mortar as a use of funds drew low interest: 24% of the respondents supported branch remodeling or expansion and only 22% felt that a renovation of the Main Library should be done.

With the results of the two recent surveys in mind, the T-LCPL administration built a levy campaign of specific promises about which they could feel very confident. Their strategy paid off when the 1987 operating levy passed by a 67% plurality. Since that time, true to the campaign promises, the library has expanded hours in several of the branches, promoted individual literary and family reading programs throughout the county, purchased hundreds of new titles and multiple copies of the most popular, provided more microcomputers and other new technology throughout the system, expanded several of the busiest branches to provide more quiet study areas and to accommodate larger collections, and repaired the aging elevators and the outdated heating/cooling system at the Main Library.

While the 1987 levy outcome was being decided, an opportunity for still further assessment of library service came about. T-LCPL was one of ten Ohio libraries chosen to administer the Wisconsin-Ohio Reference Evaluation Program developed by Marjorie Murfin of Ohio State University and Charles Bunge of the University of Wisconsin. Originally developed to measure the effectiveness of reference service in academic libraries, the REP was altered to fit the needs of the public library in 1987 and T-LCPL acted as one of ten test sites. The REP measured only reference use and user satisfaction. It did not measure whether or not an answer was accurate, a fact which bothered many of the reference librarians who participated. At any rate, librarians and patrons in four Main Library departments were asked to fill out a questionnaire about every reference question received within a certain time period. The librarians were asked:

- Did the patron want a specific title or a smaller item (e.g., a poem, article, etc.) which might be in a larger publication?
- Did the patron just want a general explanation of the computerized catalog or a printed source?
- Did the patron want a short answer to who, what, when, where, or why?

• Did the patron want a longer descriptive answer and if so what parameters were voiced to the librarian: "everything on the subject," "current information," "criticism or reviews," "pro and con," a bibliography, etc.?

Then came a section on the librarian's perception of the patron's question:

• Was key information missing?
• Was the patron in a hurry?
• Was communication with the patron difficult?
• Was it difficult to find appropriate subject headings in order to research the question?
• Were there other people at the reference desk clamoring for attention?
• Was the collection in that area weak or out of date?
• What types of materials were used to answer the question?
• How long did the transaction take?

Another questionnaire was given the patron to complete and return to a neutral location, away from the reference desk. Questions were numbered so that later on the patron's perceptions could be matched with that of the librarian who had helped him/her. The patrons were asked to rank the librarian's helpfulness by answering "Yes," "Partly," or "No" to such questions as:

• Was the librarian busy?
• Did the librarian understand what you wanted?
• Were the librarian's explanations clear?
• Was the service you received courteous and considerate?
• Were you satisfied with the information or materials found or suggested? If not, why?

The results of the Reference Evaluation Program were stunning. While one of the departments tested scored the highest user satisfaction rate among all Ohio test sites, still another had the worst user satisfaction rate. While the T-LCPL administration pretty much downplayed the results of the REP as being only an experiment, the just hired manager of the department receiving the worst results asked her staff to take a hard look at the quality of the collection and its accessibility, but most importantly, at the staff's own interpersonal skills, which had weighed so negatively on the patrons' responses. In the three years since, much effort has gone into improving the department's attitude toward customer service as well as the staff's ability to use new reference sources skillfully. Some staff have been to seminars on difficult patrons, others have attended classes in computer technology or some aspect of the difficult subject matter covered in their department, and all have benefited in one way or another by mini-sessions of in-service reference training. All four departments originally involved in the experiment look forward to a day in the near future when they can participate in the Reference Evaluation Program once again and compare the findings now to those of over four years ago.

USAGE STATISTICS

Another significant way in which the Toledo-Lucas County Public Library assesses its success is through usage statistics. Over the last few years, the system's computer, TLM (The Library Machine), has not only tracked the number of items checked out but has also been able to provide a breakdown of circulated items by Dewey number, media type, and branch or department. We can also find for each individual title the number of times it has circulated, a statistic of great importance in weeding and collection development. We also know from computer statistics that total circulation has been steadily increasing during the past ten years. In 1990, we topped the five million mark and received a great deal of favorable publicity when we were ranked among the top 10% of busiest metropolitan libraries in the nation in terms of circulation per capita. In 1991, we surpassed that milestone by 800,000 additional circulated items, increasing our per capita usage from 11.8 items of the previous year to 12.7 items.

The computer's database of registered borrowers also provides users' addresses and the yearly use which each makes of his or her library card. These factors, when analyzed by software designed to show demographic trends, become of immense importance in evaluating library use. Each political division of the county can thus be analyzed for library use trends.

As suggested by ALA's *Output Measures for Public Libraries*, T-LCPL is also interested in the "in-house" use its materials and services receive. Every year during the month of April, two weeks are set aside during which prominent signs are posted to ask patrons not to reshelve materials. During that period, hourly counts are kept of materials left on the tables or carts. By projecting these measures, we find that approximately

1,009,918 in-house uses are made yearly of library materials. This translates into a 2.18 per capita usage in the county. At Main Library, which serves as more of a research library than the branches, the annual count of materials used in-house is approximately 435,422–43% of the system's total.

Supplementing the two-week item count, daily logs of reference transactions show that our staff answered 553,143 reference questions in 1991, up 100,486 over the previous year. Thirty-nine percent of these questions were fielded at the Main Library, with the Business Department ranking as the busiest department, with 46,567 questions. The Social Science and Science-Technology Departments answered over 30,500 questions each and four of the branches did as well.

The most valuable use to which we put the Reference Transaction Sheets is on the department or branch level, where the managers analyze the questions received every month. They look for parts of the collection in need of updating; they can determine by the initialed questions and responses which staff members may need additional training in certain areas; they can explore which parts of the reference collection get the most use and perhaps buy more circulating materials on those subjects; they can document the days of the week and the hours of those days which are the busiest so that additional staff can be assigned. These statistics and others can also be used to show the need for additional staffing or redeployment. The same statistics, in harder economic times, can help the managers come up with new ideas for needed self-service pathfinders for patrons, reallocation of responsibilities among librarians, clerks, and pages alike, although still within the confines of their job descriptions, and even physical rearrangement of certain areas to accommodate heavy patron use.

STAFF CHALLENGES

Although often time-consuming and difficult for staff to implement, user studies and usage statistics, when analyzed properly, give definition to the changing information needs and priorities of the citizens of Lucas County. Responding to these interests with appropriate materials and services is the next step in achieving excellence, and responding effectively requires a dedicated, committed staff. Over the past few years, T-LCPL has followed the national trend toward a greater focus on consumer satisfaction. Two essential traits required in newly hired front-line staff members are skill in communicating with the public and ability in maintaining positive interpersonal relationships under pressure.

In reference work, if given the choice between a friendly, eager-to-learn, above average library science graduate with varied life experiences and a more brilliant, but uncompromising person of narrow interests, this system will hire the former every time, even in the large subject departments at Main Library. We have learned through years of experience that good public library service demands flexibility and the ability to adapt almost instantly to a patron's education level and to "translate" what he says he needs into acceptable search terminology without intimidating him. It is very difficult to teach such interpersonal skills to an employee if he doesn't already have some tendency toward them.

Recently adopted orientation standards for training new reference librarians at T-LCPL make managers accountable for teaching a very extensive list of policies and procedures, community resources, and technology, besides standard reference materials which may vary from department to department. There are also specific performance standards required for public service, reference service, and community and professional activities. At the end of the first six weeks of training a new reference librarian, the manager files a progress report with his/her own supervisor and at the end of the first three months, the new librarian is asked to file a confidential report with that same supervisor as to the overall success of the orientation to the system. Gone are the days when a new reference librarian was left to sink or swim on his own. Adequate training of front-line staff is essential to quality service to the community.

Neither are more experienced staff neglected in terms of training. Change in the information business is a fact of life, so it is vital that all information providers be kept abreast of new developments. T-LCPL has a commitment to continuing education, including sending as many employees as possible to the regional meetings of the Ohio Library Association and encouraging participation in ALA and PLA committee work or workshops. There are also guidelines in place for educational leave and staff exchanges. Perhaps of most importance, however, are in-service training opportunities planned throughout the year on various topics ranging from use of a new CD-ROM product to AIDS in the workplace to performance evaluation measures to be used by managers to the experiences of Viet Nam veterans which may affect their use of the public library. These are all opportunities which cannot help but make information providers more responsive to the general public, and we all wish time and money could permit even more such ventures.

PUBLIC RELATIONS

Assessment and accountability at T-LCPL also mean demonstrating to the community's decision makers the library's vital role in the community. Despite the fact that our library has many users, the irony in this and many other cities is that those users may not include the "information rich" who have the money and the power to hire others to do research for them, to buy their reading material rather than borrow it, or to network with other community leaders for information they may be lacking. At Toledo, overcoming the erroneous view of some of these leaders that the library is just a quiet place for recreational reading and children's programs, has taken tremendous and on-going public relations efforts.

One way we have done this is by proving ourselves an integral part of economic development in this area. Realizing its potential as a depository of difficult-to-access government specifications, standards, and regulations, for example, T-LCPL became the first library in the nation to establish a Government Procurement Center which provides these specifications to area businesses interested in pursuing government contracts. Now well into its eighth year and expanded to locate buying histories, pricing data, qualified vendors and subcontractors, electronic bid matching, and bid counseling for clients, the Government Procurement Center brought over $17.5 million into the local economy in 1991, and over $115 million since its inception. Subsequent local and national media reports about this phenomenon have made area leaders more aware of the library.

T-LCPL is also an active member of the local Chamber of Commerce with several of our managers currently recruiting small business leaders who use the library to join the Chamber. We also work very closely with the Ohio Bureau of Employment Security in a mutual exchange of data, and we act as a distribution center for the Job Service Resume System through which white collar resumes are linked to available area employment. In addition, during this past year our Grantsmanship Center, with its invaluable reference materials listing private and corporate foundation sources nation-wide, suddenly took on new importance as city and county budgets dwindled and area agencies were forced to rely on private funding for needed programs. In all of these cases, T-LCPL listened to the number one priority of area leaders–to help the local sagging economy–and targeted our efforts there.

In order to make certain our efforts are widely known, the library administration does three very basic things to make certain the library's role in the community is known: (1) It targets significant funding for advertising; (2) It responds in writing to all significant media coverage, whether negative or positive and; (3) It seeks out all new leaders in the community and invites them individually to lunch and an in-depth tour of the library's operations.

In 1991, over fifty different ads, some focusing on T-LCPL system successes and others marketing special aspects of our service or collection, were placed in the *Toledo Blade*, our local newspaper. Many of these ads ran more than once. Other photographs and articles about library activities were printed in neighborhood papers, and we had television and radio coverage on several occasions as a result of hundreds of press releases. Letters to the editor or to certain columnists recorded T-LCPL official responses to publicity. For example, on one occasion, the library director, Clyde Scoles, wrote to thank *The Blade* for its editorial on the library's phenomenal circulation record. In another smaller incident, assistant director Margaret Danziger's letter was partially quoted by a local columnist who had compared the silence of empty shopping malls to "echoing footsteps" at the downtown library. Mrs. Danziger had politely reminded the columnist that over 1,500 people visited the Main Library every day and that it was not a tomb-like institution. In the end, the columnist, to his credit, retracted his remarks and said she was absolutely right to point out his faulty analogy.

Newly elected or appointed officials in the community ranging from the new school superintendent to the new head of the convention center have had VIP tours of Main Library and many of its branches in the past few years. This practice is intended to plant the role of the community library firmly in the minds of these individuals. Our director is also very much involved with our state legislators in an ever-increasing effort to keep them abreast of the library's activities.

THE FUTURE

In the spring of 1991, forty community leaders from all over the county were asked to serve on a Task Force to look into the needs of the Toledo-Lucas County Public Library system over the next twenty years. For several months, the Task Force, broken down into three committees, examined the building, grounds and community use of each of the eighteen branches and Main Library. In a document released in June 1991, the Task Force made specific recommendations regarding the renovation and expansion of several of our libraries experiencing tremendous gains in usage by the public and those not complying with the terms of the 1990

American with Disabilities Act. The Task Force also said that more electronic technology should be utilized to link the branches to the resources at Main and Main to database resources throughout the world. Finally, the Task Force also covered such important topics as literacy, adequate staff training for the new technologies, preservation of rare local history materials and other important documents, etc. The total price tag attached to the twenty-year plan was $55 million.

Shortly thereafter, the Board of Trustees voted to place a .96 mill bond levy on the November ballot to pay for these renovations. Over the summer and fall months, the library staff and volunteers worked tirelessly on behalf of the levy. But in the end, the issue went down to defeat. In its annual retreat, the Board of Trustees analyzed the campaign and the mood of the voters. They decided that several factors were responsible for the unfortunate outcome:

1. Interest in "bricks and mortar" was still of low interest among the voters, just as it had been in the 1986 users survey. The system had done perhaps "too good" a job of masking space needs at Main Library by keeping all of the unseemly parts of the collection in two basement levels and allowing only staff members in their depths. Maintenance had also done perhaps "too good" a job of making cosmetic changes at several of the branches.
2. There were five other money issues on the ballot by the time election day rolled around. The taxpayers felt drained and obligated to pick and choose among the issues. Four issues, in which the voters sensed greater urgency and need, were approved.
3. The *Blade*, in an editorial which it said it regretted, came out against the library's levy, saying that it was asking for too much in harsh economic times and that the library could survive without immediate renovations. Many fence-sitting voters agreed with the editor's view in the end.

In analyzing these findings, the Board agreed that we should try again for the levy in the future. The next campaign should focus more on the harsh realities of accessing library service–the horrible parking situation at Main; the lack of room to tutor some of the 50,000 illiterates in our county through the Read for Literacy program, which the library supports; the sheer numbers of people that crowd our small Sanger branch, leaving no place to sit and no place to study quietly; the huge volume of periodicals and invaluable government documents such as patents and census data off limits to the browsing patron because of lack of space; the lines that form at the reference desks because staff are busy retrieving materials for patrons when their time would be better spent answering their information needs.

The Board also approved another survey, this one of people who have not used their library cards in the last two years. Perhaps there is something they need of us that we are not providing. And, the Board wants individual community groups around the county to get more involved with their neighborhood libraries so that we can learn from them what they need for better service and vice versa.

In conclusion, assessment of the Toledo-Lucas County Public Library's achievements and role in the community is an on-going venture. Gone are the days when a library intuitively "knew" what the public wanted and needed. Now, we must listen to our public and change when they change. In a time of budget restraints, we must get what the public asks for first and find new, more efficient ways of providing good service with the friendliest, most knowledgeable staff possible. The ultimate goal of a public library is to provide barrier-free access to information. Public financial support is a vital component as we continually strive to meet this end. In all of these endeavors, The Toledo-Lucas County Public Library is not a silent agency as it makes itself accountable to the people it serves.

Special Libraries Assessment
or Marketing the Special Library

Mary L. Strife

SUMMARY. Unlike many reference librarians, special librarians have always found themselves in the position of having to prove the value of their information centers, information services, and even themselves. Now, more than ever, it is important for the special librarian to be prepared to document the worth of the provided services to ever cost conscious management while updating services and facilities to satisfy both the user and the administrators.

Assessment, evaluation, accountability are the buzz word of the 90s. Academic libraries are scrambling to justify their worth and the value of their collections and services after budget reductions have caused collection re-evaluations. Librarians in specialized/corporate library centers have been dealing with these issues for some time. However, as corporations are downsizing at all levels, the skill of justifying the value of an information center is more important than ever.

WHAT IS THE LIBRARY WORTH?

Technical information centers (libraries) have always been under pressure to prove their worth to the organization. In organizational settings, technical information centers are part of the entire company and are therefore vulnerable to the same cuts that other departments face in budget crises. Often libraries are not seen as profit centers or as producing a product to sell. Some of these libraries do not charge for services; there-

---

Mary L. Strife is Public Services Coordinator at the S.U.N.Y. Institute of Technology Library, Utica, NY 13504-3051, and former Laser Lab and Geology/Map Librarian at the University of Rochester, NY.

fore their product is seen as having less value because the information was given away for free (Sirkin, 1991). Budget cutters will look at the library staffing, collections and services when belt tightening is needed.

Money is not the only concern for special librarians. When there is a space crunch the information center may appear to be the only expendable operation. Therefore, special librarians have become experts in marketing themselves and the services in the library. They make management aware of what time and money is saved when the library provides information through online or document delivery services, or the efforts of manual searches by the staff. Librarians make sure the information is accessible and presented in an easily readable form. These steps are necessary because the clientele of special libraries has different demands and expectations of services. If they want information, they want it now. Two days or a week is too long. Document delivery and online services are more expensive but are worth the cost if the information need is met. SDI, copying and table of contents services are often essential in a specialized library. A sharp special librarian uses the data of such services to his/her advantage.

Some corporate libraries have decided to charge back to departments for services. Charging back can consist of recovering direct costs such as an online use fee or document delivery cost or may include direct costs plus a fee for the professional/staff time spent in the retrieval of the information or any percentage of that cost. There isn't any approved method (Warner, 1989). Special librarians must consult with and have the support of their management before implementing such a fee structure. Companies seem to place more value on the information when there is a dollar amount attached to it. When these services are needed, the librarian must be well informed about the best services at the best price to provide the needed information. It is very important to use best judgment about which services are the most cost effective for the needs of the clients or organization. All departments are budget conscious and will appreciate all efforts to retrieve the needed information at the lowest cost possible.

Constant re-evaluation of all types of information services is necessary to justify the information center and its cost to management. Since money is important to organizations, saving money is something all departments are encouraged to do. If a special librarian can prove the benefits of the center's services and show how departments saved time and money through their use of the library, another point has been scored in favor of the library (Cloyes, 1991). Statistics from actual cost studies or user survey results are needed to prove to management the actual benefits to the company. Words of praise from the satisfied clients can help but are no substitute for hard facts and dollar amounts.

IS THE USER SATISFIED?

User satisfaction is a key to evaluating library services.Unsatisfied users can be a reason to cut the technical information budget or eliminate it entirely. Management is very sensitive to complaints from employees. This is especially true if a mistake is made or an experiment delayed or ruined because needed information was gathered incorrectly or was not delivered soon enough. A survey can be done to determine user satisfaction. Once information services and delivered information are evaluated, the results can be analyzed, allowing the librarian to re-evaluate the services to make sure that all current needs are being successfully met. One survey is not enough. There must be continuous communication between the information provider and the user (Basch, 1991).

User satisfaction can always change as new information needs are presented. The company's goals are connected with user satisfaction and the constant reappraisal of services. The special librarian must be aware of the company structure, goals, competitors and weaknesses and strengths on all levels (Eddison, 1990). This is not only good politics. One misstep could cost a job. The mission of the special library should reflect the goals of the organization (Christou, 1988). Keep yourself well informed by reading all the information put out by the public relations department. Have lunch with people from other departments to keep yourself in the information loop. Know what the organization's competitors or partners are doing. Develop good communication with your clients. By doing these things you will avoid being surprised by changes within the company and will be better able to meet the information needs of your company. As you keep abreast of changes and news you will only enhance your reputation and that of the information center.

HOW DOES THE LIBRARIAN CONNECT?

Networking will keep you informed as well as help make you well known among your users. If you gain the support of your management and the people you serve, you help insure the survival of the information center in the organization (Paris, 1990). This support can mean adequate staffing and materials budget for the library. It may also mean that the library may escape some budget slashing or may be able to get the extra money for a special project. By keeping communications open and asking for suggestions, you are proving your willingness to be a team player in the organization.

Last but not least is enhancing the image of the library. Image can be improved and strengthened by having a distinctive logo designed for the information center that is used on all correspondence and all promotional items (Tumey, 1991) or adding brochures, newsletters or acquisition lists to your repertoire (Mills, 1991). It is up to all information center staff to project a positive, technologically up to date image. Each member needs to be flexible and capable of answering all information needs of the organization.

It is important for the special librarian to do the best job possible in providing needed information to clients in an efficient and attractive manner. By concentrating on client need, organizational focus, communication and the image of the library, the ground work is laid for the inevitable need to justify information services to the company.

III. PATTERNS OF ASSESSMENT

Assessment in Higher Education

Nancy Allen

SUMMARY. An overview of outcomes assessment in postsecondary education is presented, including attention to legislative and accreditation mandates, assessment methods commonly used, and the controversies associated with the implementation of outcomes assessment programs. In examining the results of institutional curriculum assessment programs, the author looks at the ways academic libraries can become involved in university and college level assessment programs in ways which benefit libraries, in addition to looking at ways libraries can assess their instructional programs.

Everybody's doing it. Data from the American Council on Education cited in *Change*[1] show that 82% of all colleges have assessment activities underway. Forty-two percent of the respondents say their states require assessment, and over half say their activities are part of self-studies for regional accreditation.

THE MANDATE

Concern about the quality of higher education, particularly undergraduate education, was trumpeted in the early 1980s. The 1983 work *A Nation*

Nancy Allen is Assistant Director for Public Services, Colorado State University Libraries, Fort Collins, CO 80523.

at Risk: The Imperative for Educational Reform caught the attention of not only people affiliated with education, but also the general public. Several other key studies appeared at about the same time, which called for the improvement of undergraduate education and an assessment of student learning. Secretary Bennett worked toward federal mandates for assessment, and the Council on Postsecondary Education, the national body coordinating the regional accreditation agencies, called for action. In turn, regional accreditation agencies made statements by the late 1980s mandating assessment. One example of such a statement was issued October 27, 1989 by the North Central Association of Schools and Colleges, and approved by the Commission on Institutions of Higher Education. It reads as follows:

> The Commission affirms that the evaluation/accreditation process offers both a means of providing public assurance of an institution's effectiveness and a stimulus to institutional improvement. The Commission's criteria require an institution to demonstrate the clarity and appropriateness of its purposes as a postsecondary educational institution; to show that it has adequate human, financial, and physical resources effectively organized for the accomplishment of those purposes; to confirm its effectiveness in accomplishing all of its purposes; and to provide assurance that it can continue to be an effective institution. A variety of assessment approaches in its evaluation processes strengthens the institution's ability to document its effectiveness.
>
> The Commission reaffirms its position that assessment is an important element in an institution's overall evaluation processes. The Commission does not prescribe a specific approach to assessment. That determination should be made by the institution in terms of its own purposes, resources, and commitments. Assessment is not an end in itself, but a means of gathering information that can be used in evaluating the institution's ability to accomplish its purposes in a number of areas. An assessment program, to be effective, should provide information that assists the institution in making useful decisions about the improvement of the institution and in developing plans for that improvement. An institution is expected to describe in its self-study the ways that it evaluates its effectiveness and how those results are used to plan for institutional improvement.
>
> The Commission wants to make clear that all institutions are expected to assess the achievement of their students. With this statement we make explicit the Commission's position that student

achievement is a critical component in assessing overall institutional effectiveness. Our expectation is that an institution has and is able to describe a program by which it documents student academic achievement.

Many legislatures have also required assessment, either through the commissions or boards on higher education, or directly through legislation. Much concern was expressed when Tennessee linked funding for higher education to student outcomes assessment results. (Bonus funding for assessment activities adds up to more than $5 million per year for the University of Tennessee at Knoxville.) And, finally, processes resulting in the accreditation of individual programs is increasingly involving measurement of student outcomes.

THE CONTROVERSY

It is clear why assessment should be a good thing. The university identifies its goals, and then designs one or more mechanisms for finding out if it has met its goals. Then, why has the topic of outcomes assessment caused such heated debate and controversy over the last ten years?

One reason faculties have objected to mandated assessment is that they feel they already do it. Assignments and tests, as well as the evaluation of teaching and research built into the promotion and tenure process are ways faculty constantly assess and are assessed. This initial misunderstanding of institutional assessment activities has been generally overcome, and in fact, many assessment programs incorporate course, departmental, college, and program testing measures into a larger whole. Any observer of academe knows that faculty do not like to be told what to do by any outside agency, and certainly not governors, legislatures, or accreditors. Was assessment a new threat to academic freedom? As the president of the Association of American Colleges said in 1986, "American higher education is distinctive and even unique in the degree of autonomy enjoyed by individual institutions. They make their own decisions about who is admitted, who teaches, how much faculty members are paid, and what students must do to graduate. The faculty, as the core of the university, cherishes its own special freedom, and the typical individual faculty member is vigilant against interference from outside the university as well as from non-academic components within the university."[2]

Another objection to assessment has to do with its expense. In the midst of the controversy, a key study determined that it would cost from

$30,000 for a small college to at least $130,000 in incremental expenses for a research university to undertake a solid program of institutional measurement.[3] And of course, colleges and universities seldom receive special funding to accomplish an externally mandated assessment program; in hard times it has been difficult to support pilot projects or ongoing activities.

But perhaps most of the debate, research, and writing on outcomes assessment relates to the many methods tried and the many efforts to determine what, exactly, works.

THE METHODS

To over-simplify, outcomes assessment is a three step process: set institutional goals, measure outcomes to match against goals, and cycle feedback into the institutional planning process to ensure improvements.

All colleges and universities do not have current, concise goals. It is generally accepted that the very first step of an institutional evaluation is to establish such goals. This kind of self-analysis often takes a year or more, and once accomplished, should be followed by an attempt to find out if the university or college is meeting its goals.

One of the best ways to get a grasp of the variety of methodologies is to read case studies. Much of the literature on this topic consists of case studies. Among the most frequently cited cases are Alverno College, Northeast Missouri State University, University of Tennessee, University of Virginia, and Harvard University.

The University of Virginia conducted a longitudinal study, with a long questionnaire and an interview process given to freshmen with the intent to repeat data collection throughout the students' time in school, and thereafter as alumni. UVa recently decided to follow on that by adopting the Harvard model. The Harvard Assessment Seminars are described in Harvard's first report, in 1990.[4] This model, one of a committee structure designed to instigate wide-ranging discussions throughout campus about assessment and about outcomes, uses small group interviews and conversations to explore issues related to undergraduate education such as faculty availability, satisfaction with teaching methods, and student attitudes toward social factors influencing academic success. Alverno College, with one of the very longest assessment histories, reorganized their curriculum, building in a wide variety of methods of monitoring student learning. This integrated approach involves all faculty, and all teaching activities, with feedback to students, and cycles of changes initiated by the information discovered.

The University of Tennessee at Knoxville administers the ACT-COMP exam to freshmen and seniors, and has done so since 1983. About half of the academic programs on campus have been giving their students other standardized exams, but the other half have designed their own instruments and methods. All this is supplemented by a set of annual surveys, directed at such groups as dropouts, alumni, and employers. Northeast Missouri State's assessment program involves three parts: a value-added component to measure increases in student knowledge between freshman and sophomore years, the comparative component, to find out how students compare to students nationally using standardized instruments in each field, and an attitudinal component, using a variety of measures of student perceptions of their own university experience. These three parts together counter the many challenges made by assessment experts who warn about the pitfalls of basing a measurement program solely on the freshman and senior years administration of a standard test such as ACT-COMP, or College-Level Examination Program (CLEP), or College-Level Academic Skills Test (CLAST).

These case studies demonstrate application of most of the major methods: longitudinal analysis of educational experience and outcomes, application of standard tests, application of customized program outcomes instruments, attitudinal surveys of students, alumni surveys, and the generation and coordination of small-group based measures. Another methodology, that of using unobtrusive measures, is also used, and can even involve the library as a partner: one school measured student interest in coursework in part through looking at the number of students who used reserve readings in the library.

There are several handbooks on outcomes assessment, giving guidance about both the goals-setting and measurement processes. Some focus on such issues as the validity of various measurement instruments and other technical issues such as the construction of questionnaires.[5] James O. Nichols has written an overall "how-to" guide[6] to the entire process of looking at institutional effectiveness, in a plan which would take at least four years from onset to analysis of feedback. A concise description of more than 25 instruments for measuring cognitive outcomes can be found in a description of an approach called the "talent development" method.[7] A thorough guide to the self-study, whether it is at the institutional or program level is presented by H.R. Kells, and published in association with the American Council on Education.[8]

The Condition of Education is an annual report compiled by the National Center for Education Statistics to Congress about education, and includes figures about all levels of education. But, as Clifford Adelman says, these

data ''are limited to mechanical measures (e.g., numbers of degrees award-
ed, persistence rates, changes in educational aspirations, trends in applications to graduate and professional schools), none of which indicate what
students actually learn in college.''[9] To solve this problem, Adelman proposes a discipline-based assessment approach, and offers examples in computer sciences, mechanical engineering, biology, physics, and chemistry.

ANSWERS?

Does education make a difference? In the prologue of a history of the
application of the great variety of outcomes measures, Robert Pace[10] says,

> If one asks the question "What?" rather than "Why?", there are
> a lot of simple answers–clear, straightforward, and consistent over
> time. Do students learn anything in college? Yes. Do they them-
> selves believe that they have made progress toward such ends as
> critical thinking, acquiring a body of facts and knowledge of a spe-
> cial field, personal and social development, tolerance, broadened
> literary acquaintance, and so on? Yes. Do most college graduates
> find professional, semiprofessional, or managerial jobs? Yes. Is their
> income, on the average, higher than that of adults who did not grad-
> uate from college? Yes. Do they in their communities participate to
> a greater extent than others in a variety of civic and cultural affairs?
> Yes. Do college alumni, in retrospect, feel generally satisfied with
> their college experience? Yes. If they could do it over again, would
> they? Yes. Have colleges and universities studied themselves as
> institutions–their administration, organization, finance, the efficiency
> and effectiveness of the operations and programs? Yes. Do many
> colleges make such studies of themselves? Yes. The primary de-
> scriptive evidence is strong and consistent. Students change during
> the college experience; and the status of college graduates is demon-
> strably different from that of nongraduates in many respects.

Although much of the literature on institutional and outcomes assessment in higher education focuses on methods of finding out how students
are doing, perhaps more should be made of designing feedback systems
to inform institutional goals. Kells notes that ''Self-study should yield
improvement and it should form the basis of a planning process that follows
on its heels. Study and planning, then implementation and more study and

planning, should be part of ongoing management. They should not be seen as special or externally related events. Accrediting agencies should not be the prodders for study, as unfortunately, state coordinating boards are for planning processes. These activities should flow naturally and continuously; the leaders of the institution should make them happen."[11]

WHAT ABOUT LIBRARIES?

How can libraries be involved in the institutional planning and assessment process? If libraries and information centers of other kinds are incorporated into the college or university's goals, then questions can be asked and answers analyzed to find out if libraries are meeting these goals. But there are some key problems with bringing library and information issues into the institutional goals for education, and these problems have almost entirely prevented even the mention of libraries in assessment questionnaires or testing instruments.

Perhaps foremost among these problems is the fact that libraries are regarded as support organizations rather than instructional organizations. Libraries seldom offer fully developed curricula for teaching information retrieval and use skills. Libraries traditionally work with individual courses or individual faculty members to teach information seeking methods or research methods, and if they do work independently, libraries seldom have more than one or two credit courses. There are, of course, notable exceptions to this in the literature, but it is true in general. As has been proven over and over again in the hundreds of assessments published, students learn what they study. It is rare for students to actually *study* library use skills. They are almost always oriented to the library, and they may have a library exercise to do, or a library component in a writing course to complete, but library use, research skills, and the structure of information, indexing, the organization of knowledge, etc. are not issues studied at the undergraduate level. If a university has a program in library science, there may be undergraduate coursework, but it is then not generally offered by the library, but by an academic department. Therefore, libraries are left out of the college or university's systematic plan to measure instructional outcomes.

Libraries in colleges and universities with strong core curricula or general education programs where there are some university-wide requirements may stand a better chance of having research skills education integrated into the curriculum, and therefore of having a chance of participating in a university/college level assessment program. The Library must make the effort to be integrated into this kind of educational requirement, and once it is thoroughly involved, often faces very real budgetary and planning challenges caused by the fact that libraries are generally not staffed to handle an instructional program aimed at hundreds or even thousands of students each term. Pedagogical principles may be sacrificed to some extent, or alternatives to the traditional faculty/student relationship must be sought, resulting in, at best, automated or computer-based teaching programs.

Despite these facts, academic libraries with library instruction programs invariably feel a professional responsibility for teaching the use of the library. Hampered by the lack of a curriculum, these efforts often go unrecognized by the university administration. All librarians do not have faculty status, and the teaching activities of librarians who are not faculty may be discredited by being uninvolved with this system of recognition and reward so integral to campus life. Even if librarians do have faculty status, despite a great deal of new thought on the topic, teaching is not as well rewarded in today's colleges and universities as research is. This would not be the case if Ernest Boyer had his way. He has recently proposed[12] that the professorate be divided into four separate and related categories: the scholarship of discovery, of integration, of application, and of teaching. Librarians must give considerable thought to the ways they can and should fit into these flexible and potentially invigorating ways of looking at scholarship.

A search of the literature on evaluation of library instruction will yield much discussion of methods and cases, but little on linking such efforts with the overall institutional effort to measure instructional outcomes. A notable exception was declared recently by the Middle States Commission on Higher Education. In 1989, Howard Simmons, executive director of the Commission, placed new emphasis on bibliographic instruction, and convened a workshop to discuss methods of evaluating bibliographic instruction programs as part of the accreditation process. Librarians are members of most site visitation teams, and various aspects of the self-study process involve an examination of the extent to which faculty emphasize and require the use of libraries.[13]

If the regional accreditation association does not mandate a college/university look at bibliographic instruction, the library needs to look for ways to fit into the assessment process. What are colleges and universities assessing? In general, the categories include knowledge outcomes; skills, including cognitive skills; attitudes and values; and behavioral outcomes. Jonathan Warren's competencies[14] are: communication, analytical thinking, synthesizing ability, and awareness. The standardized tests are efforts to measure these kinds of general outcomes. How can libraries fit into this?

Pace[15] refers to a number of studies which identify the most commonly set goals for various categories of institutions of higher education. One of these which libraries should help meet is to "train students in methods of scholarship and research" or to "carry on applied research."

Another category of goals is centered around lifelong learning. Most alumni surveys have questions aimed at finding out how respondents are meeting the institution's goals on fostering lifelong and independent learning. College graduates definitely see lifelong learning as a key educational outcome. In a survey of 1975 graduates, 93% said that acquiring new skills independently was important, and 92% agreed that their college experience helped with this.[16] Can libraries fit into this goal? The ability to find and use information is clearly key to successful lifelong learning, and as the workforce is increasingly composed of "knowledge workers" rather than those occupied in manufacturing, information management skills are central.

Yet another of the goals on the list which matches the mission of most research libraries is to serve as a center for the preservation of the cultural heritage, or to provide community cultural leadership.

In summary, libraries must analyze institutional goals, and ensure that library goals support and link with them. This library goal-setting process must be done in association with college or university goals-setting rather than in isolation, published only in a library policy and procedure manual, the master copy of which sits in the director's office gathering dust.

Once library goals are in sync with institutional goals, and library processes for planning are part of the broader institutional planning processes, libraries can participate in university or college outcomes assessment programs.

Has this been done? Yes, but it is not often done. A look at the published examples of alumni assessment questionnaires shows that libraries are not usually mentioned. If the library is mentioned, it is in a question which asks for evaluation of the library's collections and resources, rather than for an evaluation of the library's instructional programs. The library on each campus must work to change this situation, since questions can be designed to measure the success of the library in supporting or meeting institutional goals. The design of questions on survey instruments is key to involving libraries in outcomes assessment. For example, the University of Tennessee, Knoxville survey of student opinions asks about the quality of the library collection related to the major. Are the results from this question valid? Librarians know enough about the information seeking skills of undergraduates to realize that if the student answering the survey did not learn information retrieval or library use skills, he or she would likely answer negatively about the quality of collections, largely because he or she did not know enough about how to use libraries to *find* the needed resources. The question might unintentionally say more about instructional programs than collections, but there is no good way to know.

Do libraries really want to know how well they teach information use and retrieval? What if it turns out that students who have had instruction by librarians do not retain what they learned, or that they do not integrate information-seeking skills into their papers, or that there is no substantial difference in performance between those students who had a library lecture and those students who did not.[17] Can libraries improve their instructional programs, or are limited funds, and the institutional charge to libraries as service rather than instructional units at the heart of an inability to change? There are many examples of librarians assessing their instructional efforts published in the literature. One of the benefits of being involved in the institutional goals-setting process, and the institutional measurement process might be a greater recognition of the issues involved in library-based instruction. Although Braskamp[18] does not specifically mention libraries, he discusses the ideal assessment environment as being one where the "triple-A perspective" is adopted: assessment, analysis, and action. The consequences of information gained through assessment actually end up making a difference. One concrete example of this has been related about the Northeast Missouri State assessment program, where the power of negative evidence was shown. "Institutions fear the impact of negative findings, but emerging experience suggests that negative findings are most likely to induce positive action."[19] The library at NEMO used poor student ratings of the library as ammunition for a capital budget request for library facilities, and succeeded in gaining support for the funding request. Perhaps the same result could be achieved when emphasis is placed on bibliographic instruction.

Another method the library can take to link to institutional planning is to undertake a self-study. Self study does not have to be mandated by an accreditation agency, it can be self-generated. The Association of Research Libraries has been furthering a self-study methodology for libraries, and facilitates self study processes as well as strategic planning and goals-setting processes. A review of this and other self-study methods for academic libraries was done by Edward Johnson.[20] However, if the library can participate in the university or college accreditation by being a focal point through a self-study, there is a guaranteed link with campus planning. Colleges and universities which do not use standard tests as an assessment method have often adopted a coordinated plan of program assessment and self study, with each program responsible for establishing the most appropriate measures. The library, like any other academic program, can participate fully in this campus-wide effort.

Fortunately, the library profession is good at devising and publishing standards, and there are published standards for all types of academic libraries, as well as performance measures listing areas to be addressed in creating and assessing any library's goals. Each library has to decide on how to place emphasis, set priorities, and then, how to measure outcomes in such a way that the campus will understand and involve such outcomes assessments in its own efforts.

REFERENCES

1. "Watching Assessment: Questions, Stories, Prospects" *Change*, September-October 1990, p. 14.

2. Chandler, John W., "The Why, What and Who of Assessment: The College Perspective" in *Assessing the Outcomes of Higher Education: Proceedings of the 1986 ETS Invitational Conference*, Princeton, New Jersey: Educational Testing Service, 1986.

3. Ewell, P. and D. Jones. "The Costs of Assessment." in C. Adelman (ed.) *Assessment in American Higher Education: Issues and Contexts*. Washington: U.S. Office of Education, Office of Educational Research and Improvement, 1986.

4. Light, Richard J. *The Harvard Assessment Seminars: Explorations with Students and Faculty about Teaching, Learning, and Student Life*, Cambridge: Harvard University Graduate School of Education and Kennedy School of Government, 1990.

5. *Performance and Judgement: Essays on Principles and Practices in the Assessment of College Student Learning*, U.S. Department of Education, Office of Education Research and Improvement, 1988.

6. Nichols, James O. *Institutional Effectiveness and Outcomes Assessment Implementation on Campus: A Practitioner's Handbook*. New York: Agathon Press, 1989.

7. Jacobi, Maryann, Alexander Astin and Frank Ayala, Jr. *College Student Outcomes Assessment: A Talent Development Perspective* (ASHE-ERIC Higher Education Report No. 7), Washington, D.C.: Association for the Study of Higher Education, 1987. pp. 37-59.

8. Kells, H.R. *Self Study Processes: A Guide for Postsecondary and Similar Service-Oriented Institutions and Programs*, New York: Macmillan, 1988.

9. Adelman, Clifford, ed. *Signs and Traces: Model Indicators of College Student Learning in the Disciplines*. Washington: U.S. Department of Education, Office of Research, 1989. p. 3.

10. Pace, Robert C. *Measuring Outcomes of College: Fifty Years of Findings and Recommendations for the Future*, San Francisco: Jossey-Bass, 1979.

11. Kells, *Self Study Processes*, p. 146.

12. Boyer, Ernest L. *Scholarship Reconsidered: Priorities of the Professorate.* Princeton, N.J.: The Carnegie Foundation for the Advancement of Teaching, 1990.

13. Lutzker, Marilyn. "Bibliographic instruction and accreditation in higher education" *C&RL News,* January 1990, pp. 14-18.

14. Warren, Jonathan, *The Measurement of Academic Competence,* Berkeley, California: Educational Testing Service, 1978.

15. Pace, *Measuring Outcomes of College,* p. 147.

16. *Ibid.,* p. 94.

17. Eadie, Tom, "Immodest Proposals: User Instruction for Students Does Not Work," *Library Journal,* October 15, 1990, pp. 42-45/

18. Braskamp, Larry A., "So, What's the Use?" in Peter J. Gray, ed., *Achieving Assessment Goals Using Evaluation Techniques,* (New Directions in Higher Education, no. 67) San Francisco: Jossey-Bass, 1989.

19. Ewell, Peter T., "Implementing Assessment: Some Organizational Issues" in Trudy W. Banta, ed., *Implementing Outcomes Assessment: Promise and Perils* (New Directions for Institutional Research, no. 59) San Francisco: Jossey-Bass, 1988, p. 22.

20. Johnson, Edward. "Academic Library Planning, Self-Study and Management Review," *Journal of Library Administration,* v. 2, nos. 2-4, 1981.

The Librarians' Role
in Academic Assessment
and Accreditation:
A Case Study

Susan Griswold Blandy

SUMMARY. Federal Regulations published in 1988 require colleges to demonstrate the difference they have made to students. The accrediting agencies such as the Middle States Association have combined frameworks for outcomes assessment with the long established requirement that college students demonstrate the ability to retrieve and use information. Hudson Valley Community College librarians work with the faculty in a liaison program to shape the collections, library use and student success. As faculty the librarians serve on college committees; at the state level the library subscribes to the SUNYLA student library competencies statement. All this is drawn on as librarians collaborate with faculty on college and departmental accreditation self study and visits. As the focus shifts from accreditation to assessment, librarians undertaking self-study must decide who will use the information and what library roles must be justified. Illustrations include an accreditation visit checklist, the Curriculum Committee LRC fact sheet and the SUNYLA Recommended Library Skills and Competencies for Graduates of Community Colleges.

Big notebooks are set aside in the Learning Resources Center, waiting for the State Education Department accreditation visit, waiting for the 1994 visit from the Middle States Association of Colleges and Schools. These notebooks are full of documents that attest to the performance of

Susan Griswold Blandy is Professor and Assistant Librarian at Hudson Valley Community College, Troy, NY 12180.

the Library/Media Center in the education of our students (Illustration 1). There are the usual resumes of the staff, samples of publications, and analysis of the Library using the ACRL/AECT Standards for Community College Learning Resources Programs. There is a collection of faculty-generated library research assignments and winning papers from the Excellence in Student Research Awards.

Although it looks very much like the documentation we had ready for the last Middle States visit, in fact the focus of accreditation has changed dramatically over the past five years. This change was accelerated in part by the publication in the *Federal Register* for July 1, 1988 of regulations

ILLUSTRATION 1. Learning Resources Center Library Self Evaluation Report

```
                        Prepared for
            New York State Education Department

  I. Self Evaluation Report, based on ACRL/AECT Qualitative performance standards

 II. Staff
     A. List of fulltime faculty/staff
     B. Resumes
     C. Job Descriptions: general and specific
     D. Organization Chart

III. Course Information
     A. Catalog pages for department
     B. Bibliographic Instruction
        1. Outline for English Composition
        2. Follow up assignment
        3. LRC Student Guide
        4. Examples of subject library instruction sessions
        5. Bibliographic Instruction annual report, 1989-90, 1990-91
     C. Library Assignments
     D. Student Research Awards with winning papers, 1989-91
     E. Interactive videos
     F. 20th Century Video Encyclopedia
     G. High School Research Field Trips: flyer

 IV. Departmental Information
     A. Policies and Procedures manual/mission statement, revised 1989
     B. Collection Development Policy
     C. Annual Reports: 1988-89, 1989-90, 1990-91
     D. Advisory Committee agendas, minutes, roster, by-laws
     E. Departmental meetings: agendas, minutes, 1989-91

  V. Resource Sharing
     A. Direct Access Program (Capital District Library Council) brochure
     B. Capital District Library Council member libraries list
     C. OCLC

 VI. LRC Publications
     A. Faculty Handbook
     B. Student Guide
     C. Newsletter
```

for educational criteria which accrediting agencies must use (see Introduction for the Regulations). These regulations include whether the college, with supporting data: has a mission statement, documents "in verifiable and consistent ways" the educational achievements of students, admits students who can benefit, and systematically takes steps to enhance student achievement. The purpose of the regulations was to close down diploma mills, to make sure student athletes got an education, to make sure that schools that took a student's dollar (a Federal dollar) gave that student a benefit. But suddenly a lot of desirable programs such as minority recruitment, critical thinking, multicultural/multinational diversity, cultural literacy, technological literacy, each with its staunch supporters, had to find their niche within campus-wide mission statements and assessment programs. Whereas we used to prepare for accreditation visits by documenting the resources of the school such as faculty degrees, lab equipment, library resources, student transfer rates and articulation agreements, we now have to concentrate on assessing student outcomes (which implies assessing student "in-comes"). Now we have to find niches within the mission statement and the assessment process for recognition of these other goals and resources. How are we going to define cultural literacy? How will we know if the student "got it"?

THE ASSESSMENT MANDATE

Colleges and voluntary accrediting associations decided not to fight the regulations they had had no role in writing since it seemed fairly obvious that the alternative was Federal government takeover of the accreditation process and a much diminished decision-making role in the process for the institutions affected.

By December 1988, State University of New York Provost Joseph Burke had asked all campus units to submit preliminary plans on assessment. Reminding the campuses that assessment not only demonstrates institutional effectiveness but is also used to improve performance, Provost Burke stated that the project has very practical uses as an honest public relations tool with the state legislature and prospective students. Most important, the assessment process was to be "campus-based and tailored to the particular mission and goals of each SUNY unit . . . assessment in SUNY must reflect this marvelous multiplicity and not a monolithic model mandated from Albany" (Burke, 1). These preliminary plans were then shared among campuses so that we could learn about the assessment process from each other, sharing what worked, what didn't.

By May 1990 the Middle States Commission on Higher Education had drafted a framework for outcomes assessment which, based on the Middle States Standards for Accreditation, blended the Teaching/Learning/Assessment/Improvement loop with the more familiar accreditation standards. Since assessment implies measuring how students are affected by their time in college, the colleges turned to standardized testing services for nationally validated instruments to measure institutional effectiveness and student readiness, tests for reading, writing, mathematics and critical thinking. Whereas the American College Testing program corporation had stated that abilities to acquire information could not be tested with a standardized test, and this moved the library out of a position of importance, perhaps even relevance, the Middle States framework said (p.14):

> Of particular interest to Middle States is the extent to which students have mastered the ability to retrieve and use information. Most often, learning in this area begins with the courses offered in the general education program, and is refined as students move into the more specialized curricula. The following questions might be asked of the syllabi for all courses. They are particularly crucial to the general education programs:
>
> How many syllabi include library-based assignments? What is the nature of those assignments? Are they appropriate for the program and its students? Do they show evidence of thought and creativity? Do they promote active learning? Do they take advantage of primary sources when appropriate? Do they display a knowledge of the range of resources available to students at the institution? Is there a sense that, as students progress from the beginning of the degree program to its conclusion, they are required to use increasingly complex library research skills?

As the College responded to these new requirements for assessment, it decided to rewrite the mission statement and goals, with input from across campus. The old goals had included a library skills statement:

(1982) . . . 3.   to acquire the ability to use a library/learning resources center effectively;

. . . 6.   to obtain a foundation of knowledge and culture to provide a basis for life long learning.

The new statement omitted any specific reference to the library or information-gathering skills:

(1990) Goals: to maintain and enhance academic excellence;
to maintain and enhance institutional fiscal responsibility and accountability;
to generate pluralism in the college community;
to maintain and enhance the institutional image.

The goals now reflect a very real shift in focus to multicultural diversity and fiscal efficiency. In spite of the Middle States' suggestion, the college's *Faculty Academic Assessment Handbook* does not specifically mention library use as an activity for achieving departmental goals.

This description of the new lay of the land is not meant to be discouraging; remember those big notebooks in the LRC waiting for the accreditation visits. And remember that this response to the call for assessment has involved input from across campus: faculty, department chairs, deans, advisors, administrators, trustees. The Library/Media Center may be no more explicitly recognized than computers or faculty degrees, but we remain as actively involved in instruction and assessment as before. The Librarians' role in the accreditation process is an outgrowth of our general role on campus.

LIAISON PROGRAM

For almost 20 years the Library has had a liaison program to link the library with the college departments and administration. Each of the librarians is assigned departments, with subject continuity, for instance: Technologies, Health Sciences, Business, Human Services, Liberal Arts. One librarian has direct responsibility for working with the administration. Special groups such as handicapped students and foreign students are assigned a librarian.

At Hudson Valley Community College there are more than 10,000 students registered, about 7600 FTE's, a central campus with many classes taught in other sites, about 250 full-time faculty with increasing reliance on adjunct faculty. There are some unusual programs, such as Dental Hygiene, Mortuary Science, a General Motors technician program and an affiliated Police Academy. There are articulation transfer agreements with well-respected four-year schools, and a very positive public image. Faculty are encouraged, within the constraints of a two-year school, to be creative, innovative and caring. More than 75% of the students work substantial part-time or full-time jobs. Their average age is about 28 and, as in all open admissions community colleges, they display every variety of readiness for college level work. The library has more than 100,000 circulating volumes, subscribes to about 650 periodicals and owns more than 5000 media items including interactive video. The librarians each work 10-15 hours a week at the reference desk, teach library instruction classes and have a major assignment such as Periodicals or Circulation.

Each department assigns at least one faculty member to work with the librarians and media specialist. The overall goal is to be mutually aware of what is going on in the LRC and in the classrooms. The actual activities include previewing films before purchase, sharing book reviews and recommending titles for purchase, and developing many kinds of instructional support such as research guides, bibliographies, special library instruction units, resource analysis for new courses, and two-way feedback on research assignments. The LRC resources and the liaison program are outlined in the LRC faculty handbook distributed to all faculty.

COLLECTION POLICY MANUAL

As part of the foundation for the liaison program the librarians and liaison faculty prepared a collections policy manual with a statement for each subject area. In addition to the ALA Collection Policy guidelines, we have specified a reading level and tried to indicate how integral a role library materials are expected to play. Obviously in a Phys Ed course the basketball or tennis court is more important than the improve-your-play videos. In the technologies and sciences the labs are the places where the students apply concepts learned in class, but in the liberal arts the library is, in effect, the lab. None of our students can become a professional in two years; they all need to know how to go on learning in their career area, how to find the trade and professional information: the *Merck Manual*, the *ASTM Standards, American Machinist, Alcoholism Treatment Quarterly*. We have also specified the role played by each resource type: books, periodicals, media and reference tools. We have also suggested the importance of primary documents, retrospective collections, currency, and expectations for weeding and updating the collection area. These statements are always made available to accrediting teams.

The liaison program is invaluable in a period of "budgetary restraint."

Audio-visual materials are regularly previewed by the faculty before purchase; the cataloguing includes a departmental code. Faculty recommend both specific titles and new subject areas for the circulating collection. All periodical additions and cancellations are reviewed by the liaison faculty and/or their department. It is important to show the accreditation group how the library works to support quality education when resources are limited.

LIBRARY ASSIGNMENTS

For the library's resource-providing role, involvement in shaping assignments gives the librarians very useful information about demands being placed on the collections. Faculty can be encouraged to use resources available; they should also let the librarians know what is needed, ahead of time. When the librarians and faculty confer about resources needed and available there can be feedback (both ways) about student success or bewilderment. Sometimes it's a matter of helping to rewrite the assignment to clarify the faculty expectations and/or the research steps. Other times, at the invitation of the faculty, the librarians will present a 10-50 minute library instruction session. Because these are designed to meet faculty-perceived needs, they may come as the assignment is given out or after students have had a chance to flounder. They may be a live librarian handing out research guides, a carefully structured introduction to resources on and off campus, or a free-wheeling discussion with the class about their research experiences. We prefer showing up when the students are well aware of the assignment and anxious about getting started. In spite of clearly written assignment sheets and library handouts refined over the years, there will still be times when the live librarian as an organizing force, a motivating force, can bridge the Slough of Despond or the Pond of Procrastination.

Reference work in a college is normally a response to class assignments. With the liaison program we can give faculty feedback, *before the papers are due,* on how well their students are doing. In some departments we have also been able to work with faculty to design alternatives to standard research assignments or to modify and refine existing assignments. The emphasis is on making it possible for the student to spend more time manipulating the information than on struggling to collect it. This may mean clarifying terms used in the assignment, changing the objectives, changing the collections. Faculty don't want to spend time grading dismal projects. They don't want to field interminable complaints about how the work can't be done. They do want to help students use professional and college level materials. They do want to help students master the concepts in the syllabus and see cross-disciplinary relationships and implications. They do want to see how well students can apply course concepts working on their own. They do want to give test-shy students a chance to show off what they can do. Some successful objectives for assignments have included relating engineering standards to the process-in-hand, researching topics not covered in class (real estate), analyzing primary documents (history, marketing, state and local government), integrating diverse information formats (economic geography, criminal justice), analyzing professional literature (psychology) and many others. In the accreditation process it is important to specify in the syllabus not only what the assignment is but what its successful completion is supposed to teach. Exactly what does the grade on the paper reflect? Grammar and spelling as well as content? Clarity of presentation? How do these assignment objectives relate to course objectives? To department goals? (Has anyone ever heard of Bloom's taxonomy?) Is there a sequence of increasingly complex assignments? For instance, in several courses the final project is compiled from a specified series of smaller projects whose due dates are staggered throughout the semester. It is also important for the accreditation process that we explain and justify when a research project may substitute for a timed exam. In some occupations one needs the information recalled immediately (nursing); in other jobs it's essentially an open book exam every day.

In order to recognize both the quality of faculty assignment ideas and the student performance in research, the librarians set up an Award for Excellence in Student Research. Many departments across all disciplines have submitted papers, and the winning papers are in the library's accreditation notebooks. Students have worked on topics as diverse as the New York State Mammography Law, an analysis of Budweiser advertising, a "first person account" of life on the 18th century Hudson River, chemistry lab analysis, and the transportation system in Shanghai. These papers dramatize not only student performance and departmental goals, but also the library's role in instruction.

FACULTY STATUS

The librarians have full faculty status, a responsibility they take very seriously. They serve on all campus committees, including Academic Policy, Curriculum, Assessment, the Chancellor's Award, the Center for

Effective Teaching, and the Honors Program. The Library began the Poetry Forum which brings noted poets to campus, and has sponsored seminars on the historic interface between art and technology. Individual librarians are involved in minority mentoring and teach as adjunct faculty. In the Curriculum Committee every new course proposal must be accompanied by an LRC impact form signed by both the liaison librarian and the media specialist (Illustration 2). This form suggests the existing LRC support for the new course and the dollar investment needed to support the course adequately. The process of going over the course outline and form with the faculty member gives the liaison librarian and media specialist a chance to suggest unfamiliar resources and a chance to review the research assignments. A copy of the form is filed with the library. The economics of a recession being what they are, these forms have never won us a budget increase even when it is clear the budget cannot accommodate new demands. However, they do show that the library has been put on notice the materials are needed and that the department has found out what is available. The library is part of a very close knit library consortium of regional public, academic and specialized libraries so that resources can easily be shared. Our students, all commuters, soon are comfortable in more than one library.

ACCREDITATION

Because of Hudson Valley Community College's many specialties and a tradition of quality education, we are accredited not only by the New York State Education Department and Middle States, but also by ABET (Accreditation Board for Engineering and Technology) and (pending) the Association of Collegiate Business Schools and Programs, both unusual for a two year school. Articulation agreements with four year schools are also a form of accreditation. Professional associations for curricula such as Nursing, Radiologic Technologies, Mortuary Science, and Construction Technology review and accredit these programs.

When the self-study guidelines come down from an accrediting agency there is almost always a section on the Library/LRC. Commonly we are asked for a list of books and journals supporting the curriculum. This is a chance, not to throw up our hands, but to renew the department's awareness of the library/media resources. We will prepare a list of periodicals with sample pages from the relevant indexes to demonstrate that much good material is cross-disciplinary and found in other titles. We will measure the shelf list in selected LC classifications with a note reminding

ILLUSTRATION 2

Curriculum Committee LRC Fact Sheet

This information is submitted to assist the Curriculum Committee in its responsibility to ascertain what instructional resources provided by the LRC are available in supporting this curricula.

(To be filled out by requesting faculty)

Course Title _____ Course Number _____ Dept. _____

Requesting Instructor _____ EXT. #

Faculty Liaison to LRC _____ EXT. #

Course Request Status

☐ New Course   ☐ Revision of Existing Course

Do you anticipate using LRC support materials for this course?

Print (Books or Periodicals)   ☐ Yes   ☐ No

If no, why not? _____

Media (Audio visual)   ☐ Yes   ☐ No

If no, why not? _____

Other _____

Are there Department grants available to purchase support materials for this curriculum?

☐ Yes   Amount _____   ☐ No

Please submit sheet to LRC CAPC Representative with FULL PROPOSAL ATTACHED

The librarian and media specialist in consultation with the requesting faculty member(s) have determined that LRC holdings to support this curriculum are:

	Adequate	Inadequate
Books		
Periodicals		
Media (Audio visual)		

The estimated funds needed to bring the collection to adequate status for support of this curriculum is: Print $ _____   Media $ _____

Comments _____

_____

_____

_____

_____   _____   _____

LRC Curriculum Committee   Media Specialist   Librarian   LRC Director
Representative

everyone that LC doesn't necessarily put materials where we expect them. (Mortuary Science materials show up in Psychology, Religion, History, Anthropology, Business, Law, Public Health, Anatomy, Architecture and Music, and Chemical Technology, so where is the Mortuary Science collection?)

The media list can be computer generated by department, and we also have on hand the materials prepared for instruction: bibliographies, resource guides, research assignments. For the visit itself we prepare additional bibliographies, displays, book counts, circulation analyses. We are happy to meet the team, walking the building with them and answering questions about the program as it is supported by the library/media center. Because we have been involved in the self-study process we are able to be articulate and specific about library strengths and weaknesses, regional backup support and student reactions to assignments. For instance the class rapport in Construction Tech is so strong that we simply do not lose issues or pages from the concrete journals. We have also sent over to the department offices materials for an exhibit there, and we often set up special media demonstrations. Although the librarian liaison and the media specialist are the official contacts, all public service clerical staff are briefed so that they too can be knowledgeable and helpful. All of the work done through the liaison program becomes relevant to the accreditation just as it has been relevant to instruction.

ASSESSMENT

Is past successful involvement in the accreditation process the prologue to future success when the emphasis has shifted to assessment? Certainly the task of making sure the library is an integral part of the teaching process is more difficult. We have the burden of reminding each department of our relevance because library skills are no longer singled out as a college objective. We are not part of standardized testing of incoming students or graduates. As the departments struggle with assessment projects such as capstone courses, portfolios, comprehensive exams, do they have time to listen to librarians? Should the librarians be reactive or pro-active? Responding or initiating? Is the library an information service or an instructional resource? We know that the testing corporations say library skills cannot be covered by a standardized test. The community colleges of California disagree and are working on that project, but some of the debate stems from a lack of consensus on what library skills are needed by college students and by college graduates.

We run the risk of seeing our graduates as a product, and of seeing performance assessment/institutional improvement as Total Quality Management, the delivery of carbon copy zero defect products. The college has a commitment to honoring the needs of the individual; the library must remind faculty, administration and students that we provide the easiest and most effective means for personalizing a course, for helping students work at their own pace, to their own time commitment on their own topics, at their own intellectual level. We need to remind students that there are standards for research they can attain. On the other hand, engineers will tell you that if you can't measure something, you can't improve it. If we measure what's measurable: number of volumes used, number of questions asked, numbers of papers assigned, we are not part of assessment. We need to look for correlations between library work in introductory courses and success in second level courses. We need to look at evidence in research projects that students can use a variety of library resources and information gathering ingenuity.

Assessment in courses, e.g., tests, tends to emphasize passivity: getting the one right answer. How does the library assess the role of library resources in active learning and critical thinking? How do we test what happens to the novice researcher looking for a book on suicide who is guided also to the criminology and psychology journals, the *U.S. Statistical Abstracts*, *DSM III*, and Judith Guest's *Ordinary People?*

LIBRARY COMPETENCIES

The librarians laid the foundation for library skills assessment in the Bibliographic Instruction program. In 1987 the State University of New York Librarians Association created a Task Force on Bibliographic Competencies. The group established a list of recommended library skills for community college graduates (Illustration 3). Most two year college librarians in New York State feel that these competencies are reasonable, approachable. The competencies are the educational objectives for our BI programs and for the syllabus and final exam of our one credit research skills course. They guide the educational objectives we suggest to faculty designing assignments.

In a typical semester the 6 librarians will teach almost 80 classes or more than 2500 students through the English Composition I bibliographic instruction program. Each student begins the worksheet by looking up their own name in the catalog, finding the author who is the closest match

ILLUSTRATION 3. Recommended Library Skills and Competencies for Graduates of Community Colleges in New York State

A.   Given a problem, the student will identify and analyze an information need, consulting reference librarians as needed.
  1. The student will identify and clearly state major topics in a research question (information need).
  2. The student will determine the type of information needed, i.e.:
     a. popular or scholarly
     b. primary, secondary
     c. current or retrospective
     d. overview, statistical, critical, biographical, etc.
  3. The student will translate the question into subject headings and/or key words used in reference sources
  4. The student will broaden and narrow a topic as necessary, choosing relevant subject headings.
B.   Given an information need, the student will develop a research strategy to satisfy the need.
  1. The student will identify types of sources appropriate to satisfy specific information needs, i.e. specific reference sources, indexes,etc.
  2. The student will keep a record of sources used.
  3. The student will be able to modify the search strategy as necessary.
C.   The student will demonstrate the ability to use library resources to carry out the search strategy.
  1. The student will utilize and apply the services, policies and procedures of the library.
  2. The student will be able to locate materials in the library (physical arrangement)
  3. The student will effectively utilize the library's catalog in any form (card catalog, online, COM, CD-ROM)
  4. The student will be able to locate an item in the library by using the call number.
  5. The student will use the information found in a book's table of contents, index, and/or bibliography to locate information.
  6. The student will select appropriate common reference tools such as almanacs, atlases, encyclopedias, dictionaries, etc. to satisfy an information need.
  7. The student will identify and use specialized reference books and journals and, where available, government documents in a field of study.
  8. The student will use a periodical index and interpret a citation.
  9. The student will locate a periodical in the library using a periodicals holdings list.
  10. The student will use microforms, non-print materials and/or computer software with appropriate equipment as needed to satisfy an information need.
  11. The student will recognize the availability and usefulness of both in-house and commercial databases (dependent upon library resources available).
  12. The student will consider sources outside the college library, including interlibrary loan as well as other libraries and agencies.
D.   The student will demonstrate the ability to analyze and evaluate whether the information located will satisfy his/her information need.

E.   The student will be able to define the role of the reference librarian for satisfying his/her information need(s).

and using that book, that subject for the rest of the assignment. The work is self-paced, self-correcting. Students with excellent library skills may speed through it, but by the end they have been in every corner of the library. Students who begin abysmally ignorant will also complete the assignment, much more slowly, with much more assistance from the librarians and friends, but at the end they will have used and recorded the same kinds of resources. For the purposes of accreditation it is sufficient to say what percentage of freshmen completed the program. For the students the worksheets are test-and-instruction enough, but they do not constitute assessment. For assessment we would in addition have to pre-test and post-test the students, not to benefit the students, not to advise the faculty, but to meet mechanical demands from some off-site agency.

At the same time that we are aware of the accreditation standards and the assessment process, we need to be aware of the time pressures on the faculty and the librarians so that we can target our available energy. If we choose to tie most library assessment to course assignments then we must understand the implications. If faculty working with unprepared and unmotivated students (the most common complaint) assign a five page paper they should review the draft of each paper (to prevent plagiarism and direct student efforts) and then grade each paper. For 150 students a semester one can estimate 75-90 hours of faculty work on that assignment alone. The library staff probably invested another 75-90 hours. We have to be able to document that was time well spent. For our college population the library would have to invest 3800 hours every semester to support one research project per student. We don't have that time, but just as significantly, we don't want to tie the justification for the existence of the library to our reference desk support of research assignments.

WHO IS THE AUDIENCE FOR ASSESSMENT?

The purpose of assessment is supposedly self knowledge which leads to improvement. We are to take systematic steps to enhance achievement. Who is really the audience for the library's involvement in assessment? The students? They are here only two years. Especially at a community college they present us with variables, big ones. Students range in age 5 or 6 decades; they are often poor students who may yet become good students; they may be vague or flighty but looking for commitment; they often lack confidence in anything but their ability to fail; there is cultural diversity, learning style diversity, language diversity, life style diversity;

and finally there is incredible variation in the time they have available for school work. (''No,'' said my student, ''I don't have a job. I have to take care of my invalid mother while we live in the garage until they can rebuild her house which burned down.'') Students want to believe in their futures, as defensive, lazy, cynical or messed up as some of them are. They may dismiss our estimate of how long it takes to prepare a research report, they may bristle at the suggestion that an old *Time* magazine article is inadequate, but this stems as much from lack of faith in themselves as from disrespect for The System. The students know before the grades arrive what they have accomplished. Student satisfaction helps bring in more students and helps build loyalty among local alumni, but the library assessment program is not really for them.

Who is the audience for assessment? The administration? They, after all, have to compile the reports for the accrediting agencies. Of necessity they see the faculty as interchangeable employees with limited options to increase productivity. Any improvement in student retention, in standardized test scores, in graduate employability, even in enthusiasm, certainly in enrollment is welcomed. Is the audience outside groups such as the legislature that votes on the budget, the employers, the accrediting groups who demand assessment, the local advisory groups who contribute time and expertise to make the programs more successful? Is assessment really a PR tool?

Who is the audience for assessment? The faculty who seem to the students to have been here forever, teaching the same few introductory courses over and over? The faculty are basically self-employed; the success of the transfer student or new employee helps bring in more students for the program. The faculty are those with the most at stake in assessment, and with the clearest responsibility for using the results.

But, ultimately, the real audience for library assessment is the library. We want to show that the library matters in instructional outcomes. We want faculty and administrators who may seldom if ever use the library to believe that we are important for students learning to think critically, learning to act on curiosity and enthusiasm. We need the security, the confidence that comes from documenting that we matter. Assessment provides tools we need to argue for our existence.

Generalizing from the specific may not be good research, but providing excellent one-on-one reference for administrators opens the door for our involvement in assessment. Emphasizing our course-related work may not support long-range library needs, but it does establish us as full-rank team players with a respected voice in the process.

WHAT IS THE PRODUCT?

Peter Drucker, the influential management expert, says one must in any business answer the questions: what is the product? who is the customer? Reference librarians in the process of justifying the existence of their library may find they come up with conflicting answers. The old accreditation process had us analyze the collection, highlight resumes and outreach, and show off our new technology. The new assessment process asks us how we know it is better to spend the money on fee-for-use data bases than on more journals; how do we know it is better to teach library instruction classes than to double the reference desk staff? The administration would like for us to look good so that they can concentrate their energies elsewhere; "Things are running well; Librarians work wonders." (They would say the same about computers, food service, the registrar's office, etc. if possible on any campus.) But this is our opportunity to lay out in the open the impact of administrative and academic decisions regarding space, budgets, staff, technologies. Is everything OK? Can we forecast? Are we relevant? Will we speak truth to power? Given limited time, limited resources, what actions have the greatest desirable impact on the educational outcomes for our students?

If we answer the question, what is the product? by saying the librarian is the product the library offers, then how do we measure what we do? How do we prioritize what we do, how do we assess our effectiveness? Answering the question "access to information" is our product produces a different assessment process. Answering the question as though we "manufacture" life-long learners creates yet a different constellation of assessment measures.

We cannot be, and evaluate, all possible products. While the fledgling assessment movement organizes itself we must choose what we *can* do to identify the library as a means of carrying out the institution's mandate. We must keep track of what other librarians are doing and keep the pressure on our public to view the library as an integral part of intelligent life on this planet.

BIBLIOGRAPHY

Argyris, Chris. "Teaching smart people how to learn," *Harvard Business Review* 69 (May-June 1991): 99-109.
Association of College and Research Libraries and the Association for Educational Communications and Technology. *Standards for Community, Junior and Tech-*

nical College Learning Resources Programs. Chicago, American Library Association, 1990. Also published in *College & Research Libraries News* 51 (Sept. 1990): 757-66.

Astin, Alexander W. "Why not try some new ways of measuring quality?" *Educational Record* 63 (1982):10-15.

Boyer, Ernest. *The Undergraduate Experience in America.* New York, Carnegie Foundation for the Advancement of Teaching, 1986.

Brint, Steven and Jerome Karabel. *The Diverted Dream: Community Colleges and the Promise of Educational Opportunity in America, 1900-1985.* New York, Oxford University Press, 1989.

Burke, Joseph C. *Campus Plans on Academic Assessment* (memo). Albany, N.Y. State University of New York. Office of the Provost, Dec. 12, 1988.

Cooper, Robin and Robert S. Kaplan. "Profit priorities from activity-based costing," *Harvard Business Review* 69 (May-June 1991): 130-5.

Cuesta College (San Luis Obispo, Calif.) Library. *Library Skills Instruction Program Skills Test* (in development), 1991.

Dale, Doris Cruger. "The learning resource center's role in the community college system," *College & Research Libraries* 49:3 (May 1988): 232-8.

Ewell, Peter T. "Assessment, where are we? the implications of new state mandates," *Change* (Jan.-Feb. 1987) 23-8.

_____"Establishing a campus-based assessment program: a framework for choice," in *Student Outcomes Assessment.* San Francisco, Jossey-Bass, Winter 1987. (New Directions in Higher Education, 59).

Greer, Arlene and Lee Weston, Mary Alm. "Assessment of learning outcomes: a measure of progress in library literacy," *College & Research Libraries* 52 (Nov. 1991): 549-57.

Halpern, Diane, ed. *Student Outcomes Assessment: What Institutions Stand to Gain.* San Francisco, Jossey-Bass, Winter 1987 (New Directions in Higher Education, 59).

Holleman, Margaret, ed. *The Role of the Learning Resources Center in Instruction.* San Francisco, Jossey-Bass, Fall 1990 (New Directions for Community Colleges, 71).

Joint Committee on *Standards for Educational Evaluation. Standards for Evaluation of Educational Programs, Projects and Materials.* New York, McGraw-Hill, 1981.

Middle States Association of Colleges and Schools. Commission on Higher Education. "Annual report of the Executive Director, 1990-91," *CHE Newsletter* (Philadelphia) Summer 1991.

_____*Framework for Outcomes Assessment.* Philadelphia, The Commission, 1990.

Naito, Marilyn. "An information literacy curriculum: a proposal," *College & Research Libraries News* 52 (May 1991): 293-6.

Pascarella, Ernest T. and Patrick T. Terenzini. *How College Affects Students.* San Francisco, Jossey-Bass, 1991.

Resnick, Lauren B. "Literacy in school and out," *Daedalus* 119:2 (Spring 1990): 169-85.

Schuman, Patricia Glass. "Reclaiming our technological future," *Library Journal* March 1990, reprinted in *Whole Earth Review* 73 (Winter 1991): 74-81.

State University of New York. Board of Trustees and Chancellor. *SUNY 2000: A Vision for the New Century.* Albany, New York, Sept. 1991.

State University of New York Library Association. Bibliographic Competencies Task Force. *Recommended Library Skills and Competencies for Graduates of Community Colleges in New York State.* 1987.

Wisconsin Association of Academic Librarians. *Minimum Library Use Skills: Standards, Test and Bibliography.* Madison, WI, 1985. (Jo Ann Carr, ed.)

Teaching High Schoolers About Libraries: A Message to Teachers

Harold Ettelt

As a college library director I am assumed to be an expert on "What library skills should high schools impart to college-bound students?" The questioners are usually high school people trying to increase bibliographic instruction for the college-bound, and they figure my opinion can be used as a weapon against the unbelievers. They expect I will give them a long and detailed list of library skills such students must master if they are to succeed in college.

Of course I, or any college librarian, could come up with such a list. But it would almost entirely consist of things *helpful*, not necessary. You see, almost every college now has its own bibliographic instruction program (if a college doesn't, don't go there because that won't be its only large failure). Any incoming student not already knowing how to use a library well will have the opportunity to learn in college. Those who already know much of it will simply have a head start. Thus my response, admittedly iconoclastic, is that the college-bound students are not the ones to worry about. Bend your efforts instead to those *not* going on to college. My reasoning is based upon personal experience.

Before I reached the exalted position of library director with an MLS from Rutgers, I spent some years as a high school dropout with no knowledge of libraries whatever. I lived and worked with similar people, although many of them had had the complete high school experience. We were not going to college where we'd have another shot at learning about libraries. We were going through life with only what our high schools had given us. And we had been short-changed. By and large, when it came to library instruction, our high schools had written us off, and we didn't even know what we were missing.

Harold Ettelt is Head Librarian, Columbia Green Community College, P.O. Box 1000, Hudson, NY 12354.

So my short answer to "What library skills should high schools impart to college-bound students?" is, "Less than those you impart to those students *not* going on to college." Because the use of libraries is not about getting through college, it is about getting through life.

Your students will want to have healthy babies or care for unhealthy ones, take out mortgages, buy cars, invest in mutual funds, move to other states or countries, choose careers or switch them, start businesses, comfort the grieving or handle it themselves, handle a rape, teach a kid about drugs, manage a teenager, and on, and on, and on. In short, they will live their lives with all sorts of unanticipated and changing needs for information, and if they know how to use libraries, know the *worth* of libraries, they will find that information. If they don't know libraries, they will have to muddle through. They can either tap the world's experts or not, depending on what they were taught. If you don't teach the college bound, the college will. But only you can teach those of your students not going on. You are their last shot.

That's my short answer. Of course I have a long one as well, things that *all* high school students should be taught. It gets into a bit more detail.

1. Teach them to read well. If they can't do that, nothing else matters much. By reading well, I mean getting information from the page into the brain in coherent fashion. Libraries can be very helpful in this if they stock things students *want* to read, even if it is not academic. I once "taught" a co-worker to read well enough to pass his driving test by using the driver's manual and *Penthouse* (yes, *Penthouse*). He *wanted* to be able to read those things.

2. Teach them how to use books. I mean the table of contents, index, glossary, bibliography. And not in one unit in one class and then it's over, but as a regular occurrence in their daily use of books. This might sound trivial but it is an extremely common failing, even among college students, and it costs them a lot.

3. Teach them to ask the librarians and keep asking, to keep coming back for more. Imbue them with the knowledge that they are not "bothering" the librarian. That's what we get paid for. And if one librarian can't/won't help, ask a different librarian.

4. Take them to some large library where they can *see* the world of knowledge that exists, including the vastness of the periodical literature, and explain that they can tap that world. Then bring them home and teach them how.

   A. Teach them how to figure out reference books, what's in them and how you get at it.

B. The card catalog, including related terms, synonyms, tracings, etc. Include a hefty dose about finding parts of books when you can't find entire books. If you have a computerized catalog, do the same things with that. Forget about memorizing the Dewey or the LC system, those are just addresses for the books and boring as well as useless to learn.

C. *Reader's Guide* at least. If you've got a computerized index, teach that if you've time, but make sure you start with a print index. It makes more sense if you *see* what you're searching through.

D. Basic bibliographic citation, including footnotes and the difference between research and plagiarism. This may sound useless to non-college students, but they'll be reading other people's research, and you'd be amazed at how many eventually go back to college. I did.

A Program with a View:
The Inner City High School Library

Margaret Galloway

SUMMARY. Rensselaer Middle High School has all the fiscal and social problems of a small inner city school, but critical thinking and independent learning are central to the curriculum. Learning Center programs include a grade 6-12 interdisciplinary research skills program, an automated library, and a field trip program to local public and college libraries. The hectic participation by students, the cooperation of the administration and city, and the active teaching role of the Librarian make it all work.

As you approach Rensselaer Middle High School it is no surprise that it is situated on the banks of the Hudson River. Over the rooftop of the building you can see the replica of Henry Hudson's ship, the Half Moon, perched atop the spire of the old Delaware & Hudson Administrative Building. But as you walk into the Library Information Center of the school you indeed experience an unexpected surprise. It is a spacious, well-appointed area in the very center of the first floor of the building with a stunning view of the river and the Albany skyline. I mention its physical location because it is illustrative of the significant role the Center and its resources and services play in the instructional program of the school and the district. This role has evolved through a series of decisions made by the Board of Education, the administration and the faculty of the Rensselaer City School District over the past several years. A brief background of the District seems appropriate at this point.

Rensselaer City School District is the smallest of 57 small inner city school districts in New York State. As such, it faces many, if not all, of the fiscal and social problems commensurate with an urban environment.

Margaret Galloway is School Library/Media Specialist at Rensselaer, NY Middle-High School.

93

It has a small, low to middle income tax base; many families are single-parent households which rely on local and state social programs for services. The Board of Education and the community, despite such restraints, are justly proud of the educational programs they provide for their children. Under the leadership of Superintendent Stephen Urgenson, the District is committed to spending its limited resources and using its faculty expertise to provide instructional programs that will best prepare the student population for living and working in what is now known as the Information Age. Long before a recent article in the New York Times indicated that schools are not teaching the necessary skills in the uses of technology and its applications that will ensure students a place in the work force of the 90's and beyond, the Rensselaer City School District recognized the critical role such skills in research and analysis of information must play in a student's learning environment.

At Rensselaer Middle High School, critical thinking and research skills, use of technology for information retrieval and reporting and the independent learning that is fostered by both these elements are all a crucial part of the overall curriculum of the school. Mr. Urgenson summarizes the District's on-going commitment when he says, "The District recognizes the central role information and research services and instruction play in educating for the future. Programs in Rensselaer Middle High School recognize the Information Age and this Age is changing the working reality for our students." Over the past eight years, the District has "put its money where its mouth is," to again quote Mr. Urgenson, in regard to staffing and funding programs and services offered by the Library Information Center at Rensselaer Middle High. In a time of fiscal "belt-tightening," the overall budget for the library media program and staff has not been significantly reduced and has, at times, even experienced a moderate increase. I believe this reflects the recognition on the part of the Board, administration and faculty of the success of the programs initiated by the Library Information Center staff.

These programs include a grade 6-12 interdisciplinary research skills program, a broadcast journalism course with a fully equipped video studio, an automated library catalogue and circulation system, a computer network system integrated into the classroom curriculum and CD-ROM application within the Library Information Center, a field trip program that allows students to use resources available in local college and public libraries and a new Junior/Senior Seminar Program that is designed to allow students the opportunity to create and explore their own interests in an independent learning situation. Rensselaer Middle High School Library Information Center is a vital and involved place to spend time. On any given day, one may observe a student or two conducting interviews for the school TV news program, two 8th grade students at the CD-ROM station deciding which magazine articles from a print-out are suitable for their research project and whether they need to use interlibrary loan to get them, an 11th grader using the CD-ROM Regional Catalogue to locate a book in another library that she needs for her chemistry project, four 6th graders composing a series of poems, with illustrations, for the literary magazine using computer programs in the instructional lab, two students at the telephone desperately trying to reach State Ed. for information on special programs for the handicapped, a 7th grade teacher and her class using encyclopedias as a first reference for their American History research paper, a newly licensed student, who is "labelled," looking for information on a car he's considering buying and two students who are simply daydreaming by the Hudson River.

Such a seemingly madcap use of a facility may sound chaotic to some, exciting to others and daunting to still others. Of one thing you can be sure, it is exhausting to the staff. But it should also show that students must be given the opportunity to locate information from as many sources as possible, in whatever format is most appropriate, at whatever level the student may be. Perhaps one of the most important outcomes of the use of Library Information Center as the focal point of the instructional program of the school is the flexibility it provides for different learning styles. Information, in such a technology environment, is not contained within one medium. Students with learning disabilities, as well as students in the regular program, may find information in a variety of non-print formats. They may also report their findings in non-traditional ways; a video tape, a report composed and written in a word processing program, a computer-generated program of their own design, computer graphics. One of the most exciting experiences for the Library Information Specialist in such an environment is to see students who have previously shunned the center and its services become active, involved users. We still have our share of students who "hang out" in the center. But now they watch teachers and other students use resources in entirely different ways and they can't help but become curious.

Use of technology at Rensselaer Middle High School is not an end in itself but a means by which students and faculty can view information and the use of that information and the use of that information differently. Technology is not driving the instructional program at Rensselaer Middle High School. Rather it's the research and information skills program using technology applications to teach students the inter-relationship of information sources in concert with the school curriculum that is the driving force of the program. At Rensselaer Middle High School we believe if you give students a range of sources they begin to look upon technology applications as a means to an answer. What is never lost sight of and what is consistently re-enforced throughout the grades is the value of asking the right questions. The students are asked to think about what they need to know, what sources can provide the appropriate answers and how best to present their findings in a clear, concise manner.

Obviously, the Rensselaer Middle High School information and technology skills program did not "grow like Topsy." It evolved because the Board, administration and faculty are committed to educating students for a technological future. We've all heard how important such co-operation is to any library media program. Our textbooks in Administration 101 stress it, Information Power demands it, and we all know how much effort it takes, in the field, to produce it. It is possible to develop a program without such co-operation but it is infinitely easier with it. Money, staff and administrative support, however, do not necessarily lead to a coherent, well-respected and vital library media program.

I believe one of the keys is in the hands of the School Library Media Specialist. How she views her role in the educational community is crucial. If we, as professionals, do not have our own vision of program, do not have our own agenda, we run the risk of allowing administrative enthusiasm or faculty perceptions to direct the course of our instructional program. And I am convinced of the importance of the term "instructional program." The Library Media Specialist (and let's begin to call her what she is–a Library Information Specialist) must become a co-operative instructor within the curriculum of the school. Her program must reflect the critical nature of the research process in educating students for a place in a technological future. That research process must now include not only non-print media but technology applications as well. And yes, we must begin to educate ourselves in those applications if we are not already "computer literate." We can no longer stand by while computer experts define the role of library information services for us. We need to develop our own program and agenda based on our school curriculum and our vision of the future. I am not suggesting we become computer experts in the technical sense, although that skill makes life infinitely less confusing. What I am suggesting is that we begin to design instructional programs that effectively incorporate technology and its applications into all aspects of the research process; critical thinking, resource analysis and methods of presentation. By using the reference interview to assist students in formulating good questions, by using Boolean Logic in computer applications to teach subject analysis, by exposing students to other libraries as sources of information, and by offering alternative technologies as reporting medium we can provide invaluable services to both students and staff.

Again, such services should be offered to faculty as a co-operative instructional effort in their curriculum. It is one thing to suggest such programs to an already over-worked faculty. It is quite another to offer to team-teach the necessary skills and content in the instructional program I've suggested. Admittedly, this is often not an easy task. Teachers are protective of their "class time" and their curriculum, as we are protective of our resources and facility. But it can happen; it is happening in many districts. When it does, as in Rensselaer Middle High School, the results speak for themselves.

It may appear that our library information program has reached its goal; that we have not only a wonderful physical setting, but the staffing, resources and co-operation needed to run an ideal program. For a small, inner city school district that may be close to the truth. But aspects of our program are adaptable to any educational environment. It takes administrative and faculty commitment, an instructional vision on the part of the Library Media Specialist–and a view of the Hudson River doesn't hurt.

REFERENCES

Basch, N.B. (1990). President's task force on the value of the information professional: conclusion: closing the service gap. *Special Libraries*, 81(2): 99-101.

Christou, C. (1988). Marketing the information center: a blueprint for action. *Wilson Library Bulletin*, 62(8): 35-40.

Cloyes, K. (1991). Corporate value of library services. *Special Libraries*, 82(3): 206-213.

Eddison, B. (1990). Strategies for success (or opportunities galore). *Special Libraries*, 81(2): 111-118.

McCaughan, D. (1991). Ingratiating yourself to all and sundry . . . or how I crawled my way to notoriety. *Special Libraries*, 82(3): 183-188.

Mills, C. (1991). Changing perceptions: making p.r. work for an information service. *Special Libraries*, 82(3): 189-195.

Paris, M. (1990). A management survey as the critical imperative for a new special library. *Special Libraries*, 81(4): 280-284.

Sirkin, A.F. (1991). Marketing planning for maximum effectiveness. *Special Libraries*, 82(1): 1-6.

Tumey, P. (1991). Developing a cohesive image for your special library. *Special Libraries*, 82(3): 165-170.

Warner, A.S. (1989). Special libraries and fees. *Special Libraries*, 80(4): 275-279.

Accountability for BI Programs in Academic Libraries: Key Issues for the 1990's

Craig Gibson

SUMMARY. The 1990's are seeing increased demands for account-ability and assessment in higher education. Business leaders and external evaluators are looking for evidence of problem-solving and decision-making skills in college graduates. Within this changing environment, instructional librarians have opportunities to integrate the problem-solving and decision-making skills taught in biblio-graphic instruction programs into the larger instructional goals of their institutions. These opportunities will require more accountabili-ty, knowledge, and expertise in librarians themselves, and will also necessitate the use of a wide range of practical assessment methods. Such techniques could include use of writing samples, interviews and ethnographic studies, flexible information skills matrices, and surveys of employers.

THE CONTEXT FOR ACCOUNTABILITY

Since the mid-1980's, calls for increased accountability in higher edu-cation have been heard repeatedly. Leaders in business and industry, a few activist governors, and a controversial Secretary of Education began the contemporary accountability movement. Administrators and faculty in colleges and universities have reacted in a variety of ways. Concerns about academic freedom, faculty governance, institutional control, and the potential abuse of quantitative measures are just a few of the reservations heard in academia.[1]

Craig Gibson is Head, Library User Education at Washington State University Libraries, Pullman, WA 99163.

99

Despite these concerns, pressure for accountability is likely to continue over the next decade.[2] Business leaders are increasingly concerned about the intellectual skills students are not acquiring in both public schools and college and universities, and emphasize the need for a more flexible and well-trained workforce to compete in the global economy. A recent report urges mutual accountability between employers, educators, and students, and points out that students should be taught not only the basic skills, but also "how to make decisions, to solve problems, to learn, to think a job through from start to finish, and to get a job done with and through other people."[3] The higher-order skills are increasingly in demand in a changing economy, and educators are called upon to develop innovative curricula that teach students how to apply knowledge in "real world" contexts, how to teach themselves on the job, and how to work in relatively autonomous groups to solve problems.

Assessing student learning itself–a part of the larger accountability issue–is receiving much attention. There is a great deal of discussion about developing methods of assessment that are appropriate to specific institutions, that measure what they are supposed to measure, and that are related to overall student development. Many thinkers on the subject of assessment point out that assessment should be multidimensional to get the most coherent picture of student learning. Assessment mandates by various states reflect different priorities and assumptions about the goals of assessment and of higher education itself.[4] Colleges and universities are faced with the societal demand for greater diversity and access to education, while at the same time proving that their students are indeed learning valuable skills for the workplace and for participation as citizens in society. Charting a course through these difficult waters may prove challenging, but the 1990's are already seeing these competing demands forced on higher education.

THE ROLE OF BIBLIOGRAPHIC INSTRUCTION
IN HIGHER EDUCATION

While accountability for traditional academic programs is fraught with difficulties, accountability for bibliographic instruction has ordinarily taken the form of occasional studies of student learning related to a specific library assignment, as well as quantitative measures such as number of BI sessions held and number of students reached. The often peripheral role of "library skills" in the curriculum has prevented the issue of accountability for bibliographic instruction from becoming a large one, except within libraries and among librarians.

The next ten years mark the fourth decade since the rebirth of the modern bibliographic instruction movement. Since the 1960's, with Patricia Knapp's classic Monteith College library experiment, to the present, with its controversies surrounding the information literacy movement, bibliographic instruction programs have grown rapidly, incorporated various modes of instruction, and reacted to the impact of information technologies in both positive and negative ways. In many instances, bibliographic instruction has also been evaluated, though such evaluation, as Mary George aptly points out, is often not of the highest quality.[5]

Several constraints impair the ability of the bibliographic instruction movement to make itself an established part of higher education. First, it is librarians, as George points out, who want instructional services, not students or faculty.[6] The "faculty problem" that Constance McCarthy commented on so compellingly is still very much with us.[7] The present generation of scholars and researchers have learned to use libraries, if at all, through trial-and-error, the helping hand of a friendly librarian, or through one research methods course in graduate school. Hence they project their own learning experiences with libraries onto their own students.

Second, librarians themselves often do not agree on what should be taught. Debate within the profession continues on "information literacy" as opposed to "library skills," and the controversy is likely to continue.[8] While debate is healthy, the profession will need, at some point, to put its thinking on the firmest epistemological footing possible. Libraries, academic computing, and the whole spectrum of campus information services are all intertwined in the information literacy debate, and librarians must come to understand the political implications of clinging to narrow "library-based" definitions of information-seeking skills. Professional redefinition is essential for librarians to maintain a role within academe. Within the profession itself, the old "information vs. instruction" debate continues, as if reference and bibliographic instruction were antithetical instead of complementary activities.[9] The epistemological problem of content for BI grows out of the training of librarians themselves, of course, in library school. The profession needs in the most serious and concerted way to address the issue of library education so that future information professionals have a firmer grounding in information literacy as a set of conceptual tools, and as a mode of learning appropriate for all citizens.

A third major constraint is that higher education itself is inherently conservative. New ideas such as "information literacy" are not always easy to promote because they cause unease among those with narrow discipline-based or department-based interests. The structures of traditional colleges and universities do not readily accommodate or encourage interdisciplinary or multi-disciplinary perspectives. Because of these traditional structures, nontraditional programs such as bibliographic instruction are often marginal at best.

A safe generalization to make about bibliographic instruction over the past twenty years is that it has developed from narrowly considered instruction in the use of specific tools to more conceptual teaching and learning. It especially has emphasized, in recent years, the importance of critical thinking and problem-solving. With more and more electronic tools available in libraries, these intellectual skills are considered critically important by many librarians. However, given that critical thinking and problem-solving are ordinarily not considered by many faculty as skills that can be taught outside traditional discipline-based structures, finding ways of teaching these skills within the limitations of a traditional curriculum poses a major challenge. Then, of course, the already crowded curriculum at most colleges and universities militates against any but the most cursory instruction in information skills. In such an environment, follow-up and assessment of student learning is problematic indeed, and a longitudinal perspective on students' information skills practically impossible.

OPPORTUNITIES

Because colleges and universities are now being required to demonstrate that students graduate with appropriate intellectual skills, librarians have the opportunity to promote information literacy programs. Information literacy skills, as described in the ALA Presidential Committee Report on Information Literacy,[10] are very similar to those problem-solving, decision-making, and self-teaching abilities identified as important by management and training consultants for the workplace in the global economy. Information literacy programs should be integrated into college and university curricula in a comprehensive manner; the instructional goals of such programs should be carefully tied to the overall instructional goals of the institution. Alliances with academic computing centers and other campus information agencies should be forged, so that a true campus-wide "information curriculum" can be developed–again, within the context of the overall instructional goals of the institution. There can be no accountability and no assessment of information literacy without well-thought-out and curriculum-integrated goals, as has been true of bibliographic instruction programs in the past.[11]

Institutional self-studies and the accreditation process provide another opportunity for information literacy programs to establish themselves. This is especially true, of course, if accrediting agencies themselves identify bibliographic instruction programs or information literacy as an essential part of the teaching/learning process. The Middle States Commission on Higher Education, for example, has prepared standards for institutions under its purview requiring bibliographic instruction as part of their curricula.[12] Such commitment is all too rare at the present. Librarians must work with campus administrators, faculty, legislators, governing boards, and accrediting agencies themselves to reform the teaching/learning process at their institutions. If the information literacy skills librarians believe in are to become a vital part of the curriculum in colleges and universities, then all the appropriate players must be convinced of the necessity of those skills. To date, the conceptual linkages have not been developed between the problem-solving and decision-making skills required in the workplace and the problem-solving and decision-making skills inculcated through information literacy programs. The connections and linkages must be made explicit and demonstrated clearly as part of overall assessment of student learning.

Librarians themselves must be willing to be accountable if information literacy programs are to succeed. Such accountability will require greater expertise in information management skills, instructional design, learning theory, institutional planning, and systems analysis. The professionalization of bibliographic instruction is now accepted within the library profession itself.[13] The real challenge for the 1990's is for instructional librarians to develop the necessary political skills to convince faculty colleagues and administrators that there is a coherent set of intellectual skills in information-seeking that can be taught, evaluated, and dovetailed with the larger goals of the institution. This political acumen will require a settled conviction about the importance of information skills to lifelong learning.

Accountability for bibliographic instruction programs in the past has often been only internal library accountability–that is, demonstrating to library directors and public service heads that so many students have attended BI sessions, so many handouts have been distributed, so many faculty seminars and end-user training sessions have been offered. While these quantitative measures may help show that bibliographic instruction is a "good thing," and is having an impact, such measures will not suffice for the future. Instructional librarians must demonstrate both internal accountability and external accountability–that is, they must show how the information-seeking skills students are taught support the institution's general instructional goals. This may mean, among other things, that librarians be evaluated along with their faculty colleagues as to teaching effectiveness; that they become experts on qualitative as well as quantitative assessment methods;[14] and that they be held accountable for conducting research on their own information literacy programs in order to gain tenure and promotion. Librarians should insist on a greater voice in curricular planning and assessment of student learning, but they will have to accept more responsibility and accountability in order to have that greater voice.

In a period when many colleges and universities are cutting some academic programs, consolidating others, and requiring assessment across the board, librarians will undoubtedly be expected to demonstrate effectiveness of information literacy programs to administrators and decision-makers outside the library. If retrenchment is the order of the day, however, librarians have an opportunity to show how static or shrinking budgets for collections need not lessen the effectiveness of their libraries. They need to show, instead, that an information literacy program means more intelligent use will be made of the collections available, that more innovative access and resource-sharing methods should be developed, and that the local collection can be a "window" on the larger universe of information—provided that students are taught basic principles of information structure and organization, and sound problem-solving methods for accessing that larger pool of information.[15]

PRACTICAL MEANS FOR INTEGRATION, ACCOUNTABILITY, AND ASSESSMENT

Librarians are only beginning to explore ways of proving the worth of bibliographic instruction programs in a larger institutional context. If the future promises more accountability and assessment for higher education in general, librarians will need to consider such methods as the following:

1. Work with faculty colleagues more closely in developing an "inquiry curriculum" that has "real world" connections, and emphasizing collaborative learning, critical thinking, and problem solving. Institutions such as The Evergreen State College and Hampshire College have developed curricula and academic structures that encourage the teaching of the intellectual skills called for by many leaders in society.[16] Legislators, business leaders, and accreditation officials may be very sympathetic to this kind of curriculum in the future.

2. Develop closer ties with writing-across-the-curriculum programs and critical thinking initiatives in local institutions, and link assess-

Patterns of Assessment105

ment methods for information literacy with the larger assessment goals of these programs. An example might involve having students write papers at significant points in their undergraduate careers discussing search strategies used in locating information for specific research projects. Writing used as an assessment tool may be much more revealing than objective examinations of information literacy skills because it encourages metacognition, "thinking-about-thinking," in students, and helps librarians get a clearer picture of the effectiveness of the problem-solving skills they hope to teach.

3. Design longitudinal studies of sample student populations and their competence in information-seeking over time–over a four-year undergraduate career, or after students declare a major. Such an approach would have many practical constraints, given the mobility of students, changes in curricula, and other variables. However, the qualitative assessment methods suggested by Frick,[17] including interviews and ethnographic studies, could be very useful for this approach. Students within a particular major or career path, honors students, or other populations who might have repeated, frequent experiences with bibliographic instruction, could be interviewed to assess changes in their use of information resources.

4. Work with academic departments to develop "information-seeking practicums" as part of students' coursework. These courses would require use of a broader spectrum of information sources than traditional library materials. In a field such as journalism or communications, for example, "extra-library" information sources are vital.[18] Local experts, community organizations, remote databases, municipal archives, and professional associations are just a few information sources students could tap as part of the broader "information universe." Requiring students to gain experience with both library and non-library information sources can only strengthen the institution's ability to show external evaluators that students are gaining "real world" skills.

5. Promote the idea of an "information literacy" oral examination for graduating seniors who might have to demonstrate competence in other areas through the oral exam method. Obviously, this assessment technique would be more feasible at smaller institutions. However, it could be a most revealing method if used properly. A hypothetical "information problem" related to the student's major and with potential relevance to his chosen career could be posed, and the student would be asked to discuss how, where, and why he would find information to solve that problem.

6. Design an information skills matrix similar to that developed at Penn State University Libraries,[19] and tie assessment methods to that matrix. An information literacy program requiring increasingly sophisticated skills of undergraduates over four years is highly desirable but difficult to implement because of the idiosyncrasies of curricula in local institutions and the shifting nature of undergraduate student populations (large influxes of transfer students, for example). A flexible information skills matrix could be used to determine what students should master at "basic" and "advanced" levels. A senior may function at a "basic" level, while a sophomore may have a stronger background and therefore work at an "advanced" level. Research tutorials, term paper counseling sessions, and end-user training services, already in place in many academic libraries, could be designed and offered more comprehensively to provide maximum opportunity for all students to gain at least the basic skills by the time they graduate. A variety of assessment methods could then be used to learn whether they have gained the necessary skills at those different levels. These methods could include evaluation of essays, journal writing, bibliographies, and other student projects.

7. Survey employers of graduates to obtain a better picture of the long-term effect of the information literacy skills taught to students as undergraduates. This method has been used by the Mann Library at Cornell University as a follow-up to implementation of its well-known information literacy program.[20] There is much potential in this method for demonstrating that information literacy is a continuum, a lifelong process. Relevance to the world of work and the professions will be one of the most telling points in favor of information literacy programs in 1990's.

Other assessment tools will need to be developed to get the most coherent picture possible of student learning. As in the past, working more closely with faculty will be essential. More collaboration with student services personnel–admissions, advising and counseling, special academic programs, among others–will be necessary to create a full range of assessment methods. Finally, gaining the commitment of campus administrators such as Deans and Provosts to information literacy will be necessary to institutionalize the changes.[21]

Accountability in bibliographic instruction/information literacy means greater knowledge, expertise, and responsibility will be required of librarians. They will have to create opportunities for integrating "information literacy across the curriculum," and commit themselves to working with library and information professionals in all settings–public schools, community colleges, and public and special libraries. All recognized professions, including librarianship, possess a body of knowledge, standards of behavior and ethics, and a commitment to service. In developing improved methods of assessment for student learning based on that body of knowledge and service commitment, librarians will demonstrate their own accountability and professionalism.

REFERENCES

1. Patricia Thrash, "Educational 'Outcomes' in the Accrediting Process," *Academe: Bulletin of the American Association of University Professors* 74(July-August 1988): 16-18.

2. Kenneth P. Mortimer and Sheila R. Edwards, "A President's View of the 1990's," in *An Agenda for the New Decade*, ed. Larry W. Jones and Franz A. Nowotny (San Francisco: Jossey-Bass 1990): 73-79.

3. Anthony P. Carnevale and Janet W. Johnston, *Training America: Strategies for the Nation* (Alexandria, VA: American Society for Training and Development), p.7.

4. Charles R. O'Brien and Marsha J. Hare, "Assessing Educational Outcomes: Basic Issues for Higher Education," *College Student Journal* 23(Summer 1989): 126-130.

5. Mary W. George, "Instructional Services," in *Academic Libraries: Research Perspectives*, ed. Mary Jo Lynch and Arthur Young (Chicago: American Library Association, 1990), pp.120-125.

6. George, p.107.

7. Constance McCarthy, "The Faculty Problem," *Journal of Academic Librarianship* 11(July 1985): 142-145.

8. Lawrence J. McCrank, "Information Literacy: A Bogus Bandwagon?" *Library Journal* 116(May 1, 1991): 38-42.

9. For an excellent discussion of professional models, see: Brian Neilsen, "Alternative Professional Models in the Information Age," in *Bibliographic Instruction: The Second Generation*, ed. Constance A. Mellon (Littleton, CO: Libraries Unlimited, 1987): 24-37.

10. American Library Association, Presidential Committee on Information Literacy, *Final Report* (Chicago: American Library Association, 1989).

11. A well-known example of an evaluated bibliographic instruction program is that of Ohio State University. See: Virginia Tiefel, "Evaluating a Library User Education Program: A Decade of Experience," *College & Research Libraries* 50(March 1989): 249-259.

12. Marilyn Lutzker, "Bibliographic Instruction and Accreditation in Higher Education," *College & Research Librarian News* 51(January 1990), p.14.

13. Donald J. Kenney, "Library Instruction in the 1980's: Where Has It Been and Where Is It Going?" in *Bibliographic Instruction: The Second Generation*, ed. Constance A. Mellon (Littleton, CO: Libraries Unlimited, 1987), pp.192-194.

14. Elizabeth Frick, "Qualitative Evaluation of User Education Programs: The Best Choice?" *Research Strategies* 8(Winter 1990): 4-13.

15. Patricia Breivik and E. Gordon Gee, *Information Literacy: Revolution in the Library* (New York: American Council on Education, MacMillan, 1989), p. 28.

16. A compelling statement of the Evergreen State philosophy of education, and of the role of librarians in higher education, is found in: Patrick Hill, "Who Will Lead the Reform of Higher Education? Librarians, Of Course!" *Washington Center News* 5(Winter 1991): 3-8. For a discussion of the Hampshire College philosophy, see: Frederick Stirton Weaver, "Liberal Education, Inquiry and Academic Organization," in *Promoting Inquiry in Undergraduate Learning*, ed. Frederick Stirton Weaver (San Francisco: Jossey Bass, 1989): 3-16.

17. Frick, pp. 4-11.

18. Barbara MacAdam, "Information Literacy: Models for the Curriculum," *College & Research Libraries News* 5(November 1990), p. 948.

19. Carol Wright and Mary Ellen Larson, "Basic Information Access Skills: Curriculum Design Using A Matrix Approach," *Research Strategies* 8(Summer 1990): 104-115.

20. Bill Coons, Presentation at 17th National LOEX Conference, "Coping With Information Illiteracy: Bibliographic Instruction for the Information Age," May 4, 1989, Ann Arbor, Michigan.

21. Breivik, p. 40

IV. TAKING HUMAN BEINGS INTO ACCOUNT

Humanism and Automation: Working with People in the Library Automation Process

Karen A. Nuckolls

SUMMARY. In the automation process, it is very important to keep the human factor before you at all times. People who are computer-shy need to be informed, and *kept* informed, about each step the library takes on the road to automation. It is vital not only to communicate often with the staff as each goal is reached, but to keep the public informed as well. Patrons who know what to expect from the system chosen will be able to use the system to their advantage. There are various steps that can be taken to alleviate fear and uncertainty of the future.

Webster's Intercollegiate Dictionary defines humanism as "A way of life centered on human interests or values." Incompatible as it might seem in the installation of library systems, you need to remember that the "human" aspect is your key to either success or failure in this endeavor.

Karen A. Nuckolls is Head of Technical Services, System Administrator and Associate Professor, at Skidmore College Library, Saratoga Springs, NY 12866.

109

STEPS TO IMPLEMENTATION

The process usually begins with an announcement at the first library staff meeting every fall: "We are looking at automated library systems," and moves on to "We have decided on a system; now we are waiting for the funds." The last message can be repeated at each fall meeting for several years. And then, one fall the funds are there; and then the contract is signed. A prescribed series of steps follow:

1. Demonstration of the system by the vendor
2. Documentation and forms arrive
3. Meetings with library staff
4. Meetings with the Computer Center staff
5. Orientation of System Administrator
6. Field trip(s) to a system site
7. Effective communication among staff and patrons
8. Training on-site
9. Bringing up modules:
   a. manuals
   b. brochures
   c. tutorials
   d. informal meetings

After contract signing, a representative from our vendor demonstrated the system to the library staff and anyone else on campus who was interested. There were both morning and afternoon sessions for each module that had been purchased. The documentation started arriving–and arriving. We had two volumes of forms to fill out, describing to our vendor how we wanted our search menus to look, our summary screens to look, whether we wanted the MARC or Card format–and in which modules, and so on. These had to be completed before attending the vendor's orientation session. Involving the staff in the automation process is essential to the smooth installation and running of the system. "The importance of the human factor must not be underestimated. If people respond badly to automation, the anticipated effectiveness of the system will not be achieved."[1] Successfully working with (and convincing) the staff around you that this will work gives them a good feeling about the system. It will, more importantly, affect *how* they work with the system, and their positive attitudes will carry over to the patrons they assist.

I decided to have multiple meetings devoted to one module at a time–but anyone on the staff could attend any of the meetings. Relevant sections of the forms were handed out, and as we read over the chapters, I asked for input, especially in those areas of the library daily routine I was unfamiliar with. Staff members who might have concerns should be listened to, as their concerns may become patron concerns encountered later.

INTEGRATING LIBRARY FUNCTIONS

As the system is successfully implemented, changes in the way one thinks about library functions have to occur. Traditionally, Technical Services (Cataloging) has been involved in library automation. OCLC and RLIN began as cataloging utilities and are now involved in other areas of library service. In implementing an integrated system, it is not only cataloging that is involved: there is now a module for each area of the library to design, to plan for and to call its own. Acquisitions, Circulation, Serials and Reference staff can have their say as to how a system will look and perform. Reference, in particular, should be solicited for patron feedback. Librarians in Public Service areas are the most familiar with search methods used, both by themselves and their users. A "Search Tracking Option" available in the system will tell them even more about library users' search strategies.

As each module is part of an integrated whole, each area or function of the library will be visible to others. A change made within one module will have an effect on another, bringing each function of the library together as never before. Errors in an entry can no longer hide in a card drawer, perhaps to be discovered one day. Now they are there for all to see. This can terrify (or annoy) staff. It should be emphasized that perfection should not be expected. Corrections can be made simply, no longer involving pulling and erasing of cards. Staff must realize that the CARD catalog is no more, and that THINKING in terms of a card catalog is not desirable. Users have been quick to spot problems, errors, and typos in the PAC. Forms for library staff and patrons to fill out detailing these discoveries should then be given to Cataloging for correction.

At about the same time staff meetings took place, weekly meetings began with personnel in the campus computer center who would be responsible for working with us on a day-to-day basis, setting up and maintaining our system.

Last fall, two months before Cataloging training was scheduled to begin, the staff traveled by bus to a library which had installed the system we had purchased. Touring their corresponding work areas to see how their respective modules functioned, our staff left with a very positive attitude about our automation project. Instead of watching a video or reading a manual, they had actually had valuable hands-on experience!

COMMUNICATING AND TRAINING

One of our most important communication resources on campus is our local E-Mail system. When I arrived on campus three years ago, it had just been introduced in the library. The majority of the staff did not bother to learn it, especially as they had to have access to a terminal–and not many had convenient access. However, as the funds were approved for automating the library, terminals were purchased for every staff member. These terminals would enable them to access the new system from their desks. Our VAX mail system began to be used by staff more often. When retrospective conversion took place several summers ago, reports were sent out detailing which shelflist drawers had been sent to OCLC.

Information about training schedules and requirements was passed on to the staff. Each step of the automation process was communicated via E-mail. Communication is the most effective way of making the staff feel comfortable with the system, and to eliminate "fear of the unknown." If electronic mail access is not available, then perhaps a brief weekly newsletter could be sent out, or weekly update meetings held.

Some staff members may not think it useful to sit through training sessions. One assistant in Acquisitions felt that since she worked with serials (a separate module), it was not necessary to attend the session. But after training, she was glad she did attend–there was information that she found valuable to her job. Another staff member was quite nervous about the training. We had a series of DOS workshops in the library which she had difficulty with. Training on the new system was a very different experience for her, and she really did enjoy it.

As Cataloging went "live," the staff began writing down their daily tasks. This can aid in formulating questions to ask before, during and after training. Every area of the library should have printed manuals. How can one know what to change until one knows his/her present duties? "Flexibility" is an important part of this–what is contained in the manual is not written in stone, but will no doubt change many times in the months ahead.

PUBLICITY AND THE PATRON

As time drew near, preparatory to bringing up the PAC, a brief instructional sheet was prepared–to be placed around the library for patron usage of the system. The computer center placed a tutorial online on the VAX for anyone on campus to access to learn how to use the PAC. Dial-up access was available at the same time–and eagerly used by the faculty, among others.

Publicity about the online catalog should be available through articles in the student and campus newspapers. If the library itself has a newsletter, ample opportunity should be made available to devote several issues to library automation. Careful consideration should be given to statements made about when the system will "go live"–always vaguely stated. Bringing up each module according to a firm schedule would be nice, but it rarely happens. Committing oneself to a definite date is not wise, especially in print. Then, no one will be disappointed when the date passes. Patrons will either embrace the PAC, or continue using the card catalog. Perhaps one of the most difficult facts about the online catalog for them to realize is that the amount of information, especially in a newly installed PAC, is not infinite. Most likely, the more difficult cataloging records, such as media materials, serials, government documents and special collections, will not be present. Therefore the card catalog still serves a purpose, if only (hopefully) temporary. This should be made apparent with signs placed around *both* catalogs. "One thing is clear. Computer-accessible records must contain the information the reader considers necessary, which is not always the same as that prescribed as necessary to a librarian."[2] When contemplating what to include in the card format, for example, remember it is to be used by the patron. Don't clutter it with information that will only confuse the user. And be open to suggestions, especially from the Public Services staff. There may be information to add that you may not have ever considered before. The MARC format should contain all the information a cataloger needs. Also remember to carefully work through the many HELP screens available in the PAC, and consider whether any changes should be made to enhance user-friendliness.

Before bringing up Circulation, be very thoroughly versed in your library's policies–and what your system can do; for flexibility will definitely increase here. Know what you want to change. This will usually have a bearing on your patrons. Some may be used to a looser, more convenient, circulation system. Be prepared to deal with this. You will receive complaints. Try to funnel them to one or two people on the staff, so that each patron is given the answer in the same way.

Just as each module becomes operational, a series of meetings with the staff involved should be held. Working through the menus, and deciding on changes (if any), again reinforces the workflow within the module. After one or two weeks of "liveness," additional meetings should continue, to discuss any problems or questions that might have come up (and that could wait).

It has been interesting to see how staff that "tolerated" OCLC at first now access and work in the system with such ease. *They* take the initiative and discover how a function works. They read the manuals. It is their system. And this positive attitude is passed on to our patrons.

REFERENCES

1. Hilary Dyer and Anne Morris, *Human Aspects of Library Automation* (Brookfield, VT: Gower Pub. Co., c1990), p. xii.

2. Jack Meadows, "Human Aspects of Electronically Stored Information–The Library User," *IATUL Quarterly* 2.3 (Sept. 1988): 162.

Assessing and Evaluating Diversity in the Reference Department

Deborah A. Curry

SUMMARY. Evaluation and assessment of reference services, reference collections, and reference librarians at academic libraries is a concern shared by many. New methods and criteria are debated extensively in library literature. Rarely, however, has any attention been given to the concepts of diversity and multiculturalism when planning strategies for assessing and evaluating staff and collections. Perhaps with the advent of curriculum that supports pluralism and the changing demographics of many communities and campuses, the time has come to examine the commitment reference departments are willing to make to strengthen and diversify their staff and collections.

The [library], . . . is the pivotal campus facility where all groups and interests intersect. This is an appropriate role for an academic library to fill, for by its very nature the library is a haven for diversity.[1]

Articles abound in library literature on the need for evaluation and assessment in academic libraries of reference services, reference collections and reference librarians. But what is interesting to note here is that very few make mention of criteria that might take into consideration the concepts of diversity–racial or ethnic, pluralism, and/or multiculturalism.

The purpose of this article is to (1) generate discussion of these concepts in relation to the evaluation and assessment of reference services and reference collections, and (2) where discussion has begun, to encourage implementation of passive rhetoric into progressive, constructive action.

Deborah A. Curry is Social Sciences Bibliographer/Reference Librarian at the University at Albany, 1400 Washington Avenue, Albany, NY 12222.

As institutions based within academe, especially where diversity has become a mandate, academic libraries must become change agents in the formulation of reference departments that reflect the racial and ethnic diversity of the population which they serve. By the beginning of the 21st century the racially defined protected class groups–African Americans, Hispanic Americans, Asian and Pacific Islanders and Native American Indians–will comprise nearly one-third of our nation's population. Projections for the non-white population group, of 18-24 years old, reflect a potential increase in the number of candidates for admission at our institutions of higher education. Given the fact that in 1986 over 2 million non-white students were enrolled in U.S. colleges and universities, and given the promise of phenomenal growth by the year 2025, one can speculate on the future shifting complexions of many communities and college campuses.[2] At least, they should shape not only the reference collections offered, but the complexion of the reference department as well.

REFERENCE STAFF

Although demographics indicate that the Black and Hispanic components of our population comprise nearly twenty percent of all Americans, academic libraries have been content to base their minority recruiting/retention goals at about 5% based on the pool of minority candidates available . . . [3]

Articles in library literature attest to the interest spurred by the discussion of recruitment of non-white librarians. What is more evident, however, is that although there has been and continues to be a significant amount of discussion focused on this issue, a sort of Band-Aid approach has been taken to increase the numbers of non-white librarians in the profession. Short term solutions produce short term results. Most of these solutions seem to be driven by affirmative action goals and unrealistic time tables set by administrators. If the administrative push to recruit and hire non-white librarians and staff is not supported by the rank and file, integration and acceptance into the workplace will not be a smooth one. Efforts may be confined to hiring a number and not on understanding how a non-white librarian can and perhaps should be a change agent or catalyst for the department in assessing and evaluating its attitudes, sensitivities and knowledge of multicultural values. The retention of non-white librarians/staff may depend on the level of commitment to inclusion and acceptance and to change the library and its workers are willing to make.

Although the numbers seem destined to defeat the effort, there are various ways to combat the existence of a racially homogeneous staff, and the picture is not as bleak as it would seem. Here in New York State there has been a modicum of success in courting undergraduates to the profession. SUNY Stony Brook's libraries have had some success with its internship program.[4] The University at Albany's libraries have selected three seniors to begin its new internship program this academic year. These two programs were specifically designed to create a vehicle for students interested in librarianship to gain experience in the field, and with financial commitment, afford them the opportunity to attend the University at Albany's School of Information Science and Policy.

Internships for undergraduates are one way to increase the numbers of prospective librarians. Once into the profession, however, the concern must be focused on attrition. Retaining non-white librarians continues to be a primary concern for librarianship. Issues such as lack of advancement, and the inability to create mentoring relationships with tenured librarians lead to frustration and dissatisfaction. Non-white librarians often comment that colleagues question their ability and knowledge due to affirmative action hiring. There is also the daily added pressure of enduring behavior that appears racially motivated. A combination of these factors can certainly disillusion even the most dedicated and committed librarian.

These are tough issues to discuss. Nevertheless, providing diversity in the reference staff allows for the opportunity of providing diversity in other areas of reference. Evaluating the strength of a reference department must include a thorough investigation of how serious a commitment to diversity the organization is willing to make.

REFERENCE COLLECTIONS

Multicultural understanding, diversity appreciation, and diversity awareness are all terms used to designate the movement on the nation's campuses to encourage and support in student, faculty, and staff the kinds of attitudes and outlooks that will lead to a valuing of diversity.[5]

Building reference collections that meet the changing needs of an increasingly diverse student and faculty population is challenging. Assessing curriculum needs for a given institution and keeping reference materials current can be a time-consuming task. However, when coupled with the added responsibility of acquiring materials representative of a diverse population and curricula, the effort may include not only political commitment, but perseverance and ingenuity.

Making sure the collection development policy created by the department contains a strong statement on the need to include materials that support ethnic and racial diversity in research as well as courses is essential. Allowing for flexibility in format and scope is also important. It may be necessary to include sources much more narrow in scope than would ordinarily be collected. Strengthening the reference collection by including materials relevant to multiculturalism can be problematic. The road is not paved for easy access.

Adversity does not, however, preclude the inclusion of materials that support the themes of racial and ethnic diversity and multiculturalism. Publishing trends for reference materials that support research in racial and ethnic diversity tend to be sporadic. For example, reference materials on African Americans surfaced in the late 1970's in abundance with the emergence of Black Studies programs, but standard, consistently updated materials remained scarce until the mid 1980's. With the advent of multiculturalism, the publishing industry has renewed its interest and the climate for new and varying titles has gained momentum. Much the same can be said for materials on Hispanic Americans and Native American Indians. Examples of new materials include Gale Research's *Statistical Record of Black America,* and *Who's Who Among Hispanic Americans, 1991-1992.* Praxis Publications' *1989 Guide to Multicultural Resources,* is an example of material published by a small press.

Though sources are being published, access to reviews or announcements of new reference materials is not always readily available. Of late, several small alternative presses, often racially based, have begun publishing reference sources that may never be reviewed in library literature. *Library Journal, Choice,* and *Publisher's Weekly* as well as other standard library review journals do not often include works published by non-mainstream presses. Alternative sources that focus on issues of diversity will often bring about more successful results. For example, *Black Books Bulletin* published by Third World Press, and *ABBWA Journal* published by the American Black Book Writers Association are examples of review sources not always mentioned in courses on collection development which might prove fruitful when selecting materials in support of a diverse reference collection.

However, when reviews are available, they are often not thorough enough for the librarian to evaluate quality. This, of course, poses the question of whether or not to purchase a particular source, albeit a poor one, that offers information important for diversity. Selectors need to keep in mind that reviews, after all, are often subjective and in the final analysis, patron use or lack thereof will gauge the value, if not the accuracy, of a source. It may be more prudent to purchase a source of poor quality that offers material not available elsewhere than not to have that information at all.

FINAL THOUGHTS

Just as educators have been challenged to become change agents, academic librarians must also become agents of change within their institutions. The reference department is a pivotal area at which effective change can occur.

As a potentially progressive unit, the reference department should create a clear image of its mission. It should assess as a group the need for diversity in all facets of the department. Providing a climate conducive to change and growth is vital. The department must create a vision, and then challenge colleagues to translate this vision into a plan of action with a clear set of goals–both short and long term. The department as an allied force can rally the organization in support of these goals.

Goals set forth by the reference department could easily include the efforts of everyone in the library. Such goals include the need to:

1. Strengthen efforts to increase the number of non-white librarians on its staff . . .
2. Continue to seek innovative methods to employ non-white students within the department . . .
3. Create a task force whose mandate is to challenge the assessment and evaluation of services offered by the department . . .
4. Develop a reference collection that supports the concept of multiculturalism.

When evaluating the strength of reference departments, it is imperative that academic librarians examine goals and ascertain that they reflect the task at hand–to create an environment within the library and hence, the institution itself, that is sensitive to, and futuristic in, its approach to issues of diversity.

It is necessary to surpass the tendency to maintain the status quo and progress to the stage of developing viable reference departments. The future of the profession depends upon it.

REFERENCES

1. Robert M. Warner. *Point of Intersection: the University Library and the Pluralistic Campus Community.* (Ann Arbor, MI: University of Michigan Library, 1988).

2. *1989-1990 Fact Book on Higher Education.* (Washington, D.C.: American Council on Higher Education, 1989).

3. Cliff Glaviano and R. Errol Lam. "Academic Libraries and Affirmative Action: Approaching Cultural Diversity in the 1990's." *College and Research Libraries* (November 1990).

4. Curtis Kendrick et al. "Minority Internship/Scholarship in Library and Information Science." *College and Research Libraries News* (November 1990).

5. Marilyn Shaver. *Cultural Diversity Programming in ARL Libraries.* (Washington D.C.: Office of Management Services, Association of Research Libraries, no. 165, 1990.)

Facing Personal Evaluation: A Mentoring Program Supports Professional Staff Undergoing Tenure Review

Annalisa R. Van Avery

SUMMARY. When librarians and library professionals have faculty status, they will face a rigorous evaluation for tenure or permanent appointment. Responding to a climate of higher professional standards and expectations for their faculty, the University Libraries of the State University of New York at Albany have instituted a mentoring program to support professional development and allay anxiety among untenured faculty. The Program Coordinator's task is to discover the real needs of both mentees and mentors and to provide a varied program of events and opportunities in which those needs can be met. Individual mentoring relationships and group discussions both play a role in achieving this goal.

Evaluating personnel is a crucial component of any organization's management. In a sense, the most crucial evaluation is done when the employer chooses among candidates for a position, but that is only the beginning. Working conditions and tasks are constantly changing, and people also develop and change, for better or worse. In most organizations evaluations are done more or less regularly, and they have several functions: to praise good work that has been done, to warn those who are not satisfying their employer's expectations, to ascertain employees' ambitions and plans, to encourage those with high potential to grow professionally,

Annalisa R. Van Avery is Periodicals Cataloger and Mentoring Program Coordinator at the University Libraries, University at Albany, State University of New York, 1400 Washington Avenue, Albany, NY 12222.

and generally to keep track of what human resources are available while at the same time shaping those resources to the organization's needs.

Being evaluated as a professional is at best an educational and constructive experience, but it is also anxiety-producing. In academic libraries where the professional staff have faculty status, they will go through a permanent appointment review, and the results of that review will determine whether the applicant may continue to work at that institution. Naturally a judgment that has such drastic personal, professional and economic consequences will provoke strong emotional reactions, including anxiety, suspense, foreboding, and in some cases anger or panic. This is true for all faculty, but librarians have an additional aspect to consider, and that is that when their applications have progressed from the library to a higher level of review, people will be evaluating them who may have little understanding of what librarians do, or how excellence in librarianship should be measured.

ENVIRONMENT AND HISTORY

At the University at Albany, State University of New York, librarians have faculty status. As the University itself has grown in quality and stature, standards for faculty have naturally risen, and librarians have been subject to these pressures along with their teaching colleagues.

Our mentoring program was one logical and necessary result of the gradual raising of standards for tenure-track library faculty. For years there had tended to be a sort of annual debate between the University Committee on Promotions and Continuing Appointment (CPCA) and the Library Faculty over the qualifications of the librarians coming up before the Committee for either promotions or continuing appointment decisions. The Library had its own criteria by which we evaluated our peers, but that was not an official document. The CPCA was continually trying to judge librarians by *their* criteria, which were designed for teaching faculty. They usually complained that librarians did not have enough research publications, and they belittled or overlooked many of the other professional activities which librarians consider important. Every few years the Library Academic Faculty felt compelled to revise the criteria, and those gradually became more comparable to the teaching faculty's in wording, if not in spirit, but at the same time we were always insisting that librarians are different. Particular bones of contention were always the importance of peer review as opposed to external review, publishing and research, the primacy of excellence in librarianship, and how that can be demonstrated.

As the standards became more stringent under criticism from the CPCA, the anxiety level became higher also. Many people felt the need to do more to help librarians prepare for review, to compensate for the fact that it was becoming more and more difficult to get through it. One of the ideas proposed was to have a mentoring program, and the Library's Professional Activities Committee started doing literature searches and writing letters to university libraries which purportedly had active mentoring programs. In 1987 the Committee, with considerable input from members of the Library Faculty, produced "Mentoring Goals and Guidelines" (see Appendix I). This statement has been the foundation of the Mentoring Program at the University Libraries to this day.

For several years, the mentoring program remained unimplemented, but the struggle over librarians' criteria continued. In 1989 the new Director of the University Libraries and Dean of the Library Faculty indicated that one of her primary goals was to have the Library Faculty recognized and respected as peers by the University Faculty as a whole. She called a library faculty forum, and advised the librarians that the library cannot operate independently from its environment. We needed to bring our criteria more truly in line with the rest of the University, and to accept the fact that they would become more demanding. We also needed to communicate with the University Senate and get our criteria understood and approved by them. If we do this, she said, then finally we must also inspire, nurture and support our newly hired members, so they can be successful in living up to the more rigorous standards.

During the 1989-90 academic year, the Personnel Policies Committee hammered out a sweeping revision of the criteria for promotion and tenure, and the new document was discussed and approved by the University Senate. It was quite well received, and several members of the Senate later expressed their appreciation and said that they understood the role of librarians much more clearly after the discussion. Since membership in the Senate and the CPCA is constantly turning over, there will always be the need to educate teaching faculty about the nature of librarianship. Nevertheless, we now have a good foundation for these discussions.

FORMATION OF THE MENTORING PROGRAM

Early in 1990, The Library Faculty felt an urgent need for action on the mentoring program, since there were a number of untenured librarians who would soon have to be evaluated under the more stringent criteria.

The author was elected to coordinate the program. A bibliography which had been compiled in 1989 by Albany librarian Mary Jane Brustman was very helpful in the planning of the program.[1] One very useful basic article was "Establishing a Formalized Mentoring Program," by Linda Phillips-Jones.[2] Also useful in a cautionary sense was "Take My Mentor, Please!" by Peter Kizilos,[3] which pointed out several typical problems characteristic of formal mentoring programs. Our mentoring program was designed specifically to avoid some of the situations he described. For example, Kizilos warned that assigned mentors may not welcome that duty, so we made sure that our entire program was voluntary. Also, the mentor/mentee relationship may become too close, isolating the pair from the organization, or there may be conflicts between the mentor and the mentee's supervisor, or the mentor may see the mentee as a rival. To avoid these pitfalls, we ruled that the mentor and mentee should not be in the same department, and there would be group activities also.

To begin the program, separate letters and survey forms were sent to all tenured librarians and to newer untenured librarians. There was also an interesting "in-between" group of people who were not new, but were still untenured. These were long-term part-timers and people so close to their tenure review that they probably would not benefit too much from a new mentoring program. In fact, most were so experienced that they could be mentors themselves. They were invited to join the program in any role they wished. When all the surveys came back, there were about twenty people interested in one aspect or another of mentoring. Not all wanted to be mentees or mentors–some were willing to speak on particular subjects, or help in some other way. Finally there were five people who wanted mentors, and eight tenured librarians who were willing to be mentors.

Besides the determination that mentee and mentor should be from different departments, two other assumptions influenced our actions at the time. In retrospect, it is clear that these assumptions were somewhat naive. One was that the essence of a mentoring program is in the mentor/mentee pairs, and therefore the first order of business is to form these pairs. The other assumption was that once pairs were formed, the mentors would know what to do, and the program would "run itself" without much more action on the part of the coordinator. In fact, some people thrive with assigned mentors and others do not. Also, would-be mentors need a clear idea of what is expected of them. The success or failure of a mentor/mentee relationship could affect the reputation and self-esteem of the mentor as much as the mentee.

MENTORS AND MENTEES

Optimistically, we worked on forming pairs as carefully and tactfully as we could. A get-acquainted meeting was held, and then everyone was asked to indicate their first, second, and third choice of partners. No pairs were assigned until the Coordinator had spoken privately to everyone to be sure it was OK. When five pairs were agreed upon, notices were sent out saying "your mentor/mentee is. . . ." It was constantly stressed that anyone could change partners at any time if they were not happy, but in reality that is hard to do tactfully. No one ever asked to change partners. However, one of the pairs was not too successful, and eventually stopped seeing each other. Forming pairs is truly a delicate matter, and one needs to be ultra sensitive to all clues. Some people are imbued with such team spirit that they will do their best to cooperate no matter what, but others have a more independent attitude. In a voluntary program, everyone must respect people's right to make their own choices, including the choice of leaving the program.

After mentor/mentee pairs were chosen, two more meetings were held. The mentors got together and shared ideas about what they were going to do. Then a Brown Bag Lunch Program on Professional Activities was presented for the whole library faculty. People spoke on the criteria and what is expected of library faculty, professional organizations, doing library research, writing and getting published, legislative and public interests, and University life and service. Actually each of these topics is worth a whole program, so this was really just an overview. It was designed to make the newer librarians aware of what is out there to do, and to get them thinking about what they wished to be involved in, and whom to see about it.

The mentoring program then entered the phase where the mentoring pairs were free to do their own thing at their own pace. From time to time I might ask people how it was going, but mostly I left them alone until the pairs had been active for about six months. Then I sent out an evaluation survey. The survey asked for ideas for group meetings, comments and criticisms, and ideas for improving the program. It was hoped that input from participants would reveal continuing needs and directions for the future of the program. Survey results were actually not that clear. Most of the returns agreed that the mentoring program was beneficial overall, and expressed satisfaction with partners, but there was less enthusiasm about other aspects of the program. Only one respondent had specific suggestions, yet there were indications that not all needs were being met.

In the meantime, the original intent of the Mentoring Program had included library professionals as well as librarians. At the University at Albany, professionals are also considered faculty. They go through a permanent appointment review process, and they are also expected to have some professional activities and University service. In the spring of 1991, work was started on mentoring for professionals.

PROGRAM FOR PROFESSIONALS

The mentoring program for professionals has developed quite differently from the librarians' experience. Instead of merely reading articles on mentoring myself, I sent copies of some thought-provoking articles with the preliminary interest survey. I conferred extensively with our professionals at various departments and levels, including our Library Personnel Officer, and also with the Library Director and some supervisors of professionals. My goal was to really understand their needs and experiences in this library environment. Some of our professionals are taking courses at the library school or already have their MLS. Others are not planning to become librarians at all. These two groups have some needs in common, but also have some very different plans, goals and motivations for working. At the time the professional program was taking shape, I was also meeting with librarian mentors and mentees, and as we critiqued what has been done and made plans for the future, I tried to apply to the professionals' program the lessons learned from the librarians, so as to avoid making the same mistakes again.

For example, the first get acquainted meeting with librarian mentors and mentees was very stiff and uncomfortable. People were too aware that they would be choosing partners, and they were being sized up. With this new group, I first scheduled separate meetings with potential mentees and mentors, and told both groups that we would not be pairing up for a while. We would have some group events first, and only then decide whether we want to pair up at all, or do things entirely differently. Then the get-acquainted meeting was a brown-bag lunch where all sat around one big table, and the discussion was informal and friendly. Members of the group were full of ideas for professionals, and everyone seemed to come away with a good feeling.

Another experience I did not wish to repeat was that Professional Activities presentation, in which we had tried to cover practically the whole library world in one hour. Each speaker had only five minutes, and could hardly begin to cover his subject. Members of the audience had wanted to discuss some things more fully, but there had not been time. We have learned to limit what we will cover at any one time, and give people a chance to really talk. That talk and interchange of ideas is often the most important part of a session!

One thing that came out very strongly from the first professional mentees' meeting was their anxiety about the permanent appointment process. They had heard all kinds of rumors. Those going to Library School were worried that once they got that degree, the library would not want them as professionals, and would not grant them permanent appointment, even if they wanted to stay. Yet a librarian's position may not be easy to find in the current economic climate. We scheduled a meeting, open to the whole faculty, on the permanent appointment process for professionals. Our personnel officer gave an excellent description of how the process is set up, with sample documents. Then two professionals who have received permanent appointment spoke about what professional activities they had done, and how they felt about it. Two supervisors of professionals (one a librarian, and the other a grade five professional) spoke about their role in seeing their staff people through it. There were a lot of questions, and it was a really informative meeting for everyone who attended.

CURRENT STATUS AND PLANS

This is more or less where the program stands as of August 1991. Since the program was begun with the original five mentees, the University at Albany has hired no new librarians, so we still need to work out how we will fold new people into a continuing system. Originally it was proposed that a new person would be allowed to settle into their job for perhaps three months before being assigned a mentor. At the evaluation meetings we had in the spring of 1991, librarian mentees and mentors both indicated interest in a program on doing research. Plans are being formed for a program on the types of research that library science lends itself to, current trends in the literature, and some areas where work really needs to be done, either to benefit our library or the profession as a whole. In addition, the professionals' mentoring group has been promised a program on how they can enrich their jobs and get involved in library and university service. That group will also be making some decisions on forming mentor/mentee pairs.

What can the reader learn from Albany's experience? One thing is clear: if your institution has faculty status and any kind of continuing appointment process, the newer members of your staff do have a lot of anxieties about the ordeal before them, and they do appreciate attention and nurturing. A mentoring program is not a substitute for the usual supervisory and peer relationships or for on-the-job training. It is a supplement to those. It can provide an experienced friend and guide who is not also an evaluator. It creates small informal forums where people can discuss their anxieties with persons who can really help and share ideas about professional obligations.

This paper has been written from the coordinator's point of view, and has stressed group programs, but of course the one-on-one relationship is the real heart of mentoring. Most of our survey respondents reported that they talked with their partner more than once a month, and this atmosphere of close attention and nurturing was exactly what we hoped to achieve in the mentoring program. However, I believe that those independent pairs should not be left alone too long without having some group events now and then. Each mentee will hear slightly different advice from his or her mentor and supervisor. They will get together and compare notes, and panic over the discrepancies! Group events provide an opportunity for some of these concerns to be hashed out, and everyone will hear the same thing. If questions can be answered by a person of authority, people will be reassured that they are getting the true facts. The Coordinator must create opportunities for the participants to express what they really need from the program. When asked for ideas or comments, individually or in a survey, people often can't think of anything to say, but in a small group discussion one person's comment will spark another idea, and soon a really productive session is underway.

Mentoring is never a substitute for good management and supervision, but it can create opportunities for new and more experienced employees to interact, get to know each other, and share professional activities. Thus it provides a balance to the more judgmental, anxiety-producing aspects of employee evaluation by creating an environment of support and encouragement along the road to professional success.

REFERENCES

1. Brustman, Mary Jane, *Mentoring in Academia: a Selective Bibliography*, 1989. Available from the Dewey Graduate Library for Public Affairs and Policy, University at Albany, State University of New York.
2. Phillips-Jones, Linda, "Establishing a Formalized Mentoring Program." *Training and Development Journal* 37, no. 2 (Feb. 1983): 38-42.
3. Kizilos, Peter, "Take My Mentor, Please!" *Training* 27, no. 4 (April 1990):49-55.

APPENDIX I

Mentoring Goals And Guidelines

University Libraries
University at Albany
State University of New York

Goals

The Mentoring Program's goals are to streamline the assimilation process of new employees, to promote their professional development, to help them advance in their careers, and to make their stay at the university both productive and constructive.

Mentors help to promote the professional development of their protégés and contribute to an effective and productive library operation.

Protégés and mentors benefit by exchanging viewpoints and ideas and by sharing knowledge and experience.

The University Libraries gain by a staff with improved morale, lower turnover, greater efficiency and a better understanding of each other's responsibilities.

Guidelines

1. Participation is voluntary for both mentors and protégés.

2. The program is available to existing employees as well as new employees hired at any professional level.

3. Mentors will supplement rather than replace assistance provided by supervisors and training programs.

4. Mentors will not be held responsible for the outcome of any personnel actions involving advancement, tenure, or continuing appointment of their protégés.

Participation

1. Mentors are Senior Assistant Librarians or above, or professionals employed by the University for at least three years, or those who have

gone through advancement, permanent or continuing appointment proceedings.

2. The Mentoring Program will begin after a new employee is familiar with his/her responsibilities (usually two or three months). New employees will be informed about the mentoring program on the first day of employment and will be reminded of it at evaluation time.

3. The mentor/protégé relationship will be informal, flexible and will be of specified duration (e.g., six months to two years).

What Must Be Done

1. The mentor and protégé will develop specific, written goals at the beginning of the period and evaluate the results at the end of the period by completing an evaluation form. Evaluation Forms will be developed by the Professional Activities Committee and will be distributed by the Program Coordinator who will collect them at the end of each mentoring period.

2. Mentors will:

    a. Maintain confidentiality of issues discussed with protégés.

    b. Refer protégés to established counseling programs for personal non-job-related matters if necessary (i.e., EAP).

    c. Reinforce and assist in the development of a good working relationship between protégé and supervisor.

    d. Contact the Program Coordinator on a periodic basis to discuss progress.

    e. Complete a brief evaluation at the end of the mentoring period.

3. Protégés will:

    a. Identify needs, goals and expectations at the beginning of the mentoring period.

    b. Maintain confidentiality of issues discussed with the mentor.

    c. Develop rapport with supervisor and request information from the supervisor for departmental issues.

    d. Contact the Program Coordinator on a periodic basis to discuss progress.

    e. Complete a brief evaluation at the end of the mentoring period.

4. Program Coordinator:

    The Program Coordinator will be elected from among the library faculty and does not have to be a mentor. The Nominations and Elections

Committee will solicit nominations for the office of Program Coordinator and will be responsible for holding biennial elections. The duties of the Program Coordinator will include:

a. Orientation of new mentors.

b. Matching up mentors with protégés. Mentors and protégés should be from different departments.

c. Serve as resource to mentors.

d. Rearrange assignments of mentors and protégés as requested.

e. Serve as an ad hoc non-voting member of the Professional Activities Committee.

f. Submit an annual report evaluating the Mentoring Program with suggestions for its improvement.

Privacy and Accountability
at the Reference Desk

Rosemary A. Del Vecchio

SUMMARY. The questions of expectation of privacy by the patron and the accountability of the reference librarian to ensure privacy are explored. Discussion reveals that different patron types have different expectations of confidentiality. Librarians have an ethical accountability based on ALA Codes of Ethics, but social and personal conflicts may arise. The reference librarian has no legal accountability to protect the patron's confidentiality during a reference interview. Although the Codes need to protect the librarian more and reflect the dualities, there may be no resolution to conflicts between professional and personal integrity.

INTRODUCTION

Confidentiality, privacy and accountability of reference services are not easily managed topics. Providing reference assistance is seldom routine; many differing and conflicting factors interact randomly. In the initial stages of this article it became evident very quickly that the topic was too broad. The issue of privacy intersects librarianship in a multitude of areas. As a result, it became apparent that only a narrow focus could, or should, be investigated. A literature search revealed that several articles have touched upon privacy of reference transactions, including a very intuitive article by Mark Stover. As the available material was reviewed, two questions concerning the issue of privacy at the reference desk came into focus. The questions:

What are the expectations of the patron for the protection of his or her privacy at the reference desk?

Rosemary A. Del Vecchio is Assistant Professor/Humanities Librarian, Lucy Scribner Library, Skidmore College, Saratoga Springs, NY 12866-1632.

133

How accountable are librarians for ensuring the privacy of reference transactions?

PATRON TYPES AND DIFFERING EXPECTATIONS

In eight years of academic reference experience this author has never been asked by a patron to treat his or her request as confidential. There are two logical conclusions for this: either the patron did not feel confidentiality was necessary or the patron assumed that the reference interview was a privileged conversation and would be treated as such. In academe, two primary types of patrons are served, students and faculty. It is likely that (1) the students do not expect confidentiality, and (2) that the faculty assume that their transactions will be held in confidence. These conclusions can be substantiated if one considers the attitude and needs of patrons.

Student queries are usually made in support of class assignments, whether for papers, individual presentations or group projects. With few exceptions, students are engaged in less competitive or primary research. Often times they are more concerned with getting the data, regardless of what person or agency must be consulted. The manner in which students approach the desk also provides an indication of their lack of concern for privacy. Students will wait at the desk listening to each other's questions. They arrive with friends in tow, openly discussing their needs in front of them. Students will also interrupt the librarian in mid-stride, in the center of a busy reference area, regardless of who is in the area. Students often share information freely with others in their classes. Every librarian may become aware of a student's question because the student will approach the entire reference department before he or she feels satisfied that every possibility for new information has been eliminated.

Further evidence of students' disregard for privacy was exhibited by student discussions in a credit course on the Information Revolution taught by the author. The class's general consensus was that the protection of one's privacy was not necessary. If the information collected was true, what did it matter, the individual just had to live with it. Although all agreed that information, in itself, is not evil, the class could not accept that there were moral dilemmas attached to the collection and use of data. They lacked perception on how information can be used and a realistic view of its impact on other people's lives. One student even suggested that privacy laws were for the paranoid. Another student eventually suggested to the class that they did not yet have enough life experience to recognize the benefit of privacy laws.

In addition to the lack of students' concern for privacy there is also the reality that the majority of transactions with students are simply too public, and beyond protection from eavesdropping. The very nature of their questions sometimes complicates the ability to provide confidentiality. The organization of a class assignment may affect service. If the entire class is using the same material, or demanding the same database or reference searches, it becomes necessary to compile a folder of materials and make it available to the entire class because staffing and funds prohibit the searches from being repeated over and over. In a small or medium-sized library this is not an uncommon occurrence. It is also not unusual that a librarian is aware of two or more students working on the same topic. It is at this juncture that the librarian who treats reference queries as confidential, regardless of the student's expectations, is placed in an ethical dilemma. Should the librarian feel compelled to advise the student that the topic is taken and that the material has been borrowed or used, or should the librarian continue on without indicating the student may be wasting time and effort? Would the librarian feel the same compulsion if the patrons were faculty instead of students?

From personal experiences and those witnessed at the reference desk, it is evident that librarians will tend to guide students into other areas of research without directly compromising the confidentiality of another student or the librarian's own professional or personal ethics. This can be accomplished simply by pointing out to the student that if the material is in circulation and unavailable there is an indication that someone else is working on it. Most students, unless deeply committed to the topic, will change the direction of their research. This seems based in the student's attitude towards research. They need to accomplish their class assignments and will readily adapt to get the job done. Faculty members in the same situation would be treated differently, and the reason is rooted in the differing expectations of faculty and students on the issue of privacy and research.

Students do not expect confidentiality, but faculty members assume confidentiality. This is demonstrated not only in the differing approaches to research but in the way faculty approach librarians. At many academic institutions, mine included, reference librarians are responsible for specific disciplines and departments. This results in a librarian being a subject specialist and therefore a more likely contact point for a specific topic. When faculty approach the reference desk they are usually seeking general directional information; other queries on research are often conducted over the phone to a specific librarian or by an office visit. The reference transaction becomes more in-depth and intimate because of the highly personal and individualized nature of the scholar's research. It results in a more private interaction which takes on an aspect of a privileged conversation. Confidentiality and privacy are assumed by both parties. Prior to a referral or consultation with other librarians or external sources, the librarian should be sure the faculty member is in agreement. If a librarian is aware that another faculty member is working on the same topic, they are placed in a position much different from that of two students working on the same topic. Due to the type of research conducted by faculty and the expectation of privacy, the librarian should not give either faculty member an indication that they are working on the same topic without the individual's expressed permission, preferably in writing.

It must be noted that this discussion has centered around reference ethics in academic libraries, and these conditions may be different in public and special libraries. Other types of libraries have different circumstances that affect the practices of confidentiality and privacy. As an example, a conversation with a colleague, who is a law librarian with a large firm, will be shared. When asked how confidential requests were treated, one was surprised when the law librarian replied reference questions were not treated as confidential within the library. Furthermore, they would refer an attorney with a question to another attorney if they had previously completed a search on the same topic for him or her. Time, knowledge, funds and staffing seemed to play a role in how confidential reference queries are treated. My colleague also mentioned that to protect the confidentiality of the lawyers and the clients, librarians occasionally did not identify themselves, or at the request of the lawyer, misrepresented themselves to get information necessary for litigation.[1] The obligation to protect a patron's confidentiality appears to be bound to the type of librarianship and the practices of each library to meet the patron needs. Many librarians seem to be caught between the expectations of their patrons, the demands of the job, and personal and professional codes of ethics.

Mark Stover pointed out that although confidentiality is a legal and ethical privilege in professions such as, medicine, law and religion, there has been no extension of that privilege to librarians.[2] Librarians protect the confidentiality of their patrons on the basis of a professional code of ethics. Whether our patrons are students or faculty, lawyers or priests, children or adults, librarians, as professionals, are expected to follow the standards proposed by the American Library Association's Code of Ethics. Librarians are further bound by the tradition in this country for a 'reasonable expectation of privacy.' In response to the first question posed, do patrons have expectations that their reference interchange is confidential, there is enough evidence to suggest that some patrons do have this expectation. What is uncertain is whether or not the patron has any more than a moral claim to privacy.

THE ACCOUNTABILITY OF THE REFERENCE LIBRARIAN TO PROTECT THE PRIVACY OF THE PATRON

There has been no legal recognition of privacy in library matters beyond the circulation of books. This fact had a direct reflection on the second question posed, how accountable are reference librarians for maintaining the confidentiality of a patron's question? A discussion of this question brings into light the basic paradox of reference service–personal integrity versus professional obligations.

The legal ramifications of a disclosure by a librarian that compromises a patron has not yet been tested. Discussions of the library profession's considerations of malpractice for incorrect information have appeared in literature, as has the real battle for the privacy of circulation records. So far, however, librarians appear to be only ethically and morally accountable for disclosure, not legally accountable. Still library administrators could conceivably reprimand or fire a librarian if an indiscretion has major repercussions that cause financial, physical or emotional damage to the patron. Since there has been no legal recognition of the privacy of the librarian-patron relationship these actions would be based solely on the acceptance of professional ethics.

Librarians are expected, according to professional ethics, to abandon personal beliefs and ethics for the greater belief in freedom of information. The reference librarian's role is ideally seen as a blind provider of knowledge, as well as, the guardian of the right of access to information. Librarians cannot censor information and they must ensure access to it. This idealistic goal discounts the humanity of the librarian. It is not an easy road to walk, nor a comfortable position to be placed in. How does the librarian feel after providing someone with a book such as the *Anarchist's Cookbook*? Librarians are asked to provide information without suspicion and to live with the possibility that they may have assisted someone who will use the information provided to endanger others. The reference librarian's role has an innate conflict in which individual and professional responsibilities clash. There seems no solution to this conflict and no way to levy accountability. If librarians accept legal accountability for the protection of an individual's privacy, they must accept moral accountability for what he or she does. Unlike lawyers and priests who hold the confidence after an illegal or immoral act, librarians have a confidence before the act. It is a quandary that may not have a solution that can be resolved by a set of codes that we must follow to protect the standards of our profession.

In the July/August issue of the *College and Research Library News*, a special plea was made by the Chair of the ACRL's Committee of Professional Ethics and by the President of ACRL to join a 'grassroots' effort to incorporate the ALA Code of Ethics into the 'policy and procedures' of each college and research library before the end of the year.³ Librarians need to consider the rationale for the Code of Ethics and what standards and protections the Codes provide.

Librarianship as a profession is in a continual state of growth, re-definition and discovery. To legitimize itself further, as a profession, librarianship seeks to provide itself with standards of ethics, and has done so since the beginning of the twentieth century. Our ethics are based, however, on moral rather than legal precedents. Ideally the Codes provide standards for librarians. Realistically, the Codes provide guidance. Reference librarians in all fields are faced daily with ethical dilemmas. The ALA's Code of Ethics in reference to privacy and confidentiality reads:

> Librarians must protect each user's right to privacy with respect to information sought or received, materials consulted, borrowed or acquired.

This statement sets in place the major conflict between personal and professional integrity, especially if one considers the statements made in the introduction of the Codes. The introduction to the Codes notes that we are "members of a profession explicitly committed to intellectual freedom and the freedom of access to information" but it adds later that librarians "have obligations for maintaining the highest level of personal integrity and competence."⁴ How can we always maintain personal integrity and always provide confidentiality or unquestioned access to materials?

CONCLUSIONS

It may not be possible to take the human element, our own unique personal integrity, out of reference. We can aspire to it, but should we? Stover, in his conclusions, agrees that there are no 'teeth' to the ALA's

Codes of Ethics. He suggested further statements should be added as corollaries. The suggested statements would provide more guidance and protection for the librarian in cases where privacy is not explicitly requested and when the librarian suspects criminal activity.[5] Although this would provide librarians with support and guidance in many of the areas conflict might arise, it does not solve them all. There are gray areas that may need to stay gray. As in the example of the law librarian, can we accept that different branches of librarianship must adhere to different rules of ethics. The Code of Ethics as it stands does not protect librarians legally. Although the adoption of corollaries would provide librarians with a moral solution they also do not provide librarians with a legal solution. We would still be left with the questions of whether librarians can ethically and legally not report possible criminal activity and how accountable our Codes of Ethics make us?

It is unrealistic to believe that the reference desk will ever have the privacy privilege of a confessional, yet we need to adhere to the principle as closely as possible. As a public service reference work cannot be conducted in soundproof glass booths. The patron may have an expectation of privacy, and although we may feel bound ethically to maintain it, we are not legally bound to maintain it. A colleague from eastern Europe wondered at the tradition of keeping reference transactions private, as nothing was private in his country. The only response I could provide him with was that this country is based on the idea of personal freedom and liberty. As librarians, we protect the patron because we protect the idea of freedom to information without censure or compromise.

The very nature of our dual roles, as the protector of information access and as a responsible member of the community in which we live, will, doubtlessly, keep confidentiality of the patron and the librarian's accountability in the world of grayness. There is no solution without losing personal integrity or professional standards. The Codes of Ethics, even if corollaries are added, can only be seen as a guiding light in the gray fog until they become legal standards. Until then, and even after, the librarian must use a ''mixture of instinct, tact, discretion and common sense''[6] at the reference desk.

REFERENCES

1. This conversation took place on June 27, 1991, prior to the American Library Association Annual Conference. Further discussion with my colleague revealed that although librarians were uncomfortable with some queries they make, they are generally made for public domain information but are necessary for liti-

gation. She believed it an ethical dilemma but the name of the firm and client could not be compromised prior to suits being filed. My colleague preferred not to be cited by name.

2. Stover, Mark, "Confidentiality and Privacy in Reference Service." RQ 27:2 (Winter 1987), 240-244.

3. Allison, Anne Marie and Anne Beaubien. College and Research Libraries News 52:7 (July/August 1991), 442.

4. Ibid.

5. Stover, op. cit., 243.

6. Farley, Judith. "Reference Ethics: a True Confession." Reference Librarian 4 (Summer 1982) 13-17.

V. REFERENCE EVALUATION

Reference Evaluation:
An Overview

Patricia Hults

SUMMARY. The current interest in reference evaluation has its roots in the unobtrusive testing begun twenty years ago. Evaluation before that was centered on criteria of quantity rather than quality. When unobtrusive testing began reporting accuracy rates hovering in the 50% range, reference services responded by exploring a variety of techniques to measure quality of service including unobtrusive testing, patron surveys, and peer review. Methods to improve reference service, such as training workshops, peer coaching, and changes in organizational climate are also beginning to be critically examined.

HISTORICAL PERSPECTIVE

The issue of reference evaluation is a relatively new phenomena, particularly when reference performance is considered. Murfin and Wynar identified under 40 articles concerning reference evaluation published between 1920 and 1960 (Murfin and Wynar 188-213; Altman 170). Until the late sixties virtually all assessment of reference service, other than patron

Patricia Hults is Head of Access Services, Learning Resources Center, SUNY Cobleskill, Cobleskill, NY 12043.

141

142   ASSESSMENT AND ACCOUNTABILITY

surveys, involved quantitative measurements: how many questions were answered in which category from what type of patron at what time of day. Much effort was spent in activities such as defining reference vs. directional and hammering out the intricacies of grid statistical analysis. That emphasis on data gathering was a reflection of the same emphasis evident in the broader field of evaluation, particularly governmental programs assessment. Much of the research being done at that time in performance measurement was centered on data gathering instrument refinement and statistical analysis (Cronin 6). Although current reference evaluation efforts focus on performance and qualitative measurements, the statistical information gathered was important and allowed librarians to begin to compare and evaluate the scope of their reference activities.

During this time patron surveys were another method of evaluation frequently used by libraries. However, most of these surveys suffered from the same perplexing problem. According to Rothstein "A number of studies have attempted to ascertain the opinion held by reference clientele regarding the service received, and the results could hardly be bettered by paying for testimonials" (Rothstein 464; Altman 175). Patrons were so happy with any service they seemed unable to make distinctions of quality.

In the sixties the field of performance measurement was further stimulated by the requirement that government programs contain an evaluative component. Evaluation research became more sophisticated and began to go further than simple data gathering (Cronin 6). The subject of library evaluation also began to elicit increased interest and show increasing sophistication. In 1967 Crowley conducted one of the first unobtrusive testings of reference performance (Crowley; Weech and Goldher 306).

UNOBTRUSIVE TESTING

Crowley continued his research and in 1971 Childers and Crowley published their landmark work in which they reported that reference staff correctly answered about 50-55% of the questions posed (39-51, 139). Similar figures have repeatedly appeared in subsequent studies done across the U.S., in England by House (Altman 175), and Finland by Koivunen (James 97). Hernon and McClure have furthered the research with consistent and similar results hovering around the 55% accuracy level.

The basic design of unobtrusive testing is simple. Proxies are trained to pose as library patrons and ask factual reference questions. These questions are normally designed so that they can be answered by sources held by the libraries being studied. The librarian's answer is rated as to it's "correctness." Some studies differentiated the level of correctness. Other studies rated additional factors, such as level of the librarian's education, size of the collection, or librarian's communication skills, and tried to come up with predictive factors for the accuracy rate. The results have been mixed. In general, there appears to be an insignificant correlation between collection size, library budget, demand, physical setting and correct fill rate (Gers and Seward; Crews). Professional librarians do seem to score higher than non-MLS degree holders, although not all studies report this (Crews 341-42). A study done in Maryland concluded that the highest predictive factor of success is the individual librarian's behavior such as reference question negotiation skill, librarian interest and comfort with the question, and perhaps most importantly, follow up (Gers and Seward 33).

The library community responded to these unobtrusive studies first with shock, then with denial. The common response is "yes, maybe, but not in *my* library." Charles McClure speaks of hearing that statement again and again, often from librarians who work in the very libraries he has tested and found right there at the magic 55% mark. As study after study confirmed the 55% figure, librarians then began poking holes in the methodology of unobtrusive testing. An article by Bill Bailey is typical of this response. He argues that the data was flawed because of test design errors including lack of third party observation of the interaction and controls on timing of questions and busyness at the desk. He also felt that "the point is that surreptitious observation eventually will uncover flaws in even a paragon of professionalism. Hernon and McClure could have tailed the brightest reference librarians until they finally gave out wrong answers" (281). The real point is that Hernon and McClure didn't do that. They tested librarians in their normal work situations and librarians failed.

Others have questioned the validity of the questions posed and felt that measuring a small aspect of the total picture of reference work was an inaccurate reflection of the quality of reference work (Whitlatch).

All of these responses beg the question. No method of evaluation measures the totality of a job or is free of design error. What the library community really needs to address are the questions McClure and Hernon have left us with: is a 55% accuracy rate acceptable; if not, what priority do libraries place on improving that rate; what is the cause of the rate and what is the cure? (Hernon and McClure, Library 70).

Certainly accuracy of information is not the only criteria of quality reference service, though it seems the baseline to work from. We are all familiar with the librarian who, though she may be accurate, has such a stern "bed-side manner" as to be unapproachable to the average patron. This obviously is not quality service. However, accuracy and "bedside manner" are not necessarily independent variables. The Maryland study indicates the highest predictive characteristics for reference accuracy have to do with those "bed-side manners," i.e., reference negotiation skills, interest in the question, etc. (Gers and Seward 33). This was confirmed by the improvement in accuracy experienced by the librarians in a program developed and instituted by Maryland's Division of Library Development. The program trained librarians in those positive reference communication behaviors. Follow up studies reported dramatic improvement in correct answer rates (Arthur 368). This makes intuitive sense. Librarians skilled at reference negotiation and other forms of communications with patrons have the best chance of understanding the question and thus providing accurate information. Reference evaluation does need to look at more than one facet of the reference interaction to accurately measure the service provided. The important characteristics, accuracy, reference interview negotiation skills, approachability, etc., are synergistic and work as a whole to determine quality of service.

Hernon and McClure have begun to look at what institutional climates best support quality reference service. There is some research backing their hypothesis that an institution that is innovative, supportive, democratically governed, and with high morale will provide better reference service ("Unobtrusive Testing and Library. . ." 107; "Unobtrusive Testing and the Role . . ." 74). Lowenthal reports preliminary correlations between emotional well-being (morale) and job performance in a study done in public libraries. Degree of disaffection from patron, depersonalization, anxiety, stress, etc. all had significant negative impact on reference performance (385-392).

CURRENT DEVELOPMENTS

Some libraries are responding to the challenge of these studies by beginning to develop methods to routinely assess reference service. A few libraries have conducted their own unobtrusive studies. The Cumberland County Public Library and Information Center took the bold step of using board members as their test proxies. Their risk paid off in increased board involvement and commitment to library excellence. Interestingly, as part of the study the proxies were asked if they were satisfied with the service they received. Although the overall accuracy rate was 74% and the proxies knew when the answer was incorrect, the proxies were satisfied 90% of the time, another example of the halo effect libraries seem to have (Hansel).

The Fairfax County Public Library also conducted an unobtrusive test of services. Because of lack of funding to hire outside evaluators, they developed a cooperative effort with a neighboring library system. Staff of both libraries were involved in the study plan, design, and execution. It was felt that this involvement was important to acceptance of the results by insuring that the staff viewed the test as fair and appropriate. Both libraries used their testing to identify needed policy manuals, appropriate training, and in some cases, staffing reorganization (Rodger and Goodwin).

Few libraries have the resources to conduct annual unobtrusive tests. Other methods have been developed to incorporate regular reference review. Linda Olson has broken reference service into four components and suggested methods of assessment for each. Instead of unobtrusive testing to measure the librarian's ability to provide factual and policy information, she suggests a 4 hour test administered to each reference librarian. For measurement of the staff's ability to provide instruction she suggests carefully designed user surveys.

One interesting method just developing in reference service is peer review. The Ramsey County Public Library developed a comprehensive system that included outside consultants to provide training in confrontation, nonverbal expression, and problem identification. The evaluation began with an extensive self-evaluation form that was duplicated and distributed to all reference staff. Facilitated meetings then used the peer review format to explore competency strengths, common factors affecting performance, reference objectives and duties. The entire format of the evaluation served as a training workshop for improved reference service ("Peer"). Other libraries with peer review programs include Louisiana State University Libraries, Auraria Library in Denver, the libraries at the University of Arizona, Appalachian State University in North Carolina and Bowling Green State University (Kleiner 353).

DEVELOPING A REFERENCE EVALUATION PROGRAM

Before you can begin to develop a reference evaluation program you must decide what you are going to evaluate; program quality, individual performance, or both. This choice will drive the choice of your tools of measurement. For example, unobtrusive testing is more appropriate for program evaluation than for individual assessment. The unique characteristics of your institution will also determine which evaluation tools will work best for you. Departments with large numbers of staff have much different logistical problems that those with small numbers. If your staff normally works alone, as is common with small staffs, peer review becomes more difficult to organize.

Early staff involvement is important regardless of the focus of your evaluation. Involving the reference staff in the process of developing criteria and evaluation methods will promote a democratic operation of the reference department and increase morale by insuring a much higher level of acceptance and enthusiasm for the end product. Early involvement in the development will promote staff acceptance because their philosophies and concerns will be incorporated into the structure. The process itself should also improve reference quality by ensuring that each reference librarian understands the goals of the reference department, understands what characteristics are considered good or bad reference practice, by promoting awareness and sensitivity to the issue of reference quality, and by creating a shared vision of what reference service should be.

A useful step is an examination of the goals of the reference department. You can't measure a service without a clear idea of what it is you want it to do. Bunge's article is a thorough explanation of the process of creating goals. The process is a multi-layered effort with the goals at every level being fueled by the broader institutional goals. Adams and Judd also focus on goal setting and do an excellent job of breaking down goals into specific, measurable performances.

The danger of this approach is the tendency to create goals of quantity rather than quality. Ellison and Lazeration recommend a reference evaluation method based on management by objectives whose main focus is on countable activities peripheral to the main function of reference service. An example is an objective that the librarian will contact X number of new faculty per semester. This method does not evaluate the actual reference performance.

The development of criteria to measure quality is the next step. Several checklists already exist that pinpoint specific behaviors of reference librarians such as does the librarian smile, make eye contact, take the patron to the source, acknowledge a waiting patron (Gers and Seward 34; Adams and Judd 137-43)? The reference staff can use these as jumping-off points to develop their own list appropriate for evaluation. These could be used by supervisors, peers, or for self-evaluation. They also can be used as standards and training tools to raise librarian awareness of the importance of these traits. The development of the criteria should help clarify the librarian's understanding of appropriate reference technique and promote consistency in the application of these behaviors. Once criteria have been agreed upon the method(s) of measuring those criteria must be tackled. The decision either to measure the department or the individual will determine the direction you take. Some tools appropriate for departmental evaluation are unobtrusive testing and patron survey. Hernon and McClure's articles provide good background reading for unobtrusive testing and Hansel and Rodger and Goodwin's articles outline approaches that can be taken on a relatively small scale.

Patron surveys need to be developed very carefully to be useful. These surveys need to be designed to measure specific components of instruction–did the librarian take you to the source, did the librarian explain in a logical manner how to use the source, did the librarian follow up later by asking if you had found what you needed? Hopefully these types of questions would gather more useful evaluation of instruction. Linda Olson's article is particularly helpful for survey development as well as Murfin and Gugelchuk.

If you are examining individual performances several methods have been used. The traditional one of supervisory rating may be the method most prone to subjectivity and bias. Some organizational structures require supervisory evaluation for reappointment, tenure, or promotion, but combining it with peer or self-evaluation will improve chances of accurately evaluating an individual. Articles useful when considering peer evaluation are Kleiner and "Peer Evaluation of Reference Librarians in a Public Library."

You can, of course, combine methods. The broader the information gathered about your reference service the more accurate the picture will be. The process of developing a reference evaluation program is not a trivial one. Considerable staff time and commitment are needed for the process to succeed. As the program is being developed and tried out, evaluation and revision are necessary as weaknesses and strengths of particular methods in your particular institution are identified.

AFTER EVALUATION

The literature stresses again and again the need to tie evaluation to some results. "If plans are not made to act on the results of an evaluation process, one might save the time and money involved . . ."(Green 168). One obvious response to evaluation is to provide training for areas of measured weakness. There is a whole body of literature concerning staff training, but of particular interest is some research done by McClure and Hernon.

They examined the effect of one workshop on reference accuracy rate. A library which holds a government document collection was unobtrusively pretested with questions that could be answered with basic materials from that collection. The staff then attended a 4 hour workshop on government document sources designed to increase their awareness and skill in using the government document material. The library was then unobtrusively tested again with the disheartening results that the accuracy rate had dropped.

The design of the workshop was typical of 1/2 day workshops librarians attend all the time. It probably was more carefully run than many. McClure and Hernon felt that even if it did contain serious design flaws (which they doubted), sheer exposure to the material should have raised awareness of that source of information. They conclude that awareness does not necessarily translate into skill of use and that one-shot workshops are not the answer to improving reference accuracy ("Unobtrusive Testing and Library. . ." 78-103).

An interesting program that seems to address this dilemma was developed at Temple University Libraries. They have had a long standing tradition of staff training, but became uneasy with the issue of transferability of the knowledge from workshop to work site. Drawing on the work done by the Maryland State Department of Education, Division of Library Development and Services, they instituted regular peer coaching for their reference staff. They concentrated on communication skills such as question negotiation and positive non-verbal behavior. They report "(1) greater clarification of the reference process for all staff involved in coaching; (2) increased recognition of positive communication behaviors, both through observation and feedback; (3) increased self-awareness of individual communication style and desk behavior; and (4) increased reinforcement of positive desk behaviors" (Arthur 372). It would have been interesting if they had tested accuracy rates before and after the training to see if they experienced improvements similar to those reported in Maryland.

CONCLUSIONS

Reference departments have slowly begun examining the quality of service they provide. Much work has been done in the last ten years, but much remains to be done, particularly in the assessment of training and other methods to improve reference service. Very few studies have been done that carefully examine the success of particular techniques of training, the impact of organizational structure on reference work, or the effects of morale, etc. on staff performance.

The process of developing and implementing an evaluation system is not a trivial one. It requires significant staff time and commitment. The implications of effective evaluation, particularly tied with effective staff training, are far reaching for our profession. If we can accurately measure how well we provide that service we say we provide and then improve service with training that works, we will go a long way in our quest for excellence in reference service.

REFERENCES

Adams, Mignon S., and Blanche Judd. "Evaluating Reference Librarians: Using Goal Analysis as a First Step." *The Reference Librarian* Fall/Winter 1984: 131-45.

Altman, Ellen. "Assessment of Reference Services." *The Service Imperative for Libraries*. Littleton, CO: Libraries Unlimited, 1982. 169-85.

Arthur, Gwen. "Peer Coaching in a University Reference Department." *College & Research Libraries* July 1990: 367-373.

Bailey, Bill. "The "55 Percent Rule" Revisited." *Journal of Academic Librarianship* Nov. 1987: 280-82.

Bunge, Charles A. "Planning, Goals, and Objectives for the Reference Department." *RQ* Spring 1984: 306-15.

Childers, Thomas A., and Terance Crowley. *Information Service in Public Libraries: Two Studies*. Metuchen, NJ: Scarecrow Press, 1971.

Crews, Kenneth D. "The Accuracy of Reference Service: Variables for Research and Implementation." *Library & Information Science Research* July 1988: 331-55.

Cronin, Mary J. *Performance Measurements for Public Services in Academic and Research Libraries*. Occasional Paper Number #9. Washington, D.C.: Office of Management Studies, Association of Research Libraries, 1985.

Crowley, Terence. "The Effectiveness of Information Service in Medium Size Public Libraries." Diss. Rutgers, 1968.

Ellison, John W., and Deborah B. Lazeration. "Personnel Accountability Form for Academic Reference Librarians: A Model." *RQ* Winter 1976: 142-48.

Gers, Ralph, and Lillie Seward. "Improving Reference Performance: Results of a Statewide Study." *Library Journal* 1 Nov. 1985: 32-35.

Green, Louise Koller. "Accessing the Effectiveness of Reference Services: A Difficult But Necessary Process." *Catholic Library World* Jan./Feb. 1988: 168-71.

Hansel, Patsy. "Unobtrusive Evaluation for Improvement: The CCPL&IC Experience." *North Carolina Libraries* Summer 1986: 69-75.

Hernon, Peter, and Charles R. McClure. "Library Reference Service: An Unrecognized Crisis–A Symposium." *Journal of Academic Librarianship* May 1987: 69-80.

_____*Unobtrusive Testing and Library Reference Services.* Norwood, NJ: Ablex, 1987.

_____"Unobtrusive Testing and the Role of Library Management." *The Reference Librarian* Summer 1987: 71-85.

House, David E. "Reference Efficiency or Reference Deficiency." *Library Association Record* Nov. 1974:222-23.

James, G. Rohan. "Reference: Analysis, Management and Training." *Library Review* Summer 1982: 93-103.

Kleiner, Jane P. "Ensuring Quality Reference Desk Service: The Introduction of a Peer Process." *RQ* Spring 1991: 349-61.

Koivunen, Hannele. *LISA* 81/2514. Cited in James 97.

Lowenthal, Ralph A. "Preliminary Indications of the Relationship between Reference Morale and Performance." *RQ* Spring 1990: 380-393.

Murfin, Marjorie E., and Gary M. Gugelchuk. "Development and Testing of a Reference Transaction Assessment Instrument." *College & Research Libraries* July 1987: 314-31.

Murfin, Marjorie E., and Lubomyr R. Wynar. *Reference Service: An Annotated Bibliographic Guide*, Littleton, CO: Libraries Unlimited, 1977.

Olson, Linda M. "Reference Service Evaluation in Medium-Sized Academic Libraries: A Model." *Journal of Academic Librarianship* Jan. 1984: 322-29.

"Peer Evaluation of Reference Librarians in a Public Library." *Library Personnel News* Fall 1987: 32-33.

Rodger, Eleanor Jo, and Jane Goodwin. "To See Ourselves as Others See Us: A Cooperative, Do-It-Yourself Reference Accuracy Study." *The Reference Librarian* Summer 1987: 135-47.

Rothstein, Samuel. "The Measurement and Evaluation of Reference Service." *Library Trends* Jan. 1964: 456-72.

Weech, Terry L. "Who's Giving All Those Wrong Answers? Direct Service and Reference Personnel Evaluation." *The Reference Librarian* Fall/Winter 1984: 109-22.

Weech, Terry L., and Herbert Goldhor. "Obtrusive Versus Unobtrusive Evaluation of Reference Service in Five Illinois Public Libraries: A Pilot Study." *The Library Quarterly* 52.4 (1982): 305-24.

Whitlatch, Jo Bell. "Unobtrusive Studies and the Quality of Academic Library Reference Services." *College & Research Libraries* March 1989: 181-94.

Young, William F. "Methods for Evaluating Reference Desk Performance." *RQ* Fall 1985: 69-75.

Wrong Questions, Wrong Answers: Behavioral vs. Factual Evaluation of Reference Service

David A. Tyckoson

SUMMARY. Due to the public nature of reference work, librarians need to be accountable to the patrons that they serve. A high level of performance at the reference desk generates good public relations and creates an atmosphere in which patrons are encouraged about returning to the library, whereas poor performance reflects poorly on the library as a whole. In addition to this direct accountability to patrons, reference librarians should be measured on their account- ability to their colleagues, the library administration, and the profes- sion as a whole.

Several methods have been developed to evaluate the performance of reference librarians. Most such methods concentrate on the ac- curacy of the response to the patron's question and neglect the pro- cess involved in obtaining that answer. Unfortunately, this method of fact-based evaluation does not reflect the needs of patrons at most reference desks. This paper proposes a method for evaluating refer- ence performance based upon behavioral factors. In addition, some specific behaviors which correlate to positive or negative experienc- es during the reference transaction are discussed.

ACCOUNTABILITY FOR REFERENCE LIBRARIANS

In most libraries, the reference librarian represents the primary public image of the library. By dealing directly with patrons, reference librarians are the principal persons within the organization who are known to library users. Although a library may employ the majority of its professional

David A. Tyckoson is Head, Reference Department, University Libraries, Uni- versity at Albany–SUNY, 1400 Washington Avenue, Albany, NY 12222.

151

librarians in a variety of other administrative, technical, and support services, patrons often generate their views of the library as an institution based upon the performance of the staff of the reference department. Patrons who have had a successful reference transaction have a tendency to think more highly of the library as a whole, while patrons who experience a less successful transaction will take this to represent the quality and level of service of the entire library. The work of an excellent technical services department may be disregarded if library patrons do not find the public services to meet their standards and expectations. Alternatively, a good reference librarian may be able to cover for inadequate resources or performance in other areas. In many ways, the reference transaction has become more than a search for specific information–it is also a powerful public relations tool.

Because of this public nature of reference service, it would be expected that reference librarians would be directly accountable for their performance. A function that reflects directly upon the entire organization would seem to warrant constant scrutiny. In practice, however, this is rarely the case. Most reference librarians do not undergo objective evaluations of their performance at the public service desks. While some librarians may receive performance reviews on a regular basis, these reviews tend to concentrate on managerial and administrative functions or on the accomplishments of specific projects. Very few librarians receive constructive feedback directly related to their desk performance.

This is not to say that librarians and administrators in most institutions are totally unaware of the performance of reference department staff. Most of us have definite opinions about the reference librarians that we have known. Some librarians have developed excellent reputations as knowledgeable and helpful staff members, whereas others may be known for less impressive reasons. However, these opinions are usually based upon relatively isolated encounters at the desk and do not reflect a statistically valid sample of the performance of that librarian. While we may think that one librarian is knowledgeable and another friendly and a third intimidating, those opinions are based upon our own interactions with the librarian and are tainted by our own biases and expectations. Unfortunately, much of this subjective evaluation becomes part of the folklore of a given library, making objective evaluation even more difficult to achieve. Such folklore may even become self-fulfilling prophecy, with the librarian who is thought to do a poor job actually doing so over time because no one is willing to believe that he or she could achieve otherwise.

What is needed in reference service are objective measures of performance that can be used to provide feedback to librarians regarding their strengths and weaknesses. A few libraries have begun to undertake such programs, although these are the exceptions rather than the rule. Bill Young[1] and Lynn Westbrook[2] have summarized many of the methods and programs currently in use. In times of tight budgets, new technologies, and an increased emphasis on access to information, reference librarians need to be accountable to the forces that shape the library and its parent institution. The two primary questions that need to be answered are: To whom should reference librarians be accountable? and: How should this accountability be measured?

ACCOUNTABILITY TO PATRONS

Since reference librarians provide direct service to the users of the library, they must be held accountable for the quality of service that they provide those users. As the primary resource available to patrons for answers to questions, assistance in using materials, instruction in research tools, advice on sources to consult or read, and information about the library and its community, the reference librarian must be responsible for both the information provided to the user and the manner in which that information is conveyed. Reference librarians must be able to respond to user demands in such a way that the user will continue to be a patron of the library. It is the responsibility of the reference librarian to ensure that patrons are pleased with the library and its services. Without accountability to users, the library would soon fail in its mission to provide information to its user community. As in all other reference service policy development, the patron must be the first consideration in the evaluation of reference librarians. Service to the patron should be the foremost issue in measuring the performance of reference librarians.

ACCOUNTABILITY TO OTHER LIBRARIANS

Reference librarians should also be held accountable to the other librarians within the institution. The great wealth of materials and formats within even the smallest library have made it impossible for a single reference librarian to know all sources in all subject areas. Effective reference service is done as a team, building upon the individual strengths of each librarian. To perform in this team environment, librarians must be accountable to each other as professionals. A librarian whose performance is not accountable to his or her peers can destroy the team environment and become a drain upon the resources and energy of the rest of the organization. The interaction between a librarian and his/her peers should be a major factor in the evaluation of reference staff.

ACCOUNTABILITY TO ADMINISTRATORS

Reference librarians must also be accountable to the administrators who manage the library and its parent institution. As policy makers, the administrators will establish the environment in which reference service takes place. However, by its very nature reference service is not a cost-effective function of the library. It is a highly labor-intensive activity that requires high level staff and which does not tangibly add to the library's collections. From a budgetary perspective, reference service is superfluous to many of the goals of the library. From an administrative viewpoint, reference service could be seen as a drain upon funds that could otherwise be used to purchase and process materials. While providing reference service, librarians do not select, catalog, or shelve books or other materials. Although many reference librarians serve multiple roles and perform other functions in areas such as collection development and technical services, reference service in and of itself adds nothing to the production value of the library.

Fortunately, the administration of virtually every library does in fact place a high level of value on the service and public relations function of reference librarians. Administrators see reference as providing the professional services sought by library patrons and also use reference as a public relations tool to interact with the community served by the library. Reference librarians must remain accountable to the administration in order continue to receive an adequate level of support. Another factor in the evaluation of reference staff should be the ability of the reference librarian to contribute to, support, and uphold the policies of the library as a whole. The skill of the librarian in lobbying the administration for support for reference is included in this aspect of accountability.

ACCOUNTABILITY TO THE PROFESSION

Finally, reference librarians must also be accountable to the profession at large. Techniques or concepts developed at one institution should be shared with librarians throughout the nation and the world. To function effectively, reference librarians must interact with their peers within the library, at state and regional levels, and through national organizations. Reference librarians should also observe the ethical guidelines and performance objectives established by state and national professional organizations. Whenever possible, reference librarians should contribute to the collective knowledge of the field by writing reports, serving on committees, or presenting papers on developments at their institution. In addition to the direct provision of service, reference librarians should also be evaluated on their contributions to the profession.

EVALUATION TECHNIQUES

Many different methods of evaluating reference service have been tested, including goal setting, obtrusive evaluation, qualitative measurement, and unobtrusive testing. Although each of these methods takes into consideration at least some of the accountability levels mentioned above, almost all are based upon the concept of accountability to the patrons of the library. Whether using statistical analyses of questions asked at a reference desk or planting test questions with patrons, the goal of most evaluation initiatives has been to determine the degree to which reference service satisfies its public. Keeping in line with the patron-oriented nature of reference service, accountability to the patron lies at the core of most reference evaluation techniques.

Unfortunately, reference librarians do not have a great reputation for such accountability. The failure of reference librarians to adequately perform their jobs has been well-documented in the library literature. The 55% rule identified by Hernon and McClure[3] has become somewhat of a standard for measuring the success (or failure) of reference service. According to several unobtrusive studies on reference effectiveness,[4] reference librarians in libraries around the nation are able to completely and accurately answer questions only slightly more than one-half of the time. Although reference librarians have argued for years that these studies do not reflect the service in *our* libraries and that we know that *our* performance is really at a higher level than 55% accuracy, study after study has arrived at almost the exact same figures. Because of these results, the 55% rule has become a part of the lore of reference service.

At the same time that our own research indicates that we are failing in our accountability to our patrons almost one-half of the time, those same patrons continue to rave about our performance. User surveys in libraries of all types have found that an overwhelming majority of patrons are highly satisfied with the services that they receive. Patrons are generally very pleased with the helpfulness of reference librarians and the assistance that they offer. In most libraries, user surveys indicate an extremely high rating for reference service, frequently surpassing the 90% satisfaction level. In the eyes of our patrons, our performance level is viewed as very high.

These two accounts provide two distinctly different views of the performance of reference librarians. On the one hand, unbiased research indicates that we are correctly serving only 55% of our users. On the other hand, over 90% of our users tell us that they are pleased with the service that they receive. Even if all of the 10% who are not satisfied received incorrect answers to their questions, we are still faced with the apparent contradiction of 35% of our patrons who seem to be quite happy with wrong information. How do we justify such statistics with the reality of reference service? Do we give away wrong answers to seemingly unknowing or uncaring patrons? Or is there some other factor that can account for high patron satisfaction and low answer accuracy? What is really happening across our reference desks and how should this be measured? These apparent discrepancies can be explained when the underlying assumptions behind these two evaluation methods are examined and compared.

FACT-BASED EVALUATIONS

Much of the existing research on evaluating reference service is based upon the factual nature of reference questions. In these studies, questions with specific known answers are posed to reference librarians. The librarians are judged on the basis of the number of questions that they answer correctly or incorrectly. By using a large enough pool of questions, a statistical analysis may be made of the effectiveness of either individual librarians or of the library as a whole. This type of fact-based evaluation is the basis for the 55% rule. The focus of fact-based evaluation is on the answer to the question and does not pay particular attention to the methods used in obtaining that answer. This assumption underlies many reference evaluation techniques.

Fact-based evaluation may be done in any of several ways. A librarian may be given a list of practice reference questions by his or her supervisor, may be observed by a colleague at the reference desk as he or she responds to patrons, may be approached at the reference desk by patrons with questions planted by the evaluator, or may be asked test questions over the telephone. In each case, the emphasis of the evaluation is on the response to previously determined questions. The use of factual questions is intended to remove any bias of the evaluator. Since the factual responses cannot be disputed, neither the librarian nor the evaluator can interpret the results in a manner other than correct or incorrect. Current theory supports the use of less obtrusive methods to remove additional evaluator bias. Unobtrusive evaluation eliminates the chances that a librarian may change his or her performance with the knowledge that an evaluation is in progress. Unobtrusive evaluation attempts as much as possible to create a situation in which the evaluator receives the same response to factual questions as those received by any other patron of the library.

Fact-based evaluation works very well in terms of generating statistical data for analysis by the evaluators. Studies may be conducted on the number of questions answered correctly, the number and type answered incorrectly, the subject areas frequently answered correctly or incorrectly, individual librarians' responses, or the degree of accuracy achieved. In each of these cases, the evaluator is able to generate a statistical profile of the library or librarians being evaluated. By comparing the profiles of one library against that of another (or of one librarian against that of another), the evaluator is able to rank libraries or librarians on their reference effectiveness. This ranking may then be used as a motivator to press for the improvement of services in those areas where the library falls below an acceptable level.

This fact-based approach to evaluating reference service is the reference librarian's equivalent of measuring a baseball player's effectiveness based upon his or her batting average. A baseball player who gets a hit one out of four times at bat (.250 batting average) is considered an average player, whereas a player who gets a hit three times out of ten (.300 average) is considered good and a player who gets a hit four times out of ten (.400 average) is considered outstanding. Similarly, the 55% rule has come to say that a library that answers one out of four questions correctly (.250 average) is performing at a poor level, a library that answers two out of four questions correctly (.500 average) is doing an average job, and a library that answers three out of four questions correctly (.750 average) is performing at an excellent level.

The problem with such a statistical approach to evaluation in either baseball or reference service is that it does not measure the complete nature of the activity under consideration. While a batting average in baseball is a good indicator of the success of a batter, it only measures the instances in which a batter reaches base safely by getting a hit. A batter with an average or poor batting average can still contribute substantially to the team in other ways, such as by frequently reaching base on a walk or an error, by advancing runners with a sacrifice bunt, or by getting his or her hits when other runners are already on base. These factors are not measured in the single statistic of the batting average, but they must be considered when measuring the player's total contribution to the team. While the batting average is an important measure of a baseball player's performance, it must be considered only in conjunction with several other factors.

Similarly, the reference librarian who records only a 55% success rate may also be an excellent instructor, a quality on-line searcher, or a competent bibliographer. Each of these qualities must also be factored into the measurement of the success of that librarian. Reference service is a transaction which is too complex to measure in simple statistical terms. Just as the team with the highest batting average does not usually win the World Series, the library with the highest rate of answering factual questions does not necessarily provide the best reference service.

Despite these limitations, there can be little argument that fact-based evaluation does provide a useful measure of the success of one part of reference service. The questions used do have right and wrong answers, making it difficult for a librarian to argue that he or she was judged incorrectly. A quick check of the known answers against the responses of the librarian should settle any discussion on this matter. The biggest problem with this type of evaluation is that it only measures a single aspect of reference service. While we tend to think of reference librarians as providing facts to patrons seeking specific information, actual reference desk experience reveals that this is not the case. In practice, very few questions asked at most reference desks have a single, specific, verifiable answer. Estimates on the numbers of questions of this type vary considerably. In his textbook on reference work, Bill Katz[5] estimates the range as from 6% to 10% for academic, special, and school libraries. The major problem with fact-based evaluation is that it measures only a small portion of the types of transactions which occur at the reference desk.

In practice, most questions asked at the reference desk require advice rather than answers. For most questions the librarian does not provide the patron with a factual response, but counsels the patron on possible approaches to finding an answer. For example, a patron searching for basic information on the history of the United States may be given a textbook, an almanac, an encyclopedia, a newspaper index, a periodical index, or a guide to a microform collection. Each of these sources will provide the patron with a different approach to the topic and each will technically answer the question correctly. Similarly, a patron writing an opinion paper on abortion may be directed to any of several different periodical indexes, from the *Reader's Guide to Periodical Literature* to *Public Affairs Infor-*

mation Service to *Social Sciences Index* to *Religion Index* to *Index Medicus*. Each of these indexes will lead the patron to different sources that he or she may use to find information on abortion and each must be considered to be a correct answer to the question. However, not all of these sources would be the best choice for all patrons. The librarian must use the reference interview process to determine which source will be the most effective for each individual patron. The focus of any evaluation of reference service cannot rely solely on the answers to the questions, but must consider how the librarian arrives at a given response for a given patron. We must evaluate not only the answer, but the process as well.

BEHAVIORAL EVALUATION OF REFERENCE SERVICE

Several factors enter into the complex process of the reference transaction. The librarian must be available to provide service, must be able to interpret the patron's query, formulate a search strategy, identify and consult potential information sources, and communicate a response. The reference transaction is a highly complex interaction in which failure at any one point in the chain will result in the failure of the entire system. Measuring the accuracy of a librarian's responses to patrons does very little to evaluate the librarian's abilities to function in the reference environment. Most fact-based measurements of accuracy assume that the librarian is available, has correctly interpreted the question, and has effectively communicated the results. Fact-based evaluation does not even measure the search strategy, concentrating instead on the final results of that strategy. At best, fact-based evaluation provides an indicator of the ability of the librarian to identify and use specific information sources. While it is important for librarians to do so effectively, this step plays only a minor role in the overall reference process.

The other factors involved in the reference transaction, such as availability, interpretation, and communication, are all behavioral-based rather than fact-based features of the reference process. To provide a complete picture of the effectiveness of the reference librarian, any accountability measures need to evaluate these behavioral factors along with the accuracy of the final response. It is precisely these behavioral factors that lead to the satisfaction of patrons with reference service, even when the accuracy rate is relatively low. Patrons are pleased to interact with reference librarians who make themselves available for service, listen to the patron's query, guide the patron through the search process, and who can communicate the results of that search. Unfortunately, few libraries have developed objective measures for reference behavior. While most reference librarians have an intuitive feel for the types of behavior that are acceptable and unacceptable at the reference desk, the profession must develop a set of guidelines for measuring the behavior of reference librarians if it is to get a complete picture of the quality of reference service.

METHODS OF BEHAVIORAL EVALUATION

Such guidelines must take into account each of the steps in the reference transaction, from informing the patron that the librarian is available to provide assistance to communicating the final results of the search. Within each segment of the process, the method of measurement also needs to provide the librarian with feedback that can be used as a guide to improve his or her performance. Several different methods are available in order to obtain such information.

Regardless of how data is collected, the library needs to establish a set of behavioral criteria on which the librarian should be evaluated. These criteria should be specific and should indicate how the librarian functions within an established scale of behavior. For example, one attribute that could be used to measure whether a librarian makes him/herself available for service is the amount of eye contact that the librarian makes with patrons approaching the desk. Each librarian could be rated on a scale indicating the range of eye contact normally made with patrons. Assuming that a higher level of eye contact is related to a higher level of availability, feedback on this point could help the librarians to establish a greater level of eye contact (and thus a greater level of availability) with patrons. This criterion is specific in that it relates to a single behavior, but it is also generalizable in that it is an indicator of how well the librarian makes him/herself available to the public. Evaluation on this point will help librarians to function better at the first step in the reference process. Similar specific behaviors could be measured that correlate with other desirable aspects of reference service.

CHECKLIST OF ATTRIBUTES

The key to the success of such a checklist of behaviors is to select specific behaviors that can be used as indicators of the more complex components of the reference transaction. Just as eye contact is a positive indicator of availability to provide reference service, each behavior to be examined should be either a positive or negative indicator of a more complex factor of reference service. The sum total of all of the indicators will provide a fairly accurate picture of the overall behavior of the librarian. Collecting this information in a checklist of behaviors will provide both the librarian and the evaluator with clear guidelines on which behaviors to measure. See Table 1 for a sample checklist of behavioral attributes.

OBSERVATIONAL EVALUATION

In order to evaluate the behavior of reference librarians, some form of observation of the reference transaction must be conducted. As discussed above, the behavioral components of reference service cannot be measured on a purely statistical study of the answers to the patron's queries. By their very nature, behavioral factors must be observed to be measured. In addition, behaviors take place throughout the reference transaction (and beyond if the patron returns for further assistance) and must be studied throughout the entire process in order to adequately evaluate the performance of any individual librarian. Behaviors will also change somewhat from day to day or from patron to patron, requiring behavioral evaluations to be conducted over a significant period of time. All of these factors combine to make observation the method of choice for measuring behavior.

OBTRUSIVE EVALUATION BY THE SUPERVISOR

One method of measuring behavior is to have the supervisor observe the librarian at the service desk. In such a case, the supervisor would listen to the interaction between the patron and the librarian and follow the librarian throughout the process. By using the checklist of behaviors, the supervisor could watch for the specific attributes to be evaluated. After observing the reference librarian for a period of time, the supervisor would be able to make an adequate assessment of the librarian's behaviors at the reference desk. By using specific, identifiable behaviors as the keys to evaluation, the supervisor will be able to provide the librarian with concrete areas in which improvement is desired.

One of the problems with using supervisor evaluations is that a librarian may change his or her behavior if it is known that an evaluation is being conducted. This theory is used to support unobtrusive measurement in both behavioral and fact-based evaluations. For behavioral evaluations,

TABLE 1. Behavioral Evaluation of Reference Service: Checklist of Attributes

AVAILABILITY

Indicators	Always	Frequently	Seldom	Never	Comments
Arrives on Time					
Makes eye contact					
Monitors the desk					
Erects barriers at desk					
Works on paperwork at desk					
Talks to colleagues or friends while at desk					

COMMUNICATION SKILLS

Indicators	Always	Frequently	Seldom	Never	Comments
Listens to patron					
Asks patron open-ended questions					
Restates question for patron					
Explains rationale for selecting strategies and materials used					
Interrupts patron					
Speaks condescending/rudely					
Does not ask clarifying questions					
Provides response without discussing methods which achieve response					

TABLE 1 (continued)

SEARCH STRATEGY SKILLS

Indicators	Always	Frequently	Seldom	Never	Comments
Breaks query into component parts					
Selects facet(s) of query that will result in shortest search time					
Makes use of Boolean operators OR, AND, and NOT					
Begins search in source that is too detailed or too general					
Uses only a single strategy and does not try alternate search paths					
Does not make use of colleagues for suggestions					

INDIVIDUAL ATTENTION TO PATRONS

Indicators	Always	Frequently	Seldom	Never	Comments
Takes patron to sources					
Explains how to use reference tool					
Checks back with patrons after a period of time					
Makes vague referrals to areas or sources					
Interrupts one patron to receive a telephone call or to work with another patron					

this factor can be minimized in one of two ways. First, if the evaluation is being conducted over a significant period of time, the librarian will find it difficult to maintain a behavioral facade throughout the process and the true nature of that librarian's behaviors will become apparent as the evaluation proceeds. Secondly, a librarian who changes his or her behavior because he or she *thinks* that an evaluation is being conducted may continue to change that behavior even when an evaluation is not under way. In this respect, the mere fact that the behaviors are being evaluated may result in the display of more positive behaviors by the reference librarian. If this is the case, then the objective of the evaluation (to improve the behavioral aspects of reference service) will have been met without the supervisor even discussing performance ratings with the librarian.

OBTRUSIVE EVALUATION BY PEERS

An alternative to obtrusive evaluation by the supervisor is to have obtrusive evaluation by the librarian's peers in the reference department. In this case, the observations would be made in the same way as described above except that they would be made by other librarians and not the supervisor. Some librarians may feel uncomfortable with their supervisor observing their reference desk activities, but would be more receptive to the same type of observation from a peer. Libraries that have tried such an approach report a high level of success, but at somewhat of a risk. This approach should only be used in a department or library in which the staff believe that they can treat each other honestly and fairly. Peer observation breaks down when staff are afraid to report on each other or when two or more staff members are in competition with each other. In this case, either all librarians will be ranked as average or there will be quite varied opinions on the performance of each individual. The system will become ineffective in either case.

EVALUATION BY OTHER MEDIA

In order to remove staff bias, the library may wish to use another medium in order to collect information regarding reference behaviors. Audio or video tapes of reference transactions can be very revealing methods for determining how a librarian interacts with patrons. After an initial period of feeling uncomfortable with the media of choice, librarians soon forget that a camera is trained upon them and return to their usual behaviors.

Although there are some technical limitations, such as the fixed location of a "hidden" camera and the ethical problem of recording patrons' queries, evaluation by other media can be one of the most effective means of improving behavior at the reference desk. Since it captures all of the activity of the librarian, listening to or viewing such a tape will demonstrate to the librarian how he or she is perceived by others. This technique is used heavily by teachers and performers and could be very valuable for analyzing reference librarians.

UNOBTRUSIVE EVALUATION BY PATRONS

A final method for collecting observations would be to borrow from the fact-based unobtrusive studies and use patrons to observe reference behavior. Patrons could either sit at a table near the reference desk and observe the librarian or could be given queries to ask at the desk. However, instead of checking if the librarian provides the correct answer, the patron would be instructed to rate the librarian on how the answer was obtained. The same checklist of indicators could be given to a patron to fill out after the transaction. If factual questions are used, the same unobtrusive evaluator could measure both accuracy and behavior. This method of evaluation would provide the greatest range of data for evaluating the performance of the reference librarian.

MEASURING REFERENCE BEHAVIORS

Regardless of the method of observation, the evaluator must be trained to watch for a specific set of behaviors displayed by the reference librarian. Unfortunately, behavior is a highly complex feature of human existence and is impossible to measure in its entirety. Statements that a librarian exhibits "good" or "bad" behavior are much too general to provide a meaningful evaluation tool. Neither the librarian nor the evaluator will be able to use such non-specific information to improve the performance of the individual under evaluation. To avoid gross generalizations, methods that evaluate behavior must break that behavior down into its component parts. By measuring incremental features of the librarian's behavior, the evaluator will be able to make more objective judgements and the librarian being evaluated will receive feedback that may be used to improve specific aspects of his/her performance. If desired, an overall behavior rating may be based on the cumulation of the specific attribute measures.

The key to breaking down behavior into measurable components is to develop a list of attributes that may be used as indicators of good or poor performance. To be effective, each attribute must be directly measurable and should be rated on a continuous scale. Some such attributes will be generalizable to all reference situations, whereas others may relate only to specific institutions. Evaluators and librarians must agree on the list of attributes in advance and evaluators must watch for those specific attributes while observing the behavior of the reference librarian. If all parties agree to the system of evaluation, this method can be used to improve substantially the behavior of librarians working in public services.

Several attributes may be used as indicators of each component of the reference transaction. Attributes may be measured on the frequency of their occurrence or by the magnitude of their implementation. In addition, attributes may be developed to measure both positive and negative behaviors. Individual libraries may establish their own standards for the desired level for each attribute. The following lists provide several examples of attributes that may be used as indicators of positive and negative behaviors relating to several different aspects of the reference transaction. These lists do not contain all possible attributes, but are intended to serve as examples to libraries in developing checklists for their own institutions. For the purposes of this paper, both positive and negative attributes are included in each category. The staff of each library will need to decide for itself how to represent the attributes which it decides to measure.

ATTRIBUTES OF AVAILABILITY

A successful reference transaction must begin with the librarian providing some indication to the patrons that he or she is available to provide assistance. A librarian may exhibit excellent performance in all other areas, but will fail completely if patrons are unlikely to approach him or her a question. A variety of indicators may be used to measure behavior in this area. Some more common factors include:

Positive Indicators

> *The librarian arrives for reference duty on time.* A librarian must physically be available in order to provide service. On-time arrival is an indicator that the librarian is ready to offer service.
>
> *The librarian makes eye contact with potential patrons.* Eye contact

with patrons approaching the desk sends a non-verbal signal that the librarian is ready to provide assistance.

The librarian monitors the desk while assisting other patrons. A librarian who checks on activity at the desk can send both verbal and non-verbal signals to waiting patrons that they will be helped soon.

Negative Indicators

The librarian erects barriers at the reference desk. A librarian who builds barriers of books or other materials sends a message to the patron that he or she should not be bothered with questions.

The librarian works on paperwork while at the desk. A librarian who becomes heavily involved in other work sends a message to the patrons that he or she is not to be interrupted.

The librarian talks to colleagues or friends while at the desk. Patrons may be reluctant to approach a librarian who is engaged in a lengthy conversation with friends or colleagues.

ATTRIBUTES OF COMMUNICATIONS SKILLS

The librarian may be available and willing to provide service, but may not be able to adequately understand the patron's needs or communicate the proper response. The librarian who cannot adequately communicate the response to the patron will fail to satisfy needs of the user. Some indicators of communication skills are:

Positive Indicators

The librarian actively listens to the patron. The librarian who allows the patron to phrase the question is given a higher level of credibility by the patron.

The librarian asks the patron open-ended questions. The librarian who uses open-ended questions is able to gain more information from the patron without leading him/her into a specific response.

The librarian restates the question for the patron. Restating the question allows both the librarian and the patron to clarify their understanding of the query.

The librarian explains the rationale for selecting the strategies and materials used. A librarian who provides justification for the use of materials or the choice of search strategy will hold the patron's attention and may end up teaching the patron to become a more independent library user.

Negative Indicators

The librarian interrupts the patron. Librarians who interrupt the patron during the process of presenting the query may jump to initial conclusions that are not valid.

The librarian speaks in a rude or condescending tone. The librarian may correctly interpret and respond to the question, but may do so in a tone of voice that indicates to the patron that he or she is above providing this type of information.

The librarian does not ask clarifying questions. The librarian may be able to correctly answer the query as posed, but might fail to respond to the true information need.

The librarian provides a response without discussing the methods used in achieving that response. While this behavior will provide the patron with an answer, it does nothing to teach the patron how to conduct a search or to justify the selection of the material for the patron.

INDICATORS OF SEARCH STRATEGY SKILLS

In addition to being available and communicating, librarians must also be able to build strategies that will lead to likely results. A librarian may be available to help patrons and may also be a good communicator, but a lack of search strategy skills will leave both the patron and librarian fumbling in the dark. Some indicators of search strategy skills include:

Positive Indicators

The librarian is able to break a query into its component parts. A librarian must be able to factor the patron's question into pieces that can be matched with available resources. The librarian must be able to identify both significant and insignificant concepts within the patron's query.

The librarian is able to select the facet(s) of the query that will result in the shortest search time. Librarians need to be able to identify the most salient aspects of each question and to begin their searches with those aspects.

The librarian makes use of the basic Boolean operators OR, AND, and NOT. To conduct a search, the librarian must understand the relationship between the concepts within the patron's query.

Negative Indicators

The librarian begins the search in a source that is too detailed or too general. A librarian who starts a search at the wrong level will spend more time reaching material that the patron will understand and can use.

The librarian uses only a single strategy and does not try alternate search paths. Librarians who only use a single strategy will be successful when a query matches that strategy, but will fail when an alternative method is required. Librarians should be willing to change gears and approach a problem from a different perspective when the first one does not lead to the desired results.

The librarian does not make use of colleagues for suggestions. No librarian will be able to develop an effective strategy for every case. Referrals to colleagues should be a regular part of the reference process. Librarians who do not question their associates are probably not providing complete service.

ATTRIBUTES OF PROVIDING
INDIVIDUAL ATTENTION TO PATRONS

Patrons are most pleased with the library when they receive quick, accurate, personalized reference services and when they feel that the librarian has paid sufficient attention to their problem. Several indicators may be used to measure a librarian's behavior in providing such service, including:

Positive Indicators

The librarian takes the patron to the sources. Librarians who walk with the patron to the source have additional time to discuss the problem. Patrons may be more likely to reveal information if the librarian spends a longer time with the patron.

The librarian explains how to use reference tools. Many patrons are not familiar with reference sources, but may be unwilling to ask for assistance. A librarian who begins to explain the use of materials can quickly determine the level of instruction required for each patron.

The librarian checks back with patrons after they have been working for a period of time. Patrons appreciate a librarian who follows up on his/her referrals. Due to a high volume of questions, librarians are frequently required to leave patrons to search through an index or other source. A follow-up visit by the librarian will reassure the patron and indicate to the librarian if the patron is having difficulty or in need of further assistance.

Negative Indicators

The librarian makes vague referrals to areas or sources. When a librarian points or hands out a call number to a patron, there is no feedback to the librarian that the patron actually knows how to find or use the materials in question.

The librarian interrupts one patron to receive a telephone call or to work with another. The patron currently at the desk should be foremost in the librarian's mind. Librarians who interrupt working with patrons send messages to the patron that others are more important. This may discourage patrons from asking questions.

VALIDATION OF BEHAVIORAL INDICATORS

Each of the indicators of behavioral attributes listed above represents a single behavior that may be correlated with good or bad reference service. While every librarian exhibits each example (both good and bad) from time to time while working at the reference desk, behaviors measured consistently over a long period of time may be used to evaluate the quality of reference service provided by an individual librarian or department. While the examples used above may be intuitively related to service, they have yet to be validated by an objective statistical study. The next goal in the evolution of the evaluation of reference services will be to validate (or invalidate) behavioral indicators of reference service. The profession could take up this mission by conducting studies on specific behaviors and relating those behaviors to patron satisfaction. Once indicators have been validated, behavioral evaluation can become a common part of the measurement of reference services.

CONCLUSION

The biggest problem with fact-based initiatives for evaluating reference service is that they evaluate the results and not the process. In practice, the reference transaction is such a complex interaction that it is impossible for the transaction to be measured on a simple "right or wrong" basis. Patrons seek much more from the librarian than answers to factual queries. In working with reference librarians, they learn how to conduct research, how to interpret sources, and how to critically evaluate different types of information. These other factors are often much more important than a single factual answer, but they cannot be measured by looking at the answer itself.

The 55% rule does have validity, but should not be used as a measurement of the overall success of reference service. We may only answer one-half of the questions correctly, but the type of questions that we answer incorrectly represent only a minute portion of the total activity at the reference desk. By basing the evaluation of reference service on behavioral rather than factual criteria, we can not only measure the success of the transaction but can also provide direct feedback to the librarian that can be used to improve that performance. As long as we continue to ask the wrong questions, we should expect to receive the wrong answers. Measuring the accountability of reference service is too important not to ask the right questions.

REFERENCES

1. Young, William F. "Methods for Evaluating Reference Desk Performance." *RQ*, v. 25, Fall 1985, pp. 69-74.

2. Westbrook, Lynn. "Evaluating Reference: An Introductory Overview of Qualitative Methods." *Reference Services Review*, v. 18, 1990, pp. 73-78.

3. Hernon, Peter and Charles McClure. *Unobtrusive Testing and Library Reference Services*. Norwood, NJ: Ablex Publishing Co., 1987.

4. Childers, Thomas. "The Quality of Reference Services: Still Moot After 20 Years." *Journal of Academic Librarianship*, v. 13, 1987, pp. 73-74.

5. Katz, William A. *Introduction to Reference Work, volume 1*. 3d ed. New York: McGraw-Hill, 1978, pp. 11-12.

How's the Water?
The Training of Reference Librarians

Heather Blenkinsopp

SUMMARY. There has been little literature written about the on-the-job training of reference librarians. This article includes a survey of training practices in the Albany, New York area. As with a previous national survey, the findings indicate that new reference librarians are not receiving basic training components.

"When librarians begin a new position, they need training on job specifics. . . . The training of reference librarians is particularly arduous because of the breadth of knowledge required for them to be effective: apart from knowing reference sources, they must have a clear understanding of the goals, objectives, priorities, procedures, and expected behavior of members of the particular reference department."[1]

Several years ago, when Karen Stabler performed a survey of newly employed academic reference librarians, her goal was to discover the perceptions of those being trained. Little literature existed as to what training programs were being utilized, no material was available on the effectiveness of these programs, and the scant literature that was available was written from the perspective of the supervisors who provided the training. The ninety-two responses Stabler received did not paint a rosy picture of reference training practices. While a majority of new academic reference librarians received the perfunctory tour of the reference department or library, there was a lack of in-depth training on specifics of the department and a decided want of guidelines for expected behavior. Many

Heather Blenkinsopp is Assistant Head of Technical Services at Mercy College Libraries, 555 Broadway, Dobbs Ferry, NY 10522. This article was researched when she was Reference Assistant/ Weekend Supervisor, Neil Hellman Library, College of St. Rose, Albany, NY.
The author thanks Mansour Alguneh for his technical assistance.

of the librarians were critical of their training programs, citing a lack of representative questions, no time for observation of experienced librarians, and a dearth of written procedural material as major problems. Others received no training at all: "One of these librarians began the first hour on the job!"[2] As Stabler pointed out, "many programs are brief and superficial; new librarians want more grounding on specifics and more interaction with staff, including support and encouragement."[3]

Stabler's article led me to wonder about the training practices employed in the Albany, New York area, commonly known as the Capital District. Were libraries in this area utilizing well-defined reference training programs? Or were Capital District reference librarians suffering from the same lack of direction and half-hearted training that Stabler's academic reference librarians complained of? The Capital District has many specialized and small or one-person libraries; had these librarians received adequate reference training and had they been provided with documentation from their predecessors? In an attempt to answer these questions, I sent surveys to thirty reference librarians in the Capital District regarding the type of reference training they received at the start of their present employment. Unfortunately, the results of this study tend to corroborate both Stabler's findings and the feelings of those few librarians who have written on the subject of reference training practices.

LITERATURE REVIEW

There is a growing body of literature bemoaning the performance of reference librarians, who (if we are to believe the unobtrusive studies) can manage to answer correctly only slightly more than fifty percent of reference questions. These same studies decry the inability of reference librarians to interview patrons properly. They further question why librarians are not referring patrons to other libraries or information sources when a lack of library materials or a lack of librarian's knowledge make an immediate answer impossible.[4] In light of accuracy and performance concerns, the study of reference training practices becomes crucial to the improvement of reference services.

"Training programs seek to prepare new reference librarians in order that they might competently serve the public within a particular institution. . . . The obvious fact is that each library, having variations in user populations and services offered, is unique," according to William F. Young.[5] But Young's assessment of the realities of reference training corresponds to Stabler's dismal findings: "As far as can be determined, few institutions in the United States have developed formal training programs for reference librarians. . . . What passes for training programs in many institutions is in fact orientation occasionally coupled with placing the new reference librarian in the care of a more experienced colleague."[6] The main focus of Young's article is the outline of the training program for new reference librarians developed by the State University of New York's University at Albany. This program includes extensive written guidelines and much verbal support, as well as hands-on experience under the direct supervision of a qualified reference librarian.

Anne F. Roberts, also associated with the University at Albany, likens librarians to other professionals and calls for more intensive training in her effort to debunk the myth that the MLS degree is the only prerequisite needed for adequate performance at the reference desk. She contends that continuing education is just as necessary for librarians as it is for doctors or lawyers, and that adequate training and professional development are critical for librarians as we continue in the information age. Her additional suggestions for training include the use of videotape technology to help reference librarians improve their communication skills, especially in the conduct of the reference interview.[7]

Structure and innovation are key concepts to improving reference service, according to Beth J. Shapiro. Her desire for more fundamental yet creative approaches translates into half of the weekly reference unit staff meetings at Michigan State in Lansing being devoted to training, with an emphasis on " . . . current information on new resources within their own units and on resources available elsewhere in the library so that proper referrals can be made."[8]

Libraries under the jurisdiction of the Maryland State Education Department have been the most aggressive in combatting the 55 percent rule. Consultants performed unobtrusive reference studies and analyzed the data to discover the factors contributing to incorrect answers and lack of referral. When the behavioral factors of verifying a patron's question, asking a follow-up question, and using open probes were determined to be vital to librarians' provision of correct responses, the Maryland team designed workshops to teach these behaviors. An evaluation administered by outside sources verified that the workshop training combined with follow-up peer coaching greatly increased the accuracy of library reference service.[9]

METHODOLOGY

In March 1990, I sent a questionnaire regarding reference training practices to reference librarians at thirty libraries within the Capital District Library Council (CDLC). The libraries fell into the following categories: academic (15), special (7), medical (4), and public (4). Medical libraries were considered separately from special libraries because of the large concentration of hospitals within the Capital District. Special libraries included corporate or government settings. The survey packets, which included the questionnaire, a cover letter, and a stamped return envelope, were sent via the courier service provided by CDLC. No individual names nor more specific titles than "Reference Librarian" were used, a device which allowed the opener of the packet to control the completion of the form.

The ten questions on the survey were designed to seek information about: the library environment, the time devoted by the librarian to reference responsibilities, the previous training and education of the librarian, the reference training received by the librarian at their present employment, and the librarian's assessment of the training they received. Both open and closed-ended types of questions were employed. A comment area was provided to allow librarians to add more thoughts on questions asked, or to include information not directly sought.

The survey, unlike Stabler's, was not limited to academic librarians, nor was any attempt made to target newly hired reference librarians. There was no question regarding length of employment, but some librarians did include this information in the comment area. Responses represent a wide range of experience, including those newly graduated from library school to heads of departments with twenty years of service.

RESULTS OF THE SURVEY

Twenty-two of the thirty surveys were completed and returned, for a 73% response rate. All of the surveys were in usable form. Response was both quick and decisive; the surveys were sent via the Capital District Library Council courier on a Monday morning and several responses were received in the mail on Tuesday afternoon. The initial responses, as well as many of the later ones, contained lengthy comments, not only in the "comment" area, but also attached to earlier questions.

Many of the respondents worked in an academic setting (46%), followed by special libraries (27%), and medical (18%), with only two responses received from public libraries (9%). Ninety-one percent of the librarians worked thirty or more hours per week in the library, with 41% of the respondents spending more than twenty hours per week assigned to the reference desk. A vast majority (86%) had completed the MLS degree. Reference education or training was received from sources other than the library by (86%) of the respondents. Most outside training took the form of library school courses, followed by training at previous employment, continuing education workshops or seminars, and in two cases by subject area degrees. The training period for the librarians' present reference employment was most often less than one month, with only three respondents receiving more than a month's training period. Eight (36%) of the reference librarians claimed to have received no training at all. When training was provided, the trainer ranged from the director to clerical staff members, but someone associated with the reference department was usually involved.

The results tended to confirm Stabler's findings that basic reference training methods are not being utilized in a majority of libraries. The survey contained a question which asked reference librarians whether specific reference training activities had been utilized in their training. The results, in descending order of response, are as follows:

Activity	Number	Percent
Library Tour	15	68
Job Description Given	14	64
Reference Department Tour	14	64
Computer Training	14	64
Observation of Experienced Librarian	12	55
Telephone Answering Instruction	8	36
Policy and/or Procedure Manual	8	36
Reference Books Training	8	36
Scheduled Employee Evaluation	7	32
Guidance on Thoroughness of Answer	6	27
Guidance on Expected Behavior	6	27
Guidance on Reference Interview	5	23
Setting Priorities (Phone vs. Person)	5	23
When an Answer Can't be Found Information	5	23
Staff Meetings on a Regular Basis	4	18
Information About Referral Sources	4	18
Training Program Outline	3	14
Practice with Sample Reference Questions	3	14
Sample Reference Questions to Study	1	5
Unscheduled Employee Evaluation	0	0

The three non-MLS respondents received the most inclusive training, with one person indicating they had received the benefits of all of the reference training activities with the exception of unscheduled employee evaluation. All three non-MLS persons included the following activities as part of their training: guidance on thoroughness of answer, job description given, practice with sample reference questions, library tour, reference department tour, and computer training.

One surprising result of the survey was that although according to the above chart a large percentage of librarians had not received a variety of basic training activities, 41% felt their training had prepared them to provide reference service. While many of the comments centered on lack of training components and the do-it-themselves nature of their reference training, and reference librarians requested more comprehensive training modules, these complaints were not mirrored in the satisfaction rate. I'm not sure what caused this phenomenon: perhaps the small number of librarians surveyed skewed the satisfaction rate; or perhaps there is a sense of rugged individualism among reference librarians that makes them shun the benefits of on-the-job training programs. Several persons listed library school education as their training as though this served as a replacement for job-specific training. One respondent indicated that previous experience may have negated the need for training at the new employment.

A major complaint from the small, specialized libraries was the lack of continuity between the predecessor and the present reference librarian. Many wrote that they had stepped into the library as the sole librarian, with no cross-training with a predecessor nor any procedure manual available. At the one-person library, reference training was a matter of self-instruction.

Some comments were enlightening and unexpected. One heartwarming note came from a reference librarian who had been in the business for almost twenty years, but "I still consider myself learning." Another person cited the difference between the American and British library systems for reference provision; according to this person, most British libraries do not contain a reference desk at all. Another spoke glowingly of a mentor who had made sure the reference librarian received adequate training, both on a formal and an informal basis. My particular favorite came from the head of a reference department whose lack of training as an entry-level reference librarian prompted them to develop a comprehensive training program when they were in the position to train others.

CONCLUSIONS

As Young points out, "The initial training period for the reference librarian is a crucial time which may be taken advantage of. It is an opportunity. In many institutions it is the only period when the work of a reference librarian is actively and closely supervised."[10] In the Capital District, as evidenced by this study, and in many other areas, as evidenced by Stabler's study, the opportunity for reference training is not being taken advantage of. At least not if you ask those being trained. The comments of one Capital District respondent typify what new reference librarians can expect from on-the-job training. "This is my first professional position. I am struck by the difference between the idealism of library school and professional literature and the haphazard way things are done in the real world. The real way I was 'trained' was to throw me in and see whether I would sink or swim. For the most part, I trained myself."

Those being trained in the provision of reference service are seeking more structure, better written guidelines, and a more inclusive program of reference training. What most are receiving now is spotty at best, nonexistent at worst. In a time when unobtrusive reference studies find that librarians answer slightly more than half of reference questions correctly and further studies verify that this accuracy rate can be improved with proper training, more care needs to be taken to provide a sound basis for reference service in the form of systematic, well-documented thorough reference training programs. We need to include a life jacket when we toss new reference librarians into the brine of reference work.

REFERENCES

1. Stabler, Karen Y. "Introductory Training of Academic Reference Librarians: A Survey," *RQ*, Spring, 1987, p. 363.
2. Stabler, p. 367.
3. Stabler, p. 369.
4. The most widely known of these articles is Hernon, Peter and McClure, Charles. "Unobtrusive Reference Testing: The 55 Percent Rule," *Library Journal*, April 15, 1986, pp. 37-41.
5. Young, William F. "Communicating With the New Reference Librarian: The Teaching Process," *The Reference Librarian*, Winter, 1986, p. 223.
6. Young, pp. 223-4.
7. Roberts, Anne F. "Myth: Reference Librarians Can Perform at the Reference Desk Immediately Upon Receipt of MLS. Reality: They Need Training Like Other Professionals," *Proceedings of The ACRL Third National Conference*, Seattle, April 4-7, 1981, pp.400-4.
8. Shapiro, Beth J. "Ongoing Training and Innovative Structural Approaches," *Journal of Academic Librarianship*, May, 1987, pp. 75-6.
9. Stephan, Sandy et al. "Reference Breakthrough in Maryland," *Public Libraries*, Winter, 1988, pp. 202-3.
10. Young, p. 230.

What Do Faculty Want?

Susan Griswold Blandy

SUMMARY. The academic reference librarian needs to know what the college faculty expect from their library. These needs seem often to be idiosyncratic if they do not fit the librarian's conception of the generalized user, but these needs must be identified and met in order to serve the faculty appropriately. Librarians need to be as aware of information acquisition patterns as they are of information sources.

What do faculty members want from the library? Seems a simple enough question with a simple enough solution: find a gregarious faculty member with a flair for writing and ask them to find out. Perform the logically dangerous job of generalizing from the particular, support it with a bibliography and, voilà, we will all be better informed.

Or more confused. The generalities did not hold across disciplines or between schools. Granted the faculty surveyed were from two year schools, four year liberal arts schools, engineering schools and state colleges and universities so there would of course be some diversity in the interview responses, but the variety also shows up in the journal articles that are being written by faculty library users. Some authors bemoan the encroachment of microfilm on their research techniques which call for spreading a serendipitous browsing feast of print materials out on their desks (and floors and chairs). Other authors wonder why we can't do even better with databases and document delivery, why we are so slow to deliver it all through their home modems. Some academics feel it is pointless to put anything in print anymore, and others pretend not to understand copyright laws (maybe they haven't written *their* textbook yet).

Susan Griswold Blandy is Professor and Assistant Librarian at Hudson Valley Community College, Troy, NY 12180 and co-author with Anne Roberts of *Public Relations for Librarians*, Libraries Unlimited, 1989.

183

RESOURCES

To: Susan

From: Shelley

Re: Women's Studies

As we have discussed, there are several books which are essential for the library to own in order to provide materials for students. ...

This is probably the most familiar kind of faculty request to the Reference Librarian/Bibliographer, in effect "I know what libraries do: they collect information for my students; here's what I need." There is a delicate ballet here of communication as we dance around the questions: do you know what we have already? Do I (the librarian) know what you need? what you are teaching? Can I afford to get what you ask for? When? Is your bibliography complete and accurate? Do these books go on reserve? on long term loan to your office? into general circulation? Do we look for out of print titles? How many students? What will the assignments look like and how will they impact the reference librarians? the reference collection? the media and periodicals collections? At least the faculty member is talking to the librarian in an organized, collaborative, advance warning way. It helps to have a policy manual on hand as you develop a closer working relationship so that when requests come in that you can't fill you can explain why. In the current budget crunch many departments are cancelling their professional journals and would like the library to pick up the subscription. It helps if the collection policy clearly states whether the title must be indexed, under a certain price, written at the students' level, curriculum supportive. The policy also works to support joint purchase of expensive but necessary acquisitions such as the new edition of the Oxford English Dictionary.

SERVICES

At the next level faculty are interested in the process and the way students collect information.

Libraries versus Airports

Walking into an unfamiliar library I immediately find that my vision blurs, my mouth becomes dry and my body temperature rises.

I also get this feeling in an airport. Both libraries and airports enable one to get to distant landscapes, but there are rules and languages one must master first. One must know the right questions to ask and the final destination. The procedures in both places are rigid and can be extremely frustrating.

I have been an instructor in the English Department at a community college for three years and have worked with a diverse student population. In all my classes I require library research.

Many of my students who enroll in my Composition One classes have never done research. They have never ventured further into the library than the Xerox machine and water fountain. A few become fascinated by the vistas, by the information, by the imperatives, and by the purity of scholarship. Others find library work to be a chore, and unfortunately, other students get discouraged and drop the class.

A few weeks into the semester I arrange for my Composition One classes to take the library class. This is a two hour session which is designed to acquaint the student with how the library works and how to obtain materials. Again, for some students these two hours of instruction are enough, but others have trouble paying attention and when it is time to complete their library assignment (which basically asks them to locate material) they falter.

As an instructor I am a firm believer in ''hands-on learning.'' For instance, although there are only four CD-ROM index terminals available for student use and it is impractical for the library class to try to squeeze around them, I would like my students to see Xeroxes of the keyboards and screens. Perhaps some imaginative facsimile could be created for classroom use.

I would also like to see specific instruction on using the vertical files and newspaper indexes. I find that although students flock to the *Readers Guide* they shy away from these other two areas. The newspaper indexes are extremely cumbersome.

I was recently looking for a magazine article in the *Readers Guide*. After finding the listing, I took my print-out and went down to the microfilm room to find the tape. Finding the roll of film was relatively simple, but when I sat down at a viewer I realized I had no idea how to use the machine. I would very much like to see instruction in using these machines become part of the library instruction and step-by-step directions available at each machine in addition to the instructions *on* the machine.

After my students complete the two hours of library instruction and the homework sheet, they select a topic for their five page research paper. I then take the entire class to the library so that they can begin their research. Due to the large class sizes (33 students) one or two librarians are never enough. And since it is unlikely class sizes will decrease, I would like to have more librarians and/or student workers also assisting.

A few semesters ago after helping a student select a topic, I advised him to begin his research in the card catalog and began helping other students. Whenever I glanced in his direction, he seemed engaged and was writing down information. Near the end of the class hour I got a chance to sit down next to him to see what he had been finding. He had covered two pages in his notebook with the names and authors of books but had neglected to put down any call numbers. He had attended the library instruction class but had somehow not absorbed this vital piece of information. This may be another area where hands-on work with the catalogs could be incorporated into the library classes.

Later thinking about this student, I began to wonder what else he and other students weren't getting. Teaching is risky business. Perhaps we as teachers need more library training. I would welcome a workshop which would allow instructors the opportunity to learn more about the library. A faculty workshop would also be a place for instructors and librarians to share ideas on how best to help students.

Feeling comfortable in a library (which means knowing how to use it) can be a lifelong adventure. It is a place where learning can go on long after formal classroom instruction ends. Unlike an airport it costs nothing and the destinations one can reach are limitless.

–*Susan Hogan,*
Kinderhook, NY

FACULTY AS LIBRARY USERS: YES, BUT

These two most simple levels of faculty expectations for the library are probably never articulated until the faculty become library users themselves. Reference librarians need to know who constitutes their community, both the actual users and the potential users. We need to know what faculty are using in the library, how they use it, whether what they are looking for matches what they find, why they use the library and what services/collections the library could drop/should add. The shifted emphasis to access to collections rather than acquisition makes it easier for libraries to justify shaping the collection to the particular real user rather than building a general collection for some idealized user.

The Reference Librarian/Bibliographer is expected to understand what is available in what formats. It is just as important to understand information acquisition patterns (cognitive styles, etc.) and information *creation* patterns. What role does interdisciplinary browsing play? retrospective analysis? careful compilation of data? rummaging? serendipity? the faint echo of a long ago heard conference paper? Are your faculty linear thinkers? global thinkers? acting on hunches? tinkerers? documenting suppositions? illustrating lecture points? creating analogies? These are questions that perhaps can be answered with generalizations about academic research but that must be answered, for effective reference service, in the particular for the individuals who use your library. If this is pampering, so be it.

Faculty have quickly bought into the idea of interchangeable formats *except* when the format hinders browsing, hinders stuffing the carrel full of texts to read in the "near future." Faculty have gratefully bought into access rather than ownership and delivery from off-site *except* when they are in a hurry (always). Because going to the library usually means going away from their desks and labs, faculty subscribe to the Principle of Least Effort formulated more than 40 years ago by George Zipf. When library technologies and procedures are cumbersome to use in relation to the desired result faculty will often simply stop asking. The reference librarian researching the complete information for an interlibrary loan request may be annoyed–we do know what the phrase "absent-minded professor" means–and *our* Principle of Least Effort (the requestor should give us complete information) is attacked, but the more rigorous and successful our work the more reason we have to justify the personal rather than the automated touch. Remember this when the computer cannot transform a request for information on the Sistine Chapel into Capella Sistina.

Faculty do want real people in the library. They say, "we need human interaction; we evolved as social animals, interacting with the environment and people. Bringing machinery in between people and their resources can be a problem." The library people may be teaching faculty and staff classes on how to use the automated library (as at the Albany, N.Y. Medical Center College.) These people may be almost invisible, but the new issues of good journals are out on display on time. These people may be the reference librarians one can always send a student to, knowing the librarian will match the faculty enthusiasm for both the subject matter and communicating it. These real people may be the unsung heroes who keep the lights turned on and the copying machines running, the staff lounge coffee pot hot.

A FOCUS GROUP DISCUSSION

A focus group interview is a technique for eliciting from a group of people their perceptions about a situation. This is not a search for truth but for the perceptions on which people act, for the behaviors with which they deal with, respond to the situation, not what it is but how they see it. The purpose of interviewing people in a group is to illuminate patterns of use, to identify expectations and problem areas, to elicit comments on service problems, to hear misconceptions that can be dealt with later and to uncover ignorance about services, collections and processes. In the process of matching library goals to faculty goals one must first understand the relative importance of faculty library goals within their overall direction. The focus group must be large enough to offer people some protection. It must be large enough that the discussions spark ideas and interaction. It should not include people who in any way supervise other members, and at best it should be led by someone without a vested interest in the results. Detailed descriptions of setting up the focus group and conducting the interviews will be found in both the social sciences and library science literatures.

At a focus group interview of a group of engineering school biologists the following points were made. Even through the filter of the focus group format the idiosyncrasies are evident. Perhaps this is because as reference librarians we prepare for our generalized user and the faculty member is most aware of how s/he doesn't fit that mold. In this group there was a "do as I say, not as I do" pattern at work. The undergraduates did spend time in the library, often because of assignments, but also to explore the journals and develop a sense of current research.

The graduate students were simplifying their lives, wearing LL Bean or Land's End clothes rather than going shopping, expecting the library to be a one-stop service: academic library for fiction, travel guides, and historic documents to support role playing games (how were Welsh coal mines laid out?). They needed to research studies relevant to the courses they were teaching. Said one, "I just sit on the floor to browse in journals, reading the popular science magazine summaries and then looking for the original study." At Cornell he used the library every day simply because it was in the same building; here he uses it once a week. Because the graduate students are so often in a hurry, "housekeeping" bothers them, from un-reshelved books to overflowing waste baskets and malfunctioning equipment.

The senior faculty said they use the library "to teach students the textbook isn't biblical" and to teach them standards of scholarly publication ("If DNA Polymerase can proofread, so can you"). They feel reading journals on the CRT is awful; the microfilm takes too much time and trouble and the printout is unsatisfactory. They feel less pressure to keep up regularly with professional journals, and recognize that does not help libraries justify the subscriptions. Said one, "Whenever I go away I never read a newspaper and nothing really changes; we don't affect the news; our lives are local." When the senior faculty are preparing a grant application or a conference report or completing a research report they will put in library time researching all relevant leads, but they will also wander the library to ease "researcher's block" and clear the head, procrastinate a little. In Canberra, one recalled with satisfaction, faculty had a card to let them get into the library after closing and a Xerox card to make copies so they could browse at will. For the senior faculty there seem to be several styles of library use, from the targeted search for a particular item to the browsing search for a study to enliven a lecture to the rambling review of current publications to the aimless wander in hope of serendipity or delay. Said one, "How can I work without sprawling, without a cup of coffee, without the telephone?" The established faculty murmured that "publish or perish" was irrelevant and used up a good deal of paper, that attending conferences was the real method, while the graduate students leaned on journals for information and hoped to be published so they would be invited to conferences. Both groups assumed the library would have a core collection of monographs. Both groups lamented the demise of the card catalog and its contextual search style and the resulting exclusive reliance on the linear computer catalog search. In the end the library seemed so tangential to the biologists' work that I asked if the library really mattered at all, and was amazed by a passionate, unanimous "Yes! We just want it to be better!"

CONCLUSION

So how does the reference librarian react, especially when you sometimes feel one step above a French maid serving the morning cafés. We need to look at library services and materials as a means to an end, providing information for student reports, meeting accreditation: standards and providing instructional support. We then need to look at library services and materials as an end in themselves for both professional and recreational uses. Faculty will use the library to support their daily academic work but they also expect library information on selecting a used car or a mutual fund and, independent as they may be, they still want it accompanied by the warmth of an interested reference librarian. We would do well to set ourselves typical questions and follow the search through the library maze ourselves so that we are better able to understand how it looks to our users. Public librarians understand, and academic librarians must also, that the informal "unimportant" problem-solving opens opportunities for later significant service and collaboration. Is the 80/20 rule an inviolable ratio or can it be improved by more sympathetic individualized faculty-librarian interaction? Aren't Raganathan's rules still the ones to govern the library?

BIBLIOGRAPHY

Hamilton, David P. "Trivia Pursuit," *Washington Monthly* (March 1991) 36-42.
Hively, William. "How much science does the public understand?" *American Scientist* (September/October 1988) 439-44.
Kohn, Rita and Krysta Tepper. *You Can Do It: a PR Skills Manual for Librarians.* Metuchen, N.J. Scarecrow Press, 1981.
Lanning, J. A. "The library-faculty partnership in curriculum development," *College & Research Libraries News* 49:1 (1988) 7-10.
Lushington, Nolan and James M. Kusack. *The Design and Evaluation of Public Library Buildings.* Hamden, CT. Shoestring Press, 1991.
The Role of a Librarian on a Research Team. Albany, N.Y. New York Library Association. Academic and Special Libraries Section, 1988.
Sexton, Mark. "No room for troglodytes at scholarly publishers' meeting," *Publishers Weekly* (July 12, 1991) 44-45.
Thimbleby, Harold. "Can anyone work the video?" *Economist* (Feb. 23, 1991) 48-51.
Watkins, Beverly T. "Scholars, librarians and technologists urged to join in using electronic information," *Chronicle of Higher Education* (Nov. 27, 1991) A21.
Widdows, Richard and Tia A. Hensker, Marlaya H. Wyncott. "The focus group interview: a method for assessing users' evaluation of library service," *College & Research Libraries* 52:4 (July 1991) 352-9.

VI. CONNECTIONS WITH THE REST OF THE LIBRARY

Reference Librarians and Technical Services Librarians: Who's Accountable?

Marilyn K. Moody

SUMMARY. The relationship between reference librarians and technical services librarians has often been strained. In our changing technological and organizational environment, it is imperative that reference librarians and technical services librarians share responsibility for improving this relationship. One way for this to take place is for individuals to become more "accountable" to their colleagues. This article provides accountability guidelines for both reference and technical services librarians which, if followed, can result in increased communication and a better understanding of the roles, concerns, and needs of both reference and technical services librarians.

INTRODUCTION

The relationship between reference librarians and technical services librarians has been historically described as shaky, if not rocky. While

Marilyn K. Moody is Head, Technical Services, Folsom Library, Rensselaer Polytechnic Institute, Troy, NY 12180.

there may have been some improvement in this relationship in recent years, in many libraries the relationship remains an uncomfortable one. While the use of new technology has often been described as having the effect of flattening the organizational structure, blurring departmental lines, or empowering individual staff members, it has not seemed to make it any easier for reference and technical services librarians to communicate effectively with each other or to support each other in working towards their common goals.

While it is always dangerous to characterize whole groups of people, my experiences working in both the public and technical services areas in several different libraries has convinced me that there often is a difference in how librarians working in one area or the other approach their work. This does not necessarily occur because one sort of personality becomes a reference librarian and another a technical services librarian. Rather this difference seems to stem from the nature of the roles each takes, the difference in the daily work and issues they struggle with, and the difference in priorities and goals. Each librarian, no matter what their position, expects a certain degree of "accountability" from their colleagues in other areas, and are disappointed when they do not receive it in the form and manner in which they expect it. The misunderstanding of the actions needed to achieve this "accountability" can be especially acute between reference librarians and technical services librarians. As a way of illustrating the kind of communication which needs to take place, the guidelines described later in this article give examples of the areas where reference librarians and technical services librarians may differ in their accountability expectations.

IMPORTANCE OF ACCOUNTABILITY ISSUES

Why is this issue of accountability so important? Why can't reference librarians and technical services librarians continue to operate in separate departments and spheres, grumbling to themselves when they fail to live up to each other's expectations? Why is it now important to make these issues (and other similar ones) clear to one another?

The environment in which we are working has changed. The first area having a great impact is in the area of automation and the use of new technologies. This use has blurred the boundaries between reference and technical services librarians and requires them to work together to use the new technologies effectively and efficiently. This type of environment may see many librarians taking on multi-functional roles, some of which will include a combination of traditionally technical services and reference services functions.[1] Far more impact is being felt, however, by those librarians whose work remains primarily as a technical services librarian or a reference librarian. In order to do their work effectively in the new technological environment, librarians must understand the work of and issues surrounding their counterparts in other areas. While the idea of the renaissance librarian who can comfortably switch from original cataloging to reference expert at the CD-ROM station is appealing, many librarians are struggling mightily to remain experts in just one area. It is not unrealistic, however to ask for the renaissance librarian in terms of one who understands the needs of the users, the importance of different types of services for the users, a broad understanding of the impacts of new library technologies, and an appreciation of the bibliographic control structures used in libraries.[2]

Secondly, many libraries are shifting their organizational structures to ones that can thrive in a team environment. In order to work effectively in the team environment, librarians need to understand each other's jobs and roles much more clearly. It is impossible to work at solving problems and implementing new ideas together without a basic understanding of each other's concerns and future plans and goals. The team environment approach demands increased communication and cannot be implemented successfully without it. It also requires librarians who understand the big picture of what is happening not only in their own library and organization, but in the profession in general. Only those who take the time to understand one another's viewpoints will be able to successfully interact and work in this type of team environment.

How is this understanding to be achieved? What paths might be taken to achieve this accountability? While I am suggesting some personal accountability guidelines for reference and technical services librarians to follow, there are also additional ways to promote the broader viewpoint and understanding of each other's roles. One of these areas is in the cross-training of librarians to work in more than one area.[3] This can help to achieve the kind of communication and understanding that is needed. Librarians in dual-assignment roles who work in both areas can also help increase understanding of issues for both areas. Staff development programs may also be used to increase understanding of one another's job roles, using both the detailed hands-on approach, as well as programs dealing with broader, more philosophical issues.[4] Other administrators are calling for a more dramatic change in the entire organizational structure of the library as a way of integrating public and technical services staffs.[5]

Use of these accountability guidelines is one way an individual can work to improve the reference librarian/technical services librarian relationship. Using the accountability guidelines requires a change in both an individual's attitude and actions. The guidelines also are best used by the individual with the self-confidence to confront others and clearly communicate concerns when these guidelines are not being followed. These guidelines are not meant to be comprehensive, and some of the items border on the mundane. Yet, it is these type of things that often irritate and exasperate people, and ultimately wear at working relationships. In most respects these accountability issues are issues involving communication. They also involve respect and trust and require sensitivity to the other librarian's role.

ACCOUNTABILITY GUIDELINES: FOR REFERENCE LIBRARIANS

1. Remember that the Reference Department is not the only area of the library which provides user service. Providing reference service is one of the most visible functions of the library. And while it is inarguably one of the most important services a library offers, many other areas of the library are involved in making it possible to offer reference service. Technical services librarians also see their role as a major and important one in providing service to library users. Just because it is not as a direct of a one, does not lessen the importance of that role. Management of the acquisition, cataloging, automation, and other processing activities of the library by technical services librarians is an integral part of what makes basic user services possible. Technical services librarians and reference librarians are working *together* to provide service.

2. Understand the basic technical services functions of your library and how your actions impact them. Technical services librarians expect reference librarians to have a good understanding of basic processing–how items are added, or withdrawn, or how bibliographic records are added to the online catalog. That expectation is based on two lines of reasoning. First, how can a reference librarian fully help users of the library if they don't understand these processes and the points along the way where procedures may affect helping a user? Secondly, an understanding of the technical services functions helps the reference librarian avoid making errors which are time-consuming to correct and poorly serve the user. For example, consider the impact when a technical services librarian discovers that a reference librarian decided to physically transfer 10 years of the *World Almanac* from the reference area to storage, but neglected to follow the procedures necessary to change the library's bibliographic records. Certainly this kind of action doesn't impress technical services librarians as a measure of accountability, but more importantly it impacts on users of the library trying to locate materials.

3. Realize that people and resources cost money, and have some idea of how much they cost. Many reference librarians do not work extensively with budgets and staffing requirements in the same way that technical services librarians are almost always involved. Suggestions for improving or changing technical services procedures coming from reference librarians may not be based in a good understanding of staffing and resource requirements. In the shrinking budgetary environment which many libraries are now placed, realistic assessments of what the library can and cannot do are needed. Reference librarians can help in their relationship with technical services librarians by becoming sensitive to budgetary and staffing concerns.

4. Don't discount the value of the work of other librarians and library staff. This is a basic concept, but one that is a sensitive matter. Technical services librarians often feel that other librarians discount the value of their own work and don't appreciate the work that is done by the technical services staff they manage.

5. Develop a broad understanding of the issues technical services librarians are concerned with. Most "technical services" issues will affect reference librarians as well at some point. For example, with the increasing use of automation, decisions regarding the online catalog need careful attention from reference librarians. For those libraries who have mounted more comprehensive information systems which also include databases and local information files, this attention is even more crucial. The distinction between technical services issues and reference issues has become increasingly indistinct, and this trend will continue. Ignoring "technical services" issues will put the reference librarian at an increasing disadvantage when it comes to carrying out their own work, and will frustrate technical services librarians who need reference librarians to contribute their knowledge and experiences in order to design and implement these information systems.

6. When you've thought of a good idea, take ten minutes to think about what needs to happen for it to take place. How is Technical Services involved? Write down the steps and procedures you think will need to happen for this idea to take place. Who will need to do them? How many of the steps and procedures involve technical services staff? How long do you think it will take to carry out this idea? What existing procedures will need to be changed? Technical services staff sometimes feel that ideas are thought of in other areas of the library, but are left to them to figure out how to implement them. By thinking through these types of questions ahead of time, reference librarians can assure a better acceptance of their ideas and a greater willingness to talk through and evaluate possibilities.

7. *Respect technical services procedures, routines, shelving arrangements, etc.* While you may not agree on the logic or reasoning, take the time to find out why things are done a certain way. If you don't like them, work to change them, but don't just pretend they don't exist or plead ignorance of your library's established practices. Accountability means taking the time and effort to talk with your technical services colleagues about the things you don't like as well as those you do, and to work towards a solution that will be the best for the library users involved.

8. *Respect the different workstyles of your colleagues.* An original cataloger may need a large block of uninterrupted time in order to accomplish his or her work. Your slowest time of the year may be the acquisition librarian's most hectic. These needs should be taken into account.

9. *Understand the basic MARC format record structure.* The MARC formatted record has become one of the building blocks for creating library bibliographic records. An understanding of that structure is imperative to understanding the work that goes into building a library system. Reference librarians cannot adequately contribute to that library process without this basic understanding. It can also be argued that reference librarians shortchange users of the system by not adequately understanding the MARC record and by underutilizing the possibilities which the bibliographic records provide.[6]

10. *Work within the organizational structure of the technical services department or unit.* The organizational structure of a technical services department may be much more hierarchical or divide tasks much more by function than many reference departments. Even in a small library, there may be one particular person who needs to be consulted regarding a specific area. Take the time to learn who the appropriate person to take problems and concerns to. Find out a way of working with the structure which makes it easy for both you and the staff members involved to communicate and get things done.

ACCOUNTABILITY GUIDELINES: FOR TECHNICAL SERVICES LIBRARIANS

1. *Remember that you both are serving the user.* The reference librarian and the technical services librarian both have the same major goal of

serving the users of the library. The hundreds of details that go into making a technical services workflow operate can sometimes cloud one's vision. Don't lose sight of your overall goals. Reference librarians are counting on working with colleagues who share the goal of serving users in the best possible way given an individual library's resources and clientele. One way to emphasize to reference librarians that this is your goal as well is to explain technical services decisions in terms of enhancing options for the user. This assumes as part of the accountability factor, that you are thinking hard about the trade-offs that you make everyday between what is possible, practical, and desirable, and that you are thinking about how those trade-offs affect users.

2. *Realize that reference librarians have the interest of the users in mind for many of the items they question or ask you to change or implement.* Take the time to listen carefully to reference librarians when they ask for a change, and ask them to explain thoroughly why they want something to happen. If you understand what they are trying to achieve, you may realize a better or easier way of accomplishing the same objective. Technical services librarians and reference librarians need to listen to one another's ideas and work together to build bibliographic and processing systems that make sense to the users of your library.

3. *Consider training reference librarians to do some aspects of technical services.* Don't just assume that it will "take more time to undo the mess they will cause" as was the sentiment expressed more than once on a recent debate on the AUTOCAT (Library Cataloging and Authorities Discussion) ListServ. Technical services librarians often complain that they are expected to do reference work but that reference librarians don't perform technical services tasks. Don't compound that attitude by not providing ways for those who are interested to learn more about technical services in a way which will help them in their primary roles as reference librarians. This does not mean that reference librarians have to be trained to do original cataloging. More limited roles, or the use of reference librarians to do discrete technical services tasks, can still help them learn about the process by which material becomes available, or better understand the structure of the bibliographic catalogs which they are using.

4. *Process materials quickly and efficiently, and be able to locate within a reasonable amount of time any item which has been received by the library.* Reference librarians rely on technical services to not only get items to the shelves and in the catalog, but to also organize uncataloged and in-process materials so they are readily available. To the reference librarian who is on the front-line with users, this is one of the most important roles which technical services provides. Users *do* want to know right

this minute where the material is and how they can get their hands on it. An understanding of the importance of this issue to reference librarians and the implementation of policies and procedures which support the easy access of uncataloged and in-process materials can provide reference librarians with essential support.

5. Keep technical services business away from the reference desk. Most reference librarians want to concentrate on the users at the desk, rather than spending their time with other staff members. Make an appointment with the person, or find out when they have non-desk time to talk with you about a problem. Don't assume that if they aren't at the reference desk that they aren't doing anything. (A misperception that is particularly irksome to reference librarians.) If you do talk with a reference librarian at the desk, don't be offended when they stop talking with you in mid-sentence to answer a user's question.

6. Don't remove items from the reference collection without letting the reference librarians know. This one action can send even the most even-keeled reference librarian into a panic when they can't find the reference book which is needed by 30 students for a business assignment. A small thing, perhaps, but one that can waste a lot of time for the reference librarians and users. Setting up procedures for dealing with these situations in advance forestalls this type of problem.

7. Don't automatically assume that reference librarians understand your job. You may need to explain your job both in a broad sense and as to the specific tasks you do, in order for reference librarians to understand the implications of what you do and how those actions help provide service for users. Reference librarians may have had little experience and contact with the types of work which technical services librarians perform. And library school courses only touch on the complexity and diversity of technical services work. Technical services librarians can help close this gap by making sure that explanations of what they are doing and why are a routine part of their work. Don't wait for the reference librarian to ask the question–anticipate areas where clear communication can enhance understanding.

8. Respect the difficulty of doing reference work. Don't underestimate the patience and energy level needed to deal with users constantly on a daily basis. While every job has its own type of stress, public service stress tends to be immediate and unpredictable. The difficult user seems to strike on the same day that the backup reference librarian is sick and a library class assignment is due. Reference librarians are often asked to deal with a huge array of subject areas in fields of which they have no formal training or even interest. Reference librarians often feel torn in several directions, with jobs that are not easily defined and in which priorities may not be clear. Reference librarians are also facing vast changes in how they do reference work as a result of the new technologies they are now using. Technical services librarians have been incorporating new technologies in their work for years, but for reference librarians this is a somewhat new and sometimes threatening experience.

9. *Recognize that reference departments are often organized differently than technical services departments.* Reference departments are often organized less hierarchically than technical services units. The ratio of librarians to support staff is usually different from that of technical services departments. Librarians in the reference department may have certain job tasks, such as liaison or outreach work, which they do quite independently. The responsibility for particular areas in the reference department may not be as neatly defined as in technical services, and there may be more shared responsibility for some functions. For example, while one person has overall responsibility for CD-ROM work-stations, whoever is on the desk may be the one who actually troubleshoots when the workstation goes down at 9:00 on a Sunday evening. This difference in organization may be frustrating to technical services librarians who are more used to operating in an environment where roles and decision making responsibility are more clearly defined.

10. *Remember that reference librarians often work nights and weekends and their schedules are not straightforward.* I once thought I was going to witness an assault in the library when a technical services librarian made a remark to a reference librarian about having "all that time off in the afternoons." An afternoon off translates into a night on the desk. Reference librarian schedules are not going to be straightforward, but this does not mean the person is not working a full schedule.

CONCLUSION

So who's accountable? Both reference librarians and technical services librarians must take the time to clearly express their individual expectations, frame them in realistic terms, and ask their colleagues to meet those expectations. Both must also attempt to understand the special frustrations and needs that each experiences in their work. Librarians who understand how their work and the work of other librarians meshes together to contribute to serving the users of libraries can make greater strides in contributing towards this accountability. Accountability between reference and technical services librarians is no longer a luxury; it is a communication and organizational challenge which must be met.

REFERENCES

1. Gillian McCombs, "Public and Technical Services: The Hidden Dialectic," *RQ* 28(Winter 1988):141-145.

2. Gillian McCombs, "Public and Technical Services: Disappearing Barriers," *Wilson Library Bulletin* 61(November 1986):25-28.

3. Sheila S. Intner, "Ten Good Reasons Why Reference Librarians Would Make Good Catalogers," *Technicalities* 9(January 1989):14-16. See also: Pamela Bluh, "Truce or Consequences: The Relationship Between Technical Services and Reader Services," *Technical Services Quarterly*, 1(Spring 1984):25-30.

4. Tara Lynn Fulton, "Reference Librarianship: Sharing Our Knowledge With Technical Service Colleagues," *RQ* 27(Winter 1987):210-219.

5. Jennifer Cargill, "Integrating Public and Technical Services Staff to Implement the New Mission of Libraries," *Journal of Library Administration* 10(1989):21-31.

6. Jon R. Hufford, "Elements of the Bibliographic Record Used by Reference Staff Members at Three ARL Academic Libraries," *College & Research Libraries*, 52(January 1991):54-64.

Evaluating OPACs,
or,
OPACs Are Reference Tools, Too!

Lynne M. Martin

SUMMARY. The evaluation of reference service is complex and subjective, because reference service itself is complex and subjective. Reference service is more easily evaluated if its facets are judged against corresponding, known criteria. The core facet of reference service, for an automated library, is its online public access catalog (OPAC). Although the library literature contains numerous papers on the functional and performance evaluation of OPACs, as well as on the evaluation of many facets of reference service, it presents little assistance for the evaluation of OPACs as the central facet of reference service. In order to alleviate this lack, this paper evaluates OPACs as if they were any other reference tool, judging them against Norman D. Stevens' classic eighteen criteria for the evaluation of reference books. A selective bibliography of works on both OPAC and reference book evaluation is included.

OK, I know what you're thinking: "What's a technical paper about OPACs, written by a cataloger, doing in a nice reference journal like this? And, say, isn't this volume supposed to be about assessment or evaluation of reference services?"

Well, don't panic!

This paper is about OPACs, but it is not meant to be a technical paper, designed only for catalogers (describing the intricacies of MARC formats, AACR2R and LCRIs, choice of access points, etc.) or for systems personnel (describing OPAC response time, MIPS, benchmark tests, etc.).

Lynne M. Martin is Monographic Cataloger, University Libraries, University at Albany, State University of New York, 1400 Washington Avenue, Albany, NY 12222.

This paper is, instead, meant for reference librarians, catalogers and systems personnel alike, and meant to accomplish three important, interrelated tasks: (1) to provide a vehicle that will place online public access catalogs (OPACs) in a new (new to OPACs, but old as libraries go) and different light; (2) to foster increased, careful consideration of exactly what OPACs are supposed to be, and what they are supposed to do for patrons, as well as for library staff and (3) to place the evaluation of a library's OPAC at the very heart of the evaluation of any of the library's services (including reference service), or of the evaluation of the library, as a whole.

The evaluation of reference service is a subjective and complex task, at best, because reference service is, itself, subjective and complex.

THE COMPLEX

In order to adequately and more easily handle the complexities of the evaluation of reference service, as a whole, it is essential that each of its component parts or facets be evaluated individually. This concept is not new; and the library literature contains innumerable papers documenting how libraries have evaluated the various facets of reference service (such as: the evaluation of the reference interview, reference desk service, the reference librarians themselves, training, the reference collection and the individual reference books, etc.). The worth of this endeavor is not disputed, remaining of vital importance and interest to librarians, as this collection attests.

What has been overlooked in the library literature, perhaps because it is so integral and obvious, the inclusion of a library's OPAC as not just a facet of reference service, but as the central facet or heart of reference service. Of course, this is not meant to exclude libraries that have not automated. On the contrary, although this paper will consider only OPACs, a print card catalog could (and should!) also be considered in a similar manner.

Therefore, when reference service is evaluated, OPACs must be included as an integral part of the evaluation. OPACs must, however, be evaluated in the context of their integral relationship with reference service, rather than evaluated as entities of and for themselves (that is, functional and performance evaluations).

Much as been written on the evaluation of the functional aspects of OPACs, as Bland attests: "The library literature is replete with studies and recommendations regarding the functional evaluation of OPACs. . . .

[They] have done an admirable job of identifying and explaining the functions which state-of-the-art OPACs should include. This literature has such breadth and depth that even libraries with limited expertise and experience with automation should have little trouble in choosing between alternative OPACs or thoroughly evaluating a single system based on functional characteristics'' (5). Performance evaluations also fill the library and computer science literature.

Unfortunately, despite the real need for all of functional and performance evaluations, none of these evaluations addresses fully the evaluation of an OPAC as an integral part of reference service as a whole; and, perhaps Bland says it best: "These evaluations may not tell a library what it needs to know: that is, whether the complicated and expensive system it is considering or has purchased is really adequate . . . for the job intended" (5).

THE SUBJECTIVE

In order to provide a means of non-objective evaluation or assessment of reference service, it is necessary to find established criteria by which to judge the service.

Once again, much has been written on the evaluation of reference service, including the definition and application of various criteria for the evaluation of almost every conceivable facet of reference service, as well as of reference service as a whole.

The facet of reference service that has consistently been overlooked in the library literature is library catalogs, especially OPACs.

Increasingly, an OPAC forms the core facet or heart of reference service. Like a biological heart, the intricate workings of an OPAC are not directly visible or noticeable, even though the effect is great. If a heart fails to work properly, the biological body as a whole suffers and death could occur; if an OPAC fails to work properly, the information needs of patrons are not and cannot be met and, therefore, the library has failed to accomplish its primary responsibility of providing the information needs of its patrons.

It is easy enough to recognize that an OPAC is the core facet of reference service, but is not as easy to define criteria to evaluate an OPAC in this manner. The library literature, sadly, offers no direct assistance with this problem; nevertheless, specific criteria to evaluate OPACs in this manner need be defined.

OPACs ARE REFERENCE TOOLS, TOO!

In thinking about OPACs in this manner, I was reminded of my library school reference course in which I studied a range of print and online reference sources, evaluating them against of a number of given, specific criteria.

The answer is simple (perhaps too simple to be considered seriously, at least on the surface of it), but, then, a plain and simple, overlooked answer is often the best solution! The answer is: evaluate OPACs in exactly the same manner as other reference tools (after all, OPACs are reference tools, too!). In fact, the answer is even simpler than that: evaluate OPACs in exactly the same manner as reference books.

The library literature contains even more papers discussing and defining criteria to evaluate reference books, than it does to evaluate OPACs. The problem would, then, be to find the best criteria.

This line of thought reminded me of Stevens' 1989 paper, that delineates eighteen specific elements, points or criteria for the evaluation of reference books (45). Stevens' paper is classic, and, perhaps, the finest delineation of evaluative criteria for reference books that exists in the library literature today.

STEVENS' EIGHTEEN CRITERIA

Stevens' eighteen criteria for the evaluation of reference books are: accuracy, appropriateness, arrangement, authority, bibliography, comparability, completeness, content, distinction, documentation, durability, ease-of-use, illustrations, index, level, reliability, revisions and uniqueness.

Let's define Stevens' eighteen criteria and apply them to the evaluation of OPACs.

Stevens notes: "In theory, by thinking carefully about the following eighteen points [or criteria], or as many of them as are appropriate in a particular case, it should be possible to make an evaluative judgement about a particular reference work [or about an OPAC]" (45).

Stevens arranges his eighteen criteria, not in rank order, but instead in alphabetical order. At first, Stevens' alphabetical arrangement may seem simplistic or merely convenient; however, when considered further, it is evident that Stevens' arrangement reinforces an important idea regarding the relationship of each criteria to the task at hand (that is, analyzing a reference tool) and each of the other criteria. That idea is: each of the criteria are equally important; no one criteria is any more important than any of the others. Further, it is only when a reference tool is evaluated on the basis of all eighteen criteria, considered together, that a complete and reliable judgement about a reference tool can be made.

In order to accomplish the task at hand (evaluating an OPAC as if it were any other reference tool), I will: list each of Stevens' eighteen criteria, define the eighteen criteria as they relate to the evaluation of a reference tool and go on to apply the criteria to the evaluation of an OPAC, as a reference tool.

Criterion 1: Accuracy

The accuracy of a reference tool refers to the correctness and validity of the information contained in the tool. Stevens writes: "A reference book, in particular, is of little value if the information which it contains is not accurate. It is not always, of course, easy to determine how accurate [the reference tool's] information may be" (45).

Criterion 1 is as easily applicable to the evaluation of an OPAC, as a reference tool, as it is to any other reference tool; indeed, an OPAC's accuracy is of prime importance.

An OPAC's accuracy refers to the accuracy of all of bibliographic and other data contained in the MARC records that comprise the database of an OPAC (including: the accuracy of title, author/editor, publication and collation information, as well as holdings and location data and call numbers and subject headings and other data).

If, for example, an OPAC displays the incorrect location or wrong call number for a given item, that item is as good as lost, and the patron's information need may well go unmet. If the title information is incorrect, a patron may well assume that the library does not own the specific title needed, and the information need, once again, goes unmet.

An OPAC's accuracy also refers to how strictly and how well the cataloger who created the MARC records applied the cataloging standards and the MARC format. Inconsistencies and errors in the application of cataloging standards and in the use of the MARC format leads to errors in the MARC records, that can, in turn, lead to errors in indexing. For example, an incorrectly tagged MARC 100 field, with indicator errors, can cause an author's name to be indexed incorrectly or not at all; and, once again, the information needs of the patron would go unmet.

An OPAC's accuracy, further, refers to the accuracy of the underlying software program. If a software program contains errors, then an OPAC stands little chance of consistently displaying correctly information for the patrons, even if the bibliographic data contained in an OPAC is accurate.

Criterion 2: Appropriateness

The appropriateness of a reference tool refers to the delicate relational balance between the type and kind of library, the information needs/wants of the patron and the type and kind of information/data included in the reference tool itself. Stevens notes: "Some perfectly good reference books are not appropriate for a particular library or for attempting to locate a particular kind of information. Beyond that there are questions to be asked about whether or not the arrangement, the content, and, in general, the approach is appropriate for the subject" (45).

Criterion 2 is also as easily applicable to the evaluation of an OPAC, as a reference tool, as it is to any other reference tool; and, like Criterion 1, the appropriateness of an OPAC, as a reference tool, is also of prime importance.

The appropriateness of an OPAC refers to: the type, level and standards of cataloging (including: descriptive cataloging, as well as the assignment of appropriate subject headings and call numbers); the type and level of indexing and the size of the database together with: the size of the online system; the response time of the system, in correspondence with the information needs and level of sophistication of the patron.

For example, an OPAC in an academic research library that contains only records listing the title and call number of items, is little more than useless, when complex subject retrieval is required for researchers. Also, an OPAC, in a rare book library, serving the information needs of rare book bibliographers and researchers, would be useless if its records failed to list specific notes regarding collation, physical condition, publishers, illustrators, etc. In addition, an OPAC in a medical library that uses Sears subject headings, rather than MeSH, will be of little help to physicians-patrons; and conversely, an OPAC in an elementary school library that includes help screens and printed documentation for patrons written on a graduate level, will be of little help for fourth- and fifth-grade students. Further, an OPAC with a database of several hundred thousand records, operating in a PC environment, rather than in a mini- or main-frame environment, would be inoperable, lacking sufficient memory to support the database.

Criterion 3: Arrangement

The arrangement of a reference tool refers to the overall organization and structure of the tool. Stevens' writes: "A good reference book presents its information in an orderly fashion and is organized and arranged in such a way as to facilitate use'' (45).

Criterion 3, like the previous two criteria, is as easily applicable to the evaluation of an OPAC, as a reference tool, as it is to the evaluation of any other reference tool; and Criterion 3 is of prime importance.

An OPAC's arrangement refers to the overall structure of the system, as well as to the appropriate and consistent application of the classification scheme, controlled vocabulary (subject headings) and bibliographic description (use of AACR2R). An OPAC must present its information to the patron in the most orderly and easily understood manner possible.

For example, an OPAC should have clear and understandable display screens for the display of search results and bibliographic records. In addition, an OPAC should provide sufficient on-screen assistance (help screens) to guide the patrons to the search process.

Criterion 4: Authority

The authority of a reference tool refers to the expertise and experience of the people who create the tool. Stevens writes: ''The qualifications of the author, contributors, and the publisher are sometimes an important aspect of evaluating the quality of a work. If they are recognized experts in a field, and have written and/or published other works on the subject, which have been well received, then perhaps it may be presumed that they know something about the subject'' (45).

Criterion 4, like the previous three criteria, is as easily applicable to the evaluation of an OPAC, as a reference tool, as it is to the evaluation of any other reference tool; and Criterion 4 is of prime importance. Authority assumes a more important role in the evaluation of an OPAC, than in the evaluation of other reference tools.

Authority, as applied to the evaluation of an OPAC, refers to the expertise of: OPAC system programmers and designers, who create the software programs that drive an OPAC; catalogers, who create MARC records contained in an OPAC's database; catalog maintenance staff, who correct and update the OPAC's database; reference and bibliographic instruction staff, who assist and teach patrons in OPAC use and individuals who create and publish documentation to assist patrons in OPAC use, etc. The expertise and appropriate application of expertise of all of these individuals is vital. If any of these people lack expertise, or fail to do their jobs excellently, then the patron will experience varying levels of difficulty in the information search, and consequently, the patron's information need may, once again, go unmet.

Criterion 5: Bibliography

The bibliography of a reference tool refers to previous works published about the tool's subject or related subjects. Stevens notes: "Almost, but not quite, every subject has had previous work published about it. A good reference tool provides adequate bibliographic information about previous work on the same, or related, subjects that will help guide users who wish to pursue a subject further" (45).

Criterion 5, in contrast to the previous four criteria, appears, at first, not to be applicable to the evaluation of an OPAC, as a reference tool. When, however, Stevens' idea of guiding patrons to other works or sources of information on the same subject is taken into account, then Criterion 5 is as easily applicable to the evaluation of an OPAC, as a reference tool, as it is to any other reference tool, and it is of equal importance as the previous four criteria.

An OPAC should ideally lead patrons to a range of sources for the needed information. This concept includes having appropriate and adequate added subject headings for each volume included in the OPAC's database. An OPAC's subject headings should, ideally, come under authority control and provide "see" and "see also" references. In addition, the OPAC should lead patrons to other online and print databases for items that the OPAC's database does not contain.

Criterion 6: Comparability

The comparability of a reference work refers to the comparison of the reference work in hand, as Stevens explains: "It is always important to consider what similar or related reference books already exist and to compare a new reference book with those previous works. Such a comparison is a good way to check such things as accuracy and arrangement as well as to obtain a general sense of the utility of one reference work in contrast to another" (45).

Criterion 6, like Criterion 5, may not seem, at first, to be as easily applicable to the evaluation of an OPAC, as reference tools, as it is to any other reference tool. When, however, an OPAC is perused from the patron point-of-view, the criterion of comparability becomes, just as the previous five criteria, of prime importance. Comparability, in relation to the evaluation of an OPAC, refers to the specific OPAC's comparability to its print card catalog predecessor and to its rival OPACs. An OPAC need be compared to its predecessors, in terms of its ability to assist the patrons in locating the information required, in the simplest and quickest manner possible.

The transition from one catalog to another (especially from a print card catalog to an OPAC) is not always easy for patrons or for staff. Patrons need to be reassured that when he/she looks for a particular author or title that it will be as easy to find as with the print catalog. If an OPAC does its job well, then it will be easier and quicker, thus, improving the service to the patron. For example, the question of "serendipity" in searching plays a role here. OPACs allow for little serendipity, or allow it in a much different manner than in the print card catalog; this difference can easily prove to be a loss of access to information for patrons. On the other hand, an OPAC that indexes the titles contained in the contents notes (The MARC 505 field), may well provide more and better access to information, than did the print card catalog.

An OPAC must also be compared to its rival OPACs. There are many choices of OPACs available to libraries, and great care must be taken in the selection of an OPAC vendor. The best match possible must be made between the needs of the library, the needs and level of sophistication of the patrons, the OPAC system itself, the vendor and the cost of the system, among many other factors, if an OPAC is to perform its job of matching information need to patron inquiry.

Criterion 7: Completeness

The completeness to a reference tool refers to, as Stevens notes: " . . . whether or not the subject [of the reference tool], as defined by the author, has been covered completely and thoroughly" (45).

Criterion 7, like Criteria 5 and 6, seems, at first, not to be applicable to the evaluation of an OPAC as a reference tool; however, Criterion 7 is easily applicable to the evaluation of an OPAC, but in a more subtle manner than the previous six criteria.

The completeness of an OPAC as a reference tool refers to: the completeness of the database as a whole as compared to a library's collections as a whole, and the completeness of the MARC records comprising an OPAC's database.

To be a complete and effective database an OPAC should ideally contain one MARC record for each item or group of items (in the case of periodical, serial and multi-volume items) owned by a library. Often (for a variety of reasons, such as budgetary constraints that prohibit full retrospective conversion of all records or the purchase of the size of an OPAC system really needed, etc.), libraries opt to omit certain parts of the collections from an OPAC. Lack of access means that patrons' information needs will go unmet.

For example, an OPAC that has omitted all books classified with the Library of Congress "Q" (Science) Classification, is not complete, and is of little value to patrons needing information in the sciences. Also, an OPAC that has omitted all periodicals, leaves a big gap in the information retrieval on any given subject. Although the practice of omitting periodicals from an OPAC is not uncommon (many libraries provide alternative finding aids for periodicals), the OPAC is still incomplete and patrons are forced to cope with numerous systems (both print and online) to find all of the materials needed.

Further, an OPAC that does not provide complete MARC records, for each item in the database, fails to give the patron full information. Imagine, for example, an undergraduate student needing information on the topic of political reform in the Soviet Union, finding only authors, titles and call numbers listed in an OPAC. Title access alone may provide some information, but certainly the student's search would not be complete. Imagine, again, an OPAC that listed full bibliographic and subject information, yet failed to list the corresponding call numbers. A search of such an OPAC would yield an adequate bibliography, but would not allow the patron to actually locate the needed items in the library. Although the previous two examples are extreme, more subtle omissions in an OPAC database will still yield the same result: a patron's information needs may go unmet.

Criterion 8: Content

The content of a reference tool refers to the actual information or data it contains. Stevens further defines content: "It is above all the content of the book, and a general impression of the content and its overall value, that is likely to be the primary consideration in evaluating any reference book" (45).

Criterion 8, like the Criteria 1-4, is as easily applicable to the evaluation of an OPAC, as a reference tool, as it is to the evaluation of any other reference tool; and Criterion 8, like Criteria 5-7 is applicable in a more subtle manner.

Criterion 8 incorporates Criterion 1 (accuracy) and expands upon it, including the accuracy of information contained in an OPAC, as well as also the overall impression of value of the OPAC. Content may be more a matter of impression of perception or accuracy, relevance, etc. For example, if patrons perceive that an OPAC will assist them in finding the information that they need and want, then they will use the OPAC, and consequently an OPAC's contents will be affirmed. If patrons do not perceive an OPAC in that way, then they may not use it (or may not use it adequately) and may not have their information needs met.

Criterion 9: Distinction

The distinction of a reference tool refers to the special qualities and features that set the tool apart from its counterparts, making it "the authority" on a particular subject. Stevens confirms the definition and refines it: "A truly outstanding reference work has some quality about it that gives it a character of its own which is not shared by any other reference work. That distinction is the indescribable quality that not only sets the work apart but makes it an obvious purchase or the obvious source to be used for answering certain kinds of reference questions on a regular basis" (45).

Criterion 9, like Criteria 1-4, is as easily applicable to the evaluation of an OPAC, as a reference tool, as it is to the evaluation of any other reference tool. Like Criteria 5-8, Criterion 9 is applicable in a more subtle way.

Distinction, as applied to the evaluation of an OPAC, is integrally related to, and perhaps, a culmination of all of the other seventeen criteria. If all of the other seventeen criteria are met, then an OPAC has become "the authority" for all of the materials and all of the information contained in those materials for a library. Also, a library's distinctive character is certainly reflected in the materials (both individually and collectively) that comprise its collections; and a library's OPAC (as the tool to locate the materials and the information contained in the materials) is also a reflection of its library's distinctive character.

Criterion 10: Documentation

The documentation of a reference tool refers to the source of the information contained in the reference tool, and is integrally related to the authority, accuracy and reliability of the reference tool. Stevens notes: "Knowledge about the source of the information contained in the reference book and how and where that information was obtained, is a vital consideration. A reference book that provides no documentation and contains no information by which one can test its accuracy and reliability is automatically suspect" (45).

Criterion 10, like Criteria 8 and 9, is as easily applicable to the evaluation of an OPAC, as a reference tool, as it is to the evaluation of any other reference tool, but in a more subtle manner. Criterion 10 is applicable in an even more subtle manner than Criterion 8 and 9.

Documentation, as applied to the evaluation of an OPAC, refers, not to the printed system documentation (or written instructions regarding the practical use of an OPAC), but, instead to an OPAC's unique combination of: authority (Criterion 4), accuracy (Criterion 1) and reliability (Criterion 16).

Criterion 11: Durability

The durability of a reference tool refers to its physical permanence or the ability of the work to withstand the day-to-day use it will undergo. Stevens writes: " . . . every reference book should be evaluated in terms of whether its physical make up is durable enough for the intended use and likely life of the work" (45).

Criterion 11 is not a subtle criterion, it is, instead, like Criteria 1-4, as easily applicable to the evaluation of an OPAC, as a reference tool, as it is to the evaluation of any other reference tool; and Criterion 11 is also of importance.

The durability of an OPAC refers to the durability of both the hardware and the software that comprise the system. The public access terminals need to be durable enough: to handle constant use (and frequent misuse) by patrons, to be left turned on for many hours at a time, to be subject to the many atmospheric and electronic whims of most library buildings (too cold or hot; too humid or dry and too little, too much or fluctuating current).

Criterion 12: Ease-of-Use

The ease-of-use of a reference tool refers to the ability of library staff and patrons to easily find the information needed in the work. Stevens writes: "Even an organized book, and sometimes even a well-organized book, may not be easy to use. Since, for the most part, reference books are intended to provide ready access to particular pieces of information, the ability to find the information contained in a reference work easily and readily is another important quality" (45).

Criterion 12, like Criteria 1-4 and 11, is as easily applicable to the evaluation of an OPAC, as a reference tool, as it is to the evaluation of any other reference tool; and, like Criteria 1-4 and 11, Criterion 12 is of prime importance. Criterion 12 may well be the most important criterion on which to judge an OPAC.

An OPAC must be easy to use, for both patrons and staff. An OPAC that is difficult for patrons to use in any way (confusing screens, little or confusing online assistance, designed with computer experts in mind, etc.) probably will not be used, and will ultimately discourage patrons from using the system. An OPAC that is difficult for public service staff to use compounds the patron ease-of-use problem; and an OPAC that is difficult for technical services staff to use will dramatically decrease output of database updates and correction, and degrade an OPAC's accuracy, completeness and authority, and will ultimately compound the patron ease-of-use, as well.

Criterion 13: Illustrations

Illustrations refer to the uses of art work or pictures to accompany the printed materials in a reference tool. Not all reference tools are or need to be illustrated. Stevens notes: "Not all reference books need illustrations. . . . The first question is whether a particular reference work should be illustrated. . . . Only then, assuming that there are illustrations, should the question of whether or not the illustrations are adequate, representative and well-selected be considered" (45).

Criterion 13, like Criteria 5-7, may, at first, seem not to be applicable to the evaluation of an OPAC, as a reference tool, because (unless the OPAC is very unusual) it will not have illustrations, as such. When, however, the corollary of illustrations is considered (that is, the use of other printed material, such as help or search aids) then illustrations as an evaluative measure of an OPAC, becomes, like Criteria 1-4 and 11-12, of prime importance. Well-prepared search guides, etc., can prove invaluable to the new patron or to the patron who uses an OPAC infrequently. Printed signs near each terminal, explaining use of an OPAC, classification systems, subject headings, explanations of library locations, etc., are also invaluable illustrations.

Criterion 14: Index

Stevens notes the obvious: "An index is considered a *sine qua non* of a reference book and, in many cases, that is certainly true but a bad and/or incomplete index, or one that simply duplicates that basic arrangement of the text and provides no additional access points, is worse than no index at all" (45).

Criterion 14, like Criteria 1-4 and 11-12, is as easily applicable to the evaluation of an OPAC, as a reference tool, as it is to the evaluation of any other reference tool.

Index, as applied to the evaluation of an OPAC, refers to the indexing of the individual fields that comprise each MARC record contained in an OPAC. The indexing of the MARC records that comprise an OPAC's database and of the MARC fields that comprise each MARC record is, not only of prime importance, but vital to the effectiveness and worth of an OPAC. OPACs usually index author fields (MARC fields 100-110, 600-610 and 700-710), title fields (MARC fields 240-245, 4XX, 730-740, 8XX) and subject fields (MARC fields 6XX). If an OPAC's software permits relatively error-free indexing, then most items are searchable and retrievable on the OPAC by title, author and subject.

More complete access is possible when other MARC fields are also indexed. For example, when the MARC field 505 (contents note) is indexed, access to the individual titles contained in a given work is attained. Indexing by call numbers, permits subject searching by call number ranges, much like browsing the shelves of the library.

Criterion 15: Level

The level of the reference tool refers to the intellectual level of the tool, and must be considered in relationship to the intellectual level of the intended audience. Stevens writes: "Almost any subject can be dealt with in various ways depending upon the age, education, and level of understanding of the intended audience. The approach that reference work takes to a subject, including such things as the language used, and the relationship of that approach to the intended audience's capabilities and needs is worth some thought" (45).

Criterion 15, like Criteria 1-4, 11-2 and 14, is as easily applicable to the evaluation of an OPAC, as a reference tool, as it is to the evaluation of any other reference tool; and, Criterion 15 is of prime importance. Level, as applied to the evaluation of an OPAC, also incorporates one aspect of Criterion 2 (that is, the level of sophistication of the patron) and highlights and enhances it.

For example, an OPAC designed for graduate students, with instructions written on that level and with records for materials on a graduate level, would not help an elementary student. Also, an OPAC designed for research physicists, with instructions in scientific jargon and containing records for highly specialized books and journals, would be of little use to a public library patron, seeking a best-seller to read for enjoyment.

Criterion 16: Reliability

The reliability of a reference tool refers to the trustworthiness, accuracy and stability of the work. Stevens writes: "Reliability is accuracy on a larger scale . . . . The simple test of reliability is whether or not the user is likely to find the information on a subject he/she is most often looking for in a particular tool" (45).

Criterion 16, like Criteria 1-4, 11-12 and 15-15, is as easily applicable to the evaluation of an OPAC, as a reference tool, as it is to the evaluation of any other reference tool; and, Criterion 16 is of prime importance. Criterion 16 also incorporates aspects of Criterion 1 (accuracy), Criterion 8 (content) and Criterion 9 (distinction) and expands upon them.

If an OPAC has achieved reliability, it will be proven by the fact that patrons flock to it, utilizing it before consulting any other resource to supply their information needs. Patrons will only be encouraged to this if an OPAC has yielded accurate do timely information on a consistently regular basis.

Criterion 17: Revisions

Because information in any given field changes over time, and a reference tool freezes the information at a given point in time, the value of a reference tool is in its ability to be easily and adequately revised. Stevens says it best: "Few reference books endure without some regular provision for updating and revision. On the other hand revision for the sake of revision, and perhaps incidentally the ability to sell a new edition more often than is really needed, is of no real value" (45).

Criterion 17, like Criteria 1-4, 11-12 and 14-16, is as easily applicable to the evaluation of an OPAC, as a reference tool, as it is to the evaluation of any other reference tool; and Criterion 17 is also of prime importance.

Library collections tend to be intensely dynamic. For example, new items (of all types: books, audiovisuals, software, periodicals, etc.) are added to a collection on a regular, on-going basis, at the same time as other items are withdrawn (as collections are judiciously weeded or as routine loss occurs). In addition, items frequently change locations within a library. For example, a book, once designated a reference book, may be replaced by a newer edition and the older edition may be moved to the circulating collection).

Also, call numbers may change over time. As changes occur, it is of particular importance that an OPAC permit revision of the MARC records contained in its database. In addition, it is also important that the method of change be relatively easy, with minimal computer programming or data entry time. Revision of records in an OPAC should be much easier than the revision of the print catalog cards that comprised the card catalog.

The amount of time that it takes to add new records to an OPAC should be brief, and should take much less time than to file print catalog cards. Many OPACs permit the direct transmission of records from the bibliographic, while other OPACs require that MARC tapes be loaded by batch process. Loading records should require little system down-time, providing the least inconvenience to patrons (remember, while several staff could file catalog cards in the print card catalog, patrons could still use the catalog).

Criterion 18: Uniqueness

The uniqueness of a reference tool refers to the tool's distinctive distinctiveness and specificity. Stevens writes: "The last, and perhaps the truest, test of the value of a reference work is its uniqueness. An outstanding reference work somehow provides information, or access to information, in a fashion that is unlike what is found in any other reference work or on the same subject and that somehow give the work a character all of its own" (45).

Criterion 18, like Criteria 5-7 and 13 seems, at first, not to be applicable to the evaluation of an OPAC, as a reference tool; however, like Criteria 8-10, Criterion 18 is applicable, but in a much more subtle manner.

Stevens' definition of uniqueness certainly captures the true spirit of an OPAC. An individual library's OPAC should reflect the nature and character of that library, by containing records for that library's unique and individual collections. No other reference tool (aside from an OPAC) possesses the ability to capture the quintessential spirit of a library and provide such unique and complete access to a library's collections.

Library catalogs are unique. Over the years, I have heard many stories about the uniqueness and individuality, and sentimentality attached to library print catalogs! Several academic librarians have reported that professors offered to "take in" the print catalog (lock, stock and barrel) when an OPAC was introduced, because, the professors said (again and again) the print catalogs had such character and were so unique. As time passes, I think, we will feel the same way about our OPACs, and wonder how we ever got along without them.

CONCLUSIONS

Stevens makes one further comment that must be added here: "All of those [eighteen criteria or] elements of evaluating reference books must be placed eventually in a perspective that relates to a particular situation whether in selection or use in an individual library or selection for use in seeking particular information"(45).

By blending the eighteen criteria together, a complete picture regarding the success or failure of an OPAC can be compiled, and an accurate evaluation made.

A successful OPAC, ultimately, is one that provides patrons with the needed/wanted information in the easiest manner possible, and in the shortest possible time-frame. The definition of a successful OPAC is, then, the same definition as successful reference service (successful delivery of the needed/wanted information to the patron).

If the financial resources, time and effort that we, as librarians, put into the creation and operation of OPACs are to be worth it all, then we must do the very best job possible with an OPAC to successfully impact on the overall quality of reference service. If we fail in the provision of excellent OPACs, then our reference service has also failed, and our patrons are left wanting.

The evaluation of any specific facet of reference service (including the evaluation of OPACs), in the end, comes full circle back to the patron as the primary and fundamental focus of reference service, and to Ranganathan's Five Laws of Library Science: "Law I: Books are for Use; Law II: Every Reader His Book; Law III: Every Book its Reader; Law IV: Save the time of the Reader and Law V: The Library is a Growing Organism" (39).

But, that is another paper. . . . And, oh, yes, its OK to panic now!

REFERENCES

1. Adalian, Paul T.; Rockman, Ilene F. "Title-by-Title Review in Reference Collection Development" *Reference Services Review* 12: 85-88, 1985 (February).

2. Balay, Robert. "Subject Coverage of Reference Books in Reviewing Journals" *Choice* 24: 424-430, 1986 (November).

3. Barreau, Deborah K. "Using Performance Measures to Implement an Online Catalog" *Library Resources and Technical Services* 32: 312-322, 1988 (October).

4. Bates, Marcia J. "Rethinking Subject Cataloging in the Online Environment" *Library Resources and Technical Services* 33: 400-412, 1989 (October).

5. Robert N. Bland. "Evaluating the Performance of the Online Public Access Catalog: A Redefinition of Basic Measures" *North Carolina Libraries* 47: 168-173, 1989 (Fall).

6. Bonta, Bruce D. "A Desert Island Reference Collection" *Reference Services Review* 13: 7-9, 1985 (Spring).

7. Borgman, Christine L. "Why Are Online Catalogs Hard to Use?" *Journal of the American Society for Information Science* 37: 387-400, 1986 (November).

8. Carlyle, Allyson. "Matching User Vocabulary in the Library Catalog" *Cataloging & Classification Quarterly* 10: 37-63, 1989.

9. Crawford, Walt. "Testing Bibliographic Displays for Online Catalogs" *Information Technology and Libraries* 6: 20-33, 1987 (March).

10. Dwyer, Gill. "Evaluating Online Public Access Catalogues: A Checklist" *State Librarian* 32: 42-43, 1984 (November).

11. Dwyer, James R. "The Road to Access and the Road to Entropy: Using Online Catalogs to Stimulate Effective Library Use" *Library Journal* 112: 131-136, 1987 (September).

12. Edmonds, Leslie; Moore, Paula R.; Balcom, Kathleen Mehaffey. "The Effectiveness of an Online Catalog" *School Library Journal* 36: 28-32, 1990 (October).

13. Ercegovac, Zorana. "Augmented Assistance in Online Subject Searching" *The Reference Librarian* no. 23: 21-40, 1989.

14. Farley, Judith R. "Desert Island Journal" *Reference Services Review* 12: 5-6, 1984 (Winter).

15. Furniss, Peter. "A Proposed Methodology for Examining the Provision of Subject Access in the OPAC" *International Classification* 17: 85-90, 1990.

16. Hattendorf, Lynn C. "The Art of Reference Collection Development" *RQ*: 219-229, 1989 (Winter).

17. Hernon, Peter. "On an Isolated Island" *Reference Services Review* 13: 5-7, 1985 (Fall).

18. Hooten, Patricia A. "Online Catalogs: Will They Improve Children's Access?" *Journal of Youth Services* 2: 267-272, 1989 (Spring).

19. Huestis, Jeffrey C. "Clustering LC Classification Numbers in an Online Catalog for Improved Browsability" *Information Technology and Libraries* 7: 381-393, 1988 (December).

20. Issacson, David. "Literary Style in Reference Books" *RQ* 28: 485-495, 1989 (Summer).

21. Katz, William A. *Introduction to Reference Work.* 5th ed. New York, McGraw-Hill, 1987.

22. Klugman, Simone. "Failures in Subject Retrieval" *Cataloging & Classification Quarterly* 10: 9-35, 1989.

23. Knutson, Gunnar S. "A Comparison of Online and Card Catalog Accuracy" *Library Resources and Technical Services* 34: 24-35, 1990 (January).

24. Koohang, Alex A. "Increasing Users' Positive Response Toward the Li-

brary Computer System: A System Design Approach" *Library Resources and Technical Services* 11: 391-397, 1989 (October).

25. Lang, Jovian. "Evaluation of Reference Sources Published or to be Published" *The Reference Librarian* no. 15: 55-64, 1986 (Fall).

26. Lang, Jovian. "Marooned, but Resourceful" *Reference Services Review* 12: 7-9, 1984 (Fall).

27. Lynch, Clifford A. "Response Time Measurement and Performance Analysis in Public Access Information Retrieval Systems" *Information Technology and Libraries* 7: 177-183, 1988 (June).

28. McSweeney, Linda; Cassell, Marianne K. "A Bare Bones Reference Collection" *The Unabashed Librarian* no. 62: 27-28, 1987.

29. Markey, Karen. "Alphabetical Searching in an Online Catalog" *The Journal of Academic Librarianship* 14: 353-360, 1989 (January).

30. Markey, Karen. "Online Assistance in Online Catalogs" *Library Hi Tech* 8: 72-74, 1990.

31. Markey, Karen. "Subject-Searching Experiences and Needs of Online Catalog Users" *Library Resources and Technical Services* 29: 34-51, 1985 (January).

32. Mensching, Teresa B. "A Question of Need and Turf" *Research Strategies* 7: 187-189, 1989 (Fall).

33. Miller, William. "Night of the Living Dead Books" *Reference Services Review* 15: 5-7, 1987 (Summer).

34. Muncer, Joy; Hill, Carol J.; Didley, Martin P. "Raised Eyebrows: A Survey of Public Reactions to an OPAC" *Public Library Journal* 5: 71-72, 1990 (May/June).

35. Murdock, Paul R. "Cataloging Catalysis: Toward a New Chemistry of Conscience, Communication and Conduct in the Online Catalog" *Cataloging & Classification Quarterly* 10: 65-80, 1989.

36. Nielsen, Brian; Baker, Betsy K. "Educating the Online Catalog User: a Model Evaluation Study" *Library Trends* 35: 571-585, 1987 (Spring).

37. Patterson, Charles D. "Ten Reference Books: A Selfish Selection for Survival" *Reference Services Review* 14: 5-7, 1986 (Summer).

38. Peters, Thomas A. "When Smart People Fail: An Analysis of the Transaction Log of an Online Public Access Catalog" *The Journal of Academic Librarianship* 15: 267-273, 1989 (November).

39. Ranganathan, S.R. *The Five Laws of Library Science.* 2nd ed. Bombay, Asia Publishing House, 1957. p. 9.

40. Rice, James. "Serendipity and Holism: The Beauty of OPACs" *Library Journal* 113: 138-141, 1988 (February).

41. Rothstein, Samuel. "On a Crowded Desert Island" *The Reference Librarian* no. 25/26: 359-363, 1989.

42. Schlachter, Gail A. "Obsolescence, Weeding, and Bibliographic Love Canals" *RQ* 28: 7-8, 1988 (Fall).

43. Soper, Mary Ellen. "What You See May Not Be What You Get: Errors in Online Bibliographic Records for Serials" *The Reference Librarian* no. 27/28: 185-213, 1989.

44. Stanke, Nicola K. "User Satisfaction with an Online Catalog" *Iowa Library Quarterly* 24: 24-34, 1987 (Winter).

45. Norman D. Stevens. "Evaluating Reference Books in Theory and Practice" *The Reference Librarian* no. 15: 9-19, 1986 (Fall).

46. Watson-Boone, Peter G. "Collection Development and Evaluation in Reference and Adult Services Librarianship" *RQ* 26: 143-145, 1986 (Winter).

"All I Need Is in the Computer": Reference and Bibliographic Instruction in the Age of CD-ROMs

Trudi E. Jacobson

SUMMARY. In this age of CD-ROMs and other electronic technology, librarians must take their responsibility to educate patrons on the use of these popular new sources very seriously. The apparent ease of using CD-ROMs can seriously mislead students about the appropriateness of their search results. Through the reference interview and bibliographic instruction, librarians have the opportunity to familiarize students with the vast power of CD-ROMs, to teach them to harness that power, and to provide them with the critical skills necessary to question whether a particular CD-ROM database is the appropriate place to find information on a certain topic. Specific methods for doing this are included.

Working at the reference desk in the time since CD-ROMs became a major presence in the University at Albany library, I can not help but notice that many patrons, primarily students, are swamped by the results they obtain from a CD-ROM search. In speaking with other librarians, it is obvious that this is not a local phenomenon. While students have had access to large amounts of information in the past, the process of finding and transcribing citations would deter most students from becoming overloaded by the quantity of available sources. CD-ROMs have dramatically changed this scenario. Students find them exciting to use (more exciting than print sources, at any rate), irresistible in that they print citation after citation with nary more than a keystroke, and high profile in that they are well-promoted by faculty and friends alike. Because of their popularity and the effect they are having upon reference and interlibrary loan servic-

---

Trudi E. Jacobson is Bibliographic Instruction Coordinator, University Libraries, University at Albany, State University of New York, Albany, NY 12222.

es, CD-ROMs raise concerns that, while applicable to other library sources, feel more immediate. This article is written from the viewpoint of an academic librarian, but the issues are ones that are shared by most librarians, regardless of library type.

We, as librarians/educators, are responsible to our students and to other patrons (and to ourselves as professionals) to provide guidance in the use of these extremely popular tools, and we need to approach this issue from the view of both the reference desk and the bibliographic instruction classroom. As Mary Reichel has stated:

> Reference librarians need to assume explicit responsibility, shared with the other faculty, for the bibliographic knowledge of researchers on their campus. Once this responsibility is acknowledged, it follows that reference service should be active. Active reference service includes letting faculty, staff, and students know about new information sources and processes.[1]

Her article makes the point that bibliographic instruction and reference desk service, along with online searching and interlibrary loan, form a continuum of reference services and that bibliographic instruction "has increased the active nature of reference service."[2]

Librarians need to find as many opportunities as possible to familiarize students with the vast power of CD-ROMs, to teach them how to harness that power, and to provide them with the critical skills necessary to question whether a particular CD-ROM database is the appropriate place to find information on a certain topic. Students need to learn not only when and how to use a CD-ROM database, but also when not to.

In this article I limit myself to a discussion of educating students on the use of CD-ROM databases as a pressing example of our accountability[3] to them. Yet, as supercatalogs become more prevalent, and as more and varied databases become available for patron use, the problem will be compounded. Any strategies and techniques developed for use with CD-ROMs should, with modification, be applicable to other newly available forms of technology. While Mary Jean Pavelsek argues that end user instruction (other than prepared handouts and, time-permitting, individualized help) is not necessary because today's students are very computer literate,[4] Harold Shill points out:

> The risks of the electronic environment may be less apparent to patrons, though librarians should be acutely sensitive to them . . .

(One risk is) user ignorance of relevant databases, the content of such databases, and the shortcomings of their search strategies. . . . Instruction librarians have an ongoing responsibility to educate their patrons in the deficiencies, as well as the capabilities, of the new information technologies.[5]

The University at Albany CD-ROM area, located near the reference desk, is composed of 11 machines providing access to more than 20 different databases. In the center of this area is a CD-ROM information desk, and beyond that is a CD-ROM literature rack. The CD-ROMs are extremely heavily used.[6] It is not an unusual sight when providing assistance in the CD-ROM area to see students displaying or printing vast quantities of citations. Librarians need to intervene to ascertain whether these students have developed a search strategy that does justice to their topic. Indeed, it is not uncommon at this point to find that a student who is looking for material on Jane Austen is searching *ERIC*, the education database. Many of the CD-ROM databases found in libraries are, at face value, easy to search. Students type in terms and *voilà*, receive instant results (usually). They often do not know about descriptors, field searching, and Boolean searching. They frequently do their research a disservice, and unless we guide them to doing more precise searches, we are doing them a disservice. CD-ROM assistance does not mean simply showing patrons which key to press, but involves broader issues.

As with all reference interviews, interviewing patrons/students who wish to do a CD-ROM search about their needs, and knowing when to delve beyond their initial response, is paramount. When they say they are looking for material on the aged, are they looking for the psychology of the aged? Medical issues? Public policy? Do they need newspaper articles? For experienced reference librarians, these types of questions are basic tools of the trade. But in dealing with students who want to use CD-ROMs, there is sometimes another twist: they want to use a computer, whether or not there is a database that is appropriate. I occasionally wonder how many students have changed their topics to fit one of the databases we offer. They are even more adamant if their professors have recommended that they use CD-ROMs. If there is no appropriate database for their subject, it does not help to explain that their professor may have been searching a very different topic, or may only have heard about these new wonders by word of mouth, and may not be familiar with exactly what they contain.

CRITICALLY EXAMINING SEARCH RESULTS

It is not possible, or even desirable, for librarians to check every citation on every printout generated by each student using the CD-ROMs. We do not reach many students at all, simply because they do not ask for assistance as they conduct their search. But for those with whom we do interact, we must, depending on the level and requirements of their search, introduce them to such search aids as thesauruses, the availability of field searching, the benefits of Boolean searching, and the frequent necessity to use synonyms. As we examine with them the results of their searches, we should point out elements of the citations that would indicate the usefulness of the materials retrieved. Are they getting citations to scholarly journals or to popular magazines? Are they retrieving materials that address the appropriate angle of the topic, as they have defined it? Are the materials in a language they can read? We can encourage them to discover whether they are getting materials that represent different viewpoints on a topic, and suggest alternative sources that will provide these.

This is not unusual guidance for librarians to be providing. But I contend that we need to be even more vigilant about CD-ROM searches because students seem to feel that if the material comes from a computer, it can't be wrong, incomplete, or inappropriate. We have the opportunity when students request assistance in using CD-ROMs to help them develop viable, if not sophisticated, information searching skills. As librarians in an educational setting, we are accountable to our students to provide this guidance.

In working with students, and in helping them develop a search strategy, it is often useful to invoke metacognitive processes. Donna-Lynn Forrest-Pressley and T. Gary Waller explain the use of metacognition:

> We have knowledge about our cognitive (i.e., mental) processes and we use this knowledge to choose the most efficient strategy for, or ways of dealing with, any problem that we might face . . . Regardless of what the task is, as we proceed we monitor and regulate our activities.[7]

As librarians, we can give voice to our thought processes to enable students to follow why we are choosing certain tools, or how we are arriving at appropriate descriptors or subject headings to use in a search. Why are we showing them *General Science Index* instead of *Reader's Guide*? Why isn't *Newspaper Abstracts* on CD-ROM appropriate in this instance?

Which indexes, in whatever form, would provide materials that complement one another? In modeling the thought processes that are at work in developing a search strategy, we are providing students with a framework they can use when they are searching for information on another topic. We also provide more opportunities for refining the search strategy. If the reference question wasn't fully formed when it was asked, each step of the decision making process provides time for the student to say, "no, I really need. . . ."

BIBLIOGRAPHIC INSTRUCTION AND CD-ROMs

Bibliographic instruction allows us to reach many more students than at the reference or CD-ROM desks. The availability of CD-ROMs have drawn University at Albany faculty, some of whom never previously took advantage of bibliographic instruction, like a magnet. This interest presents an excellent opportunity to educate faculty members about what CD-ROMs are, what they can and cannot do. It is important to stress to faculty that these tools are not appropriate for all questions, so that they do not overemphasize them to their students. In class sessions librarians can encourage students to think critically about CD-ROMs, and can integrate them into the vast body of tools used for finding information.

Simply telling students the advantages and limitations of CD-ROM databases does not mean they have therefore learned this material. But when they can discover for themselves that *MLA* on CD-ROM won't pick up articles prior to 1981, or that *Magazine Index Plus on InfoTrac* is not providing articles from scholarly journals, they are more likely to remember to evaluate certain sources. When feasible, devise exercises for students to do either during or after class that will point out to them the strengths and weaknesses of CD-ROM databases. While hands-on exercises are most beneficial, many libraries do not have enough computers to make this possible. An example of an exercise which doesn't require actual use of a CD-ROM and which encourages students to evaluate databases and sources is to have students work in small groups to critique obviously skewed bibliographies.[8] Or students might be asked to develop a search strategy using free text terms and then again using descriptors. Either they or the librarians could then execute the searches and students can compare the results. Using exercises on which students can work, preferably in small groups where they can propose ideas and get the feedback of others, provides an active learning environment more conducive to the development of critical thinking skills.

Instruction in use of CD-ROM databases is vital. But, as Gillian Allen points out:

> There does not appear to be agreement as to which is the best methodology to use for CD-ROM training, or for bibliographic instruction in general.[9]

She later adds:

> Patron perceptions and preferences should be considered in designing bibliographic instruction programs.[10]

INSTRUCTION OPTIONS

The University at Albany has a multi-faceted program to introduce as many students and other patrons as possible to CD-ROMs. Course-related instruction plays an important part in this program, but due to the usual time limitations on individual sessions, we can often give students only a taste of the potential of CD-ROMs, and of course many classes do not come to the library. We attempt to fill these gaps in one way each semester by offering many CD-ROM instruction sessions. Students can sign up for these on their own–they are not dependent on whether their professor decides to bring their class in for instruction. We offer sessions which are generic introductions to CD-ROMs, as well as database-specific sessions for thirteen different databases. Many of the sessions allow students to gain hands-on experience. Over the course of the Spring 1991 semester, we offered altogether 43 CD-ROM instruction sessions.

One-on-one assistance is provided at the CD-ROM desk, as well as at a new search strategy desk. This latter service, which does not operate as many hours as the general CD-ROM assistance, is offered by librarians who are expert at developing search strategies, and is targeted to more sophisticated CD-ROM users, although anyone may use it. Individual assistance is also provided through Partners in Research, our term paper clinic. In this program, a librarian guides a student through the library's resources appropriate for a particular topic. When a student has a topic that would benefit from a CD-ROM search, the librarian with whom he/she is working will teach the student how to do a search (if they do not already know). The librarian will also use this time to explain searching techniques with which the student may not be familiar.

For students who prefer not to ask for help, or when no one is available to help, students may turn to the database's own tutorials and help screens, and to the information guides we have developed which are prominently displayed in the literature rack. In providing so many types of assistance and instruction, we reach students comfortable with a variety of learning styles. Those who do best working in groups can attend instruction sessions. Those who prefer individual help have a variety of options. And instruction is also provided for those who want to learn by themselves.

Many libraries now offer CD-ROMs for their patrons to use. These systems are more complex than printed indexes and abstracts. Often the CD-ROMs in a library will run on as many different software packages as there are databases. Bibliographic instruction is an established service provided by most academic libraries. For over two decades, librarians have been committed to helping patrons navigate the sometimes muddy waters of information. As bibliographic instruction moves from its second generation to what perhaps will be its third, we must provide viable and effective instruction for these glitzy new navigation tools, the CD-ROMs.

REFERENCES

1. Mary Reichel, "Bibliographic Education and Reference Desk Service–A Continuum," *The Reference Librarian* #10 (Spring/Summer 1984), p.197.

2. Reichel, p.196.

3. I use the word accountability here as defined by *Webster's Third New International Dictionary of the English Language Unabridged* (Springfield, Massachusetts, G. & C. Merriam Company, 1986.): "the quality or state of being accountable, liable, or responsible."

4. Mary Jean Pavelsek, "A Case Against Instructing Users of Computerized Retrieval Systems," *College & Research Libraries News* 52 (May 1991), pp. 297-301.

5. Harold B. Shill, "Bibliographic Instruction: Planning for the Electronic Information Environment," *College and Research Libraries* 48 (September 1987), p.446.

6. From September 1990 to April 1991, 35,555 CD-ROM searches were done. In terms of questions during that period, there were 14,216 questions relating to CD-ROMs. This compares to 45,272 non-CD-ROM reference questions.

7. Donna-Lynn Forrest-Pressley and T. Gary Waller, *Cognition, Metacognition, and Reading* (New York: Springer-Verlag, 1984), p. 1.

8. Ridgeway uses such an exercise to a slightly different end. See Trish Ridgeway, "Integrating Active Learning Techniques into the One-Hour Bibliographic Instruction Lecture" in Glenn E. Mensching, Jr. and Teresa B.

Mensching, eds., *Coping with Information Illiteracy: Bibliographic Instruction for the Information Age* (Ann Arbor: Pierian Press, 1989), pp. 33-42. Lynn Westbrook, Undergraduate Library, University of Michigan, presented a poster session at the ALA Annual Conference in Chicago in 1990 entitled, "Critical Thinking: Advanced Pieces." Her poster session literature describes two learning cycles which encourage critical thinking. In one of these cycles, groups of students determine research flaws in sample bibliographies. While not designed specifically for use with CD-ROMs, some of the suggested exercises could be adapted for that use.

9. Gillian Allen, "CD-ROM Training: What Do the Patrons Want?," *RQ* 30 (Fall 1990), p.89.

10. Allen, p.89.

Interactive Multi-Media
and Electronic Media
in Academic Libraries:
Policy Implications

Lorre Smith

SUMMARY. Electronic information formats such as optical media or multi-media used in colleges and universities present challenges for academic library policy makers. Some policy areas that should be considered for electronic and interactive formats are familiar and some are new. This paper describes areas of policy and decision points for services involving new and emerging formats such as hypermedia, interactive multi-media and full-text electronic files. Topics include: planning, staffing, collection development, security, access and services. The areas discussed were encountered by librarians in the author's library during the process of installing a 20-work-station Interactive Media Center.

INTRODUCTION: INTERACTIVE MULTI-MEDIA

Interactive media begins with a computer. Typical computer storage media include the internal memory, floppy diskettes, magnetic tape, "hard" disk, and more recently, hard disk cartridges, optical disks (also called laser disks) and compact disks. Many types of sound and visual images can be incorporated into the microcomputer programs to provide

Lorre Smith has been Director of several small libraries, both academic and public, and is currently Head of Media, Microforms, Periodicals and Reserves, University at Albany, State University of New York, 1400 Washington, Avenue, Albany, NY 12222.

The author wishes to thank Judith Hudson, Head of Cataloging at University Libraries, University at Albany, for her support and advice.

very stimulating interactive programs. Microcomputer software can be designed which provides access to information from all types of peripherally attached devices. Laser disks, which are large optical disks of 12 inches in diameter, and compact disks (commonly called CD's), can be "played" on players which will also communicate via cable with microcomputers. Video tape players can be employed by the programmer (instructional designer) as well.[1]

Educators in schools and in industry have been using programmed instruction in computers and in printed texts for quite some time.[2] Modern interactive computer programming methods incorporate the media from peripheral devices using microcomputers to provide stunning presentations of material, some of them simulations. Well-designed instruction engages the learner for significant interaction with the material in ways that reading or watching or looking alone do not.[3] For the message designer enormous intellectual and pragmatic challenges lurk behind the thrill of designing something that proves to be quite effective.

Compact disk players which can play CD-ROM reference works, such as ERIC Indexes, and other so-called "full-text" publications, such as the *Thesaurus Linguae Graecae*, are examples of the possible peripherals connected by cable to the microcomputer and used as interactive media. Compact disk players may also be able to "play" audio disks. Many compact disks are now "interactive" meaning that they provide data in response to queries or respond according to information entered (by using a keyboard or other means) by a learner, just as floppy diskettes have been used.

Interactive CD and video are commonly used for training in the professions and in industry[4] because it provides uniform quality instruction, thus eliminating to a certain extent bad or inconsistent human instruction. It also allows trainees to approach the same lesson or the same subject matter virtually an endless number of times. In many instances video sequences, or models created within the computer software provide demonstrations that are not physically possible within the resources of the ordinary training program. In the case of legal training for courtroom procedures, for instance, a courtroom scene may be enacted only a certain number of times by real human beings, but a video may be replayed any number of times. In addition interactive media provides opportunities for learners to enter responses to situations at the microcomputer keyboard, or with a touch-screen "key," or with a mouse.

Computer assisted instruction has developed from a tool used for drills or exercises to the point where peripherals which add text, illustrative motion or still material and sound can be incorporated into many types of educational or training software. Lectures can be recorded and played back on tape or videodisc with text on the same screen as text created by the programmer. The learner is engaged with not only the visual or sound images, but with the text of the instructor and the ability to repeat any portion of the learning experience for full understanding. Within certain design concepts such as the Apple program called "Hypercard," the learner makes links within the learning experience which obtain the greatest relevance, and with help or complementary experience from various portions of the learning package, whether they are text, visual images or sound. With touch-screen technology and "mouse" (a non-keyboard input device) technology the learner does not even need to learn to type in order to participate in the experience and enter information or responses to the computer program. "Hypercard," "Guide," "Authorware," "Toolbook," and "Quest" are examples of commercially produced software which allow an instructor to produce interactive programs of this type.

Many academic libraries have taken on the role of the marketplace for ideas within their institutions. Innovative information formats may be an extension of this idea, so that libraries not only provide a stimulating breadth of ideas to scholars, but stimulating ways to gain access to the wealth of reproducible texts existing in our society. Tasks that each library staff confronts are: assessment of needs and selection criteria to determine which user services are appropriate for media formats. Many service possibilities should be assessed: subject content of electronic media collections, electronic formats, loan policies, playback facilities, and support personnel.

Library innovators and change agents may need to explore and evaluate an ever-increasing breadth of machinery and electronics and provide advice to their institutions on storage and retrieval capabilities, just as computer services staff now do. Academic libraries have grappled with non-print information formats for decades and have developed services that range from having small collections to running the entire audiovisual services for the college or university. Each library staff must identify options, assess them, and use that information in making decisions.

There are many policy issues and decision points which bear reviewing as libraries embark on collecting electronic information formats such as computer files and multi-media. This paper is an attempt to present several categories of policies: planning, staffing, library instruction, collection issues, access and services, organizing the collection, and security. No single paper can guide a library through the complex processes involved in planning for the future development of services, but perhaps this paper can help with the beginning stages of assessment and decision-making.

GENERAL PLANNING

When planning services based on electronic or multi-media, feedback from funding sources or administrators, and from teaching faculty or other clientele is imperative. If it is successful, an innovative service elicits positive thought or provides excellent assistance to the user community.

An electronic or interactive multi-media collection can be an outstanding tool for training and classroom teaching. A large facility for electronic or interactive multi-media can have an enormous impact on the way a curriculum is presented to learners. If administrators are trying to interject high technology into the process of teaching and learning, certain steps must be taken in the planning process to persuade or convince faculty to change their methods.[5] Library administrators contemplating a facility for high-technology information formats must consider the acceptance of these formats within their institutions, and plan services and staffing accordingly. For instance, if the facility is to serve as an instrument of change in instructional techniques to high technology formats across the institution, staff and services will need to support users in a different way than if the institution is highly saturated with high technology and users do not need instruction in the technology itself.

Innovative information formats and collections may provoke change that is eventually good, but may be painful and stressful in surprising ways. For example, an academic department head who is enamored of interactive multi-media may decide that all classes on a particular subject will be taught using interactive multi-media. Teachers will have to change their teaching methods in fundamental ways. Teachers and students as well as information providers may suffer in the process.

The commonly-used committee can be practically employed for the purpose of defining issues. A steering group for the planning process composed of faculty from academic affairs, academic computing, financial and technical departments, library staff, library systems staff, and so forth, should be convened very early. A campus-wide group may be used to tackle general issues regarding services, to begin delineation of criteria for specific areas such as equipment selection or just to advise and discuss issues throughout the campus so that schools and departments know what is happening. A campus-wide group can discuss broad issues such as coordination of computing across the campus or faculty development and support in the area of instructional technology and computer-assisted instruction.

A group of library faculty and staff can help advise on library policies regarding issues discussed all through this paper. Representation from all library divisions and departments may be necessary. A library group can make sure that existing library policy can be applied or that policy changes are recommended to accommodate new library services and other innovations. The library group can consider more specific space planning and its effects on other library services, for instance. Either the campus-wide group or the library group could define feasible and relevant services for the campus. Subcommittees can tackle specifics such as equipment selection and purchase, circulation rules, cataloging problems, and floor plans, and so on.

The use of the committee technique requires very good communication from institutional leaders and decisions makers so that committees have specific goals and objectives. Committees require techniques for reporting committee discussion in order for decision-makers to avoid unnecessary or overwhelming information. Clear definitions of purpose go a long way in helping committees remain organized and productive.

STAFFING

Staff of all ranks are needed for multi-media services. Libraries will need to consider people who can cope with the technical ins and outs of work-stations, who have skills in communicating concepts concerning electronic information and who can make library users comfortable in a high-technology environment. Libraries embarking on services involving electronic information formats need people who can assess public service needs and deliver appropriate services, and who are willing to learn a plethora of operating systems and interface software, just as in the past librarians have had to know the subtleties of and differences between printed library materials. Good candidates may come from the fields of library and information science, computer science and education.

Clerical staff may be required to assist in user education, demonstrations, documentation of equipment, creating catalogs or other lists, production of promotional materials and other printed materials, public service at any service desk (if there is one), student training, and processing of materials for circulation. Student staff can assist with circulation, give location and directional information, and give basic user support for setting up work-stations. They can book work-stations and provide telephone service. Graduate assistants and interns may be desirable for special projects and may come from a variety of disciplines, including library and information science, computer science, and education.

EDUCATION OF LIBRARY STAFF

In the case of rather complex services implied by an interactive media facility, staff education should be among the top priorities. The committee or group process can be effectively used in this case. A representative library group can assess training needs of various departments. A committee or task forces can develop training strategies and methods of dissemination of information about new services or service changes and requirements. Collecting, processing and circulating electronic interactive multi-media will be new and different for library staff. Library public services staff (with the exception of the few curious librarians who are interested in hypertext or hypermedia) may feel uncomfortable with all the peripherals and with different operating systems. Likewise, any other library divisions or departments may discover puzzling or difficult aspects of new hardware or software.

In a large organization where library departments specialize, continuing promotional and educational efforts may be necessary. At a time when new technology is changing services on a weekly or monthly basis, the beginning of any new service may be lost in the shuffle unless it is high-lighted and several opportunities for staff demonstrations and instruction are provided. Everyone may feel that the onslaught from CD-ROM data-bases in the Reference area has been enough "professional growth" for the year. Staff, like other users, may be familiar only with computer equipment that is designed for their jobs. Do not assume, however, that they will understand the latest microcomputer technology and applications created for interactive multi-media. Staff training and familiarization of all staff with the systems and their special qualities should not be ignored if effective service is to continue and grow.

The technical services staff may not be acquainted with the materials that will be collected for high-technology applications. If they are to process and catalog the material, they will need education in advance in order to avoid major trouble spots. New methods of packaging and different shapes and sizes of labels will be needed. Cataloging expertise with the various versions of media will have to be developed. Technical services staff members of libraries with audiovisual collections may be surprised at the differences in electronic media. If audiovisual collections have been treated separately, policies for another separate treatment for electronic media may have to be created.

LIBRARY SKILLS INSTRUCTION

Librarians who invested time in the world of electronic information must begin to develop strategies to transfer such technical knowledge to library users. Users who are to use electronic sources and multi-media need to become computer literate in a sophisticated way that has not been necessary until now. Computers still prevent access for the computer illiterate. Librarians must decide how far to go in making sure that the users are computer literate enough to gain access to the information. Policy must be made for the limits of skills instruction to be accomplished by library staff.

Documentation must be developed for users who are using programs at library work-stations. If users put the diskette into the compact disk drive or accidentally reformat something or if they can't get the computer to communicate with the videodisc player they have no access to the information. Documentation for equipment and software is a tremendous investment of time and personnel. Well-written print and online documentation is difficult to produce. Librarians must devise efficient methods to train for computer use so that content training can be easily accomplished.

COLLECTIONS

For the information professional charged with collecting, storing and retrieving electronic and multi-media information formats, the challenges lie in the fragility of the materials, understanding the implications of the software and hardware, expense in maintenance and upgrades, and the development or collection of appropriate software for user levels and subject needs.

At the time of this writing the market for commercially produced "electronic publications" is changing rapidly. Scholars in many disciplines welcome the electronic versions of many of the texts they are trying to analyze with cries of delight and demand for "more! more!" as they become computer literate, but few titles are available for purchase. There are currently only a few dozen commercially produced interactive multi-media programs for higher education.

One of the challenges for electronic media and interactive multi-media collectors is to find ways to deal with the implications of full-text databases and electronic journals. The Bible, dictionaries, full-texts of ancient writings, novels, Supreme Court decisions, data sets and a wide variety of other electronic productions present the librarians with hardware, cataloging and circulation challenges. The storage challenges alone include archival copy matters, obsolescence of hardware and supporting software, and shelving or disk space or magnetic tape storage facilities. Production of portable copies, or reproduction of the information presents difficulties in the legal arena and in equipment selection and availability. Providing access to simultaneous users forces libraries to take on legal issues regarding copyright and hardware challenges.

The faculty in many institutions may enthusiastically favor producing materials locally, so that they can be tailored to specifications of the curriculum. The library or the institution may want to deal with authoring or production support for the faculty. In a library setting, that might be equivalent to running a television and video studio. Some libraries currently provide television and video services, and consider them to be as relevant to modern librarianship as other information services. Determining the scope of library services, based on the type of collection, can be a continuous process, and should involve many members of the library staff.

Commercially available programs may also require software support for users as well as maintenance. This type of support is analogous to the user support required to maintain a periodical index, such as the *Social Sciences Index*, in hard copy.

A selection committee can help librarians discuss the variety of software formats and the implications of each. Everything from the type of programs which will facilitate use, but not necessarily affect the content of the library's collection (e.g., word processing software, spreadsheets), to the full language courses on interactive video can be considered. A committee can help draw boundaries and distinctions. For instance, it may be necessary to buy word processing or other "utility" software (e.g., virus detection programs) from funds other than collection development funds. Faculty may request software for the collection that does not "play" or "run" on current equipment and the committee can help to recommend equipment purchase for highly desirable programs. A committee can make decisions against purchase for the same reason. Technical advice can be invited by appointing computing services personnel on library committees. Issues of collection content can be carried to all academic departments by liaison. If a single bibliographer is selected to handle all collection development of multi-media rather than a committee, he or she would by necessity have to be well aware of collection scope and expectations and be in constant contact with other collection development librarians.

Policy issues involving collection content are legion. The commercially-produced offerings on laser disk and compact disk are increasing each year. Collection of electronic reference works will create demands for assistance in use of hardware, systems operation and intellectual content, and librarians must be prepared to meet these needs. Full-text optical disks may contain hundreds of texts that may previously have been housed according to classification schemes that placed them in hundreds of different physical locations. Means must be found to assist users in location of and access to electronic texts that will encompass many traditional subject classes. "Utility" software for computer systems will be necessary, but it may or may not be considered as part of the library collection and may or may not be in the collection policy. Duplication of hard copy text with electronic text will require careful consideration in library policy, since the electronic versions provide possibilities of access and analysis unheard of in hard copy. Data files that require statistical software packages and that may only be published in magnetic tape format should be given policy consideration. Obsolescence of hardware and software will give new meaning to the term "up to date" when used to describe library collections. "Out of date" may also mean that the hardware is obsolete and there is no longer a machine that will run the software.

Physical access to work-stations where software is mounted must be considered as well. There must be a sufficient number of them to provide access to the information. Many libraries tackled similar problems when trying to estimate the number of terminals needed for adequate access to online public catalogs. Networking of work-stations may be one solution, but copyright problems must be resolved.

Some commercially produced compact disks in existence today store more than 400 distinct texts. Collection development policies for such items will need to consider duplication of texts across the CD format, and also duplication in other formats. Encyclopedic works may include complete musical pieces and motion pictures. One compact disk currently being published contains the whole of Beethoven's ninth symphony, but becomes another work altogether when an accompanying "Hypercard" stack is used to control it.[5] Collection managers and developers will encounter many such new configurations of intellectual content in items and policies will need to reflect a coherent philosophy or structure for their acquisition and use.

Many issues regarding electronic formats must be considered in developing statements of collection purpose. Since some library services may merely entail the provision of the passwords to databases which do not reside anywhere on the campus of the institution, access-oriented language rather than possession-oriented language may be in order. The "collecting" of electronic journals may pose policy questions regarding the location of the information. Developing policy language for information which has no location in the library will be a challenge. Assessment of user needs is necessary to determine the scope of access services.

Existing policies may encompass the collection of CD-ROM indexes, but there are many more materials which will pose problems once libraries embark on collection of electronic texts or electric multi-media. Lines that once were easy to distinguish become blurred. Some data bases on optical media or other electronic media may require a spread sheet program, a word processing program, a printer interface, a hardware board or card, or a recording device in order to be usable. A statement of collection purpose which includes support of classroom instruction might need to include materials created by faculty members.

Some electronic media can be easily changed by users, just as audio and video recordings can accidentally be erased. A replacement policy will have to take this possibility into account. Versions of electronic media occur in similar manner to editions of print media. Almost everyone who uses a microcomputer becomes aware of the versions of operating the system and basic programs for word processing, etc. that are developed. Collection adequacy may require hardware upgrades, and librarians should be prepared to face necessary software upgrades to keep current as well. Libraries will also have to face the question of whether to purchase software for which they have no hardware. There are many items that will require mainframe computer hardware support, and libraries will need to hold discussions with units on campus that "own" the mainframe(s).

Another policy issue involves the cataloging of archival copies which may have been designated only for "emergency" or "back-up" use. Counting and listing this type of item as part of the collection must be carefully considered. The library will actually have two copies. Reassessment of what is counted or how items are counted may be in order. Archival copies may not be stored within the library building for safety purposes, and making them available on lists or counting them as part of the library holdings may pose problems unless appropriate policies are in place and widely known by library staff.

ACCESS AND SERVICES

One of the challenges for librarians who provide public services involving interactive multi-media and electronic media is to find ways to deal with the implication of full-text databases and electronic serials. The implications loom large if one fixes on the scenario of full-text periodical collections on compact disk. In order to take advantage of the compactness, thousands of pages of text are stored on one compact disk. At a stand-alone work-station one person at a time will have access to all those thousands of pages. Libraries should have appropriate access policies in place to deal with such demands. Policies for dealing with demands for take-away copies of such texts should also be developed.

Many of the policy challenges for access and circulation lie in protection and preservation of the collection versus access by users. The fragility of non-print formats is widely known among constant users. In addition, copyright considerations are important for anyone who is circulating software. Possible destruction and flagrant violation of copyright by users cause many librarians to clutch expensive media within closed stacks as though users would destroy it by merely looking at it. Policies will be needed that provide not only reasonable access within copyright limitations, but reasonable access and queue management for all formats. The policies must describe all format expectations, including playback expectations. The mixed media formats, especially if they are serials that are transferring from one format to another, must be considered as well. All access tools to print collections must be assessed for their applicability to the electronic collections.

Playback equipment needs should be considered in access or circulation policy too. Sufficient numbers of machines can make the difference between timely access and no access at all.

Loan periods and questions of whether to loan certain formats need to take into consideration the type of use expected. If an instructor expects all students in a class to interact with a software package, a reserve-type service may be in order. Booking or reservations policies may provide very good access for popular items, and loans may be facilitated by site licenses which allow unlimited copying. (Librarians may wish to work with legal counsel in fashioning reasonable copying agreements with vendors.)

Fine and replacement policies in place for print materials or even for audiovisual materials may need to be revamped for software that may cost thousands of dollars to replace. As the price of print media continues to rise, the price of much electronic media looks reasonable in comparison. Carefully-drawn policies for replacement or multiple copies may provide the best access. Vendor agreements to replace physical entities at low cost may be in order. Examples of this have already cropped up in the world of CD-ROM indexes, where a vendor will happily provide replacement copies of damaged CD's for free or at low cost. It may be appropriate to set a very low fee for the user who damages such materials, rather than the higher vendor fees associated with acquisition of "the information."

ORGANIZING THE COLLECTION

Many libraries have created classification systems to be used exclusively for media, or have shelved by accession numbers or other systems rather than using classification systems common to print classification systems. Each library will encounter the need for decisions about classification of electronic media that may replicate print media, and will have to decide whether the electronic media will be treated like traditional paper, audiovisual media, or something else altogether new.

Archival considerations may cause libraries to keep at least one copy relatively inaccessible, but determining optimum accessibility may take time. For instance, if a popular diskette is continually being "wiped out," the storage location of the archival copy or back-up copy may be closer to the area of use than less used items. Electronic archives may be possible with the appropriate telecommunications. Under that method, the library maintains a file on magnetic tape in the archives instead of a file on diskettes or microcomputer hard drives. The "working copy" could be reproduced as needed by calling up the file on a mainframe terminal and downloading.

Closed or open stacks will have an impact on the need for finding aids of all sorts. If a general catalog cannot produce lists of items by format, separate lists may be needed. If users cannot browse the actual items for reasons of security, it may be helpful for covers or other packaging to be displayed. If items are displayed by format, e.g., all videocassettes together, users may need other methods for finding materials based on subject matter. Serial runs that transfer from one format to another need special consideration. If a serial has been produced in paper copy for a number of volumes and then is produced on compact disk, or a combination of compact disk and paper or diskette and paper, the organization must help users find all parts of the series if necessary.

If home-made classification schemes have been used in the past for audiovisual media, the integration of new media into the collection may cause problems. An example could be: a vinyl disk recording collection has been organized by a home-made scheme. Recordings of Beethoven's symphonies are in the collection. Multi-media versions of Beethoven's symphonies are acquired so that the library now has Beethoven's symphonies on vinyl disk, videocassette, compact disk and videodisc, plus on diskette. The library also has scores of Beethoven's symphonies classified by the Library of Congress system. Which versions should be classed by the home-made system and which by another system?

SECURITY

The staff must create security procedures which will allow the greatest access but prevent theft and vandalism. As soon as one enters the environment of floppy disks and hard drives it becomes evident that the conventional library magnetic or radio "security system" is quite insufficient to protect data and operating systems in the microcomputers. The magnetic media used for diskettes is similar to audiovisual material. The formats often do not allow placement of a concealed target. The practically invisible hard drive is certainly another matter altogether, since any operator has the potential to create and destroy files and directories. The libraries that cannot afford staff to watch all users and detect abuse must develop means of keeping data secure.

The computer virus becomes practically an everyday experience in a public-access environment. At the higher education level there are clever vandals who study such things at length and pride themselves on speed and wit. Knowledge of virus detection and immunization are necessary tools of the trade. The library's systems are susceptible to even the bumbling novice hacker unless there is sufficient staff to hover over the shoulders of all users, or software mechanisms or hardware mechanisms for security.

Hundreds of thousands of dollars in hardware can easily be packed into a 300 square-foot area. Policy should determine the optimum amount of staff time and equipment to invest in security for that hardware. The staff can watch over equipment when they are present in the area. If staff are allowed to move freely about the library and are not assigned in the equipment area, it is vulnerable to a myriad of theft and vandalism threats.

When the building is unstaffed, the security of the equipment must also be a concern. Security systems exist for computer equipment and may encompass a range of fiber-optic and sensor technology. When one is protecting $300,000.00 in computer hardware, a system for $10,000 can be seen as reasonable.

CONCLUSION

In summary, all problems that libraries encounter in the age of electronic media present challenges and they may not currently have good solutions. Many problems inherent in providing access to print formats are also obstacles in the areas of audiovisual and electronic media access, and our experience in dealing with formats of the past aids us in dealing with the electronic age. New problems are yet to be sufficiently widespread enough for our collective professional knowledge to come to bear, so the field is wide open for plenty of speculation and theory. Speculate! theorize! experiment! Pool your knowledge and common sense, and allow groups of users, computer services staff and faculty to tell you about needs and suggest their solutions. Employ all possible staff in the development of public and technical services which involve electronic formats. It will give them all an opportunity to find out what applies from past experience and what must be created in order to offer library users the best possible information. Use groups or committees efficiently and insist on appropriate communications from leaders and back to leaders so that assessment and resulting policies have been adequately formulated, and so that they can be fairly evaluated.

NOTES

1. Johnston, Jerome. *Electronic Learning: From Audiotape to Videodisc.* Hillsdale, NJ : Lawrence Erlbaum, 1987.

2. *Interactive Multimedia: Visions of Multimedia for Developers, Educators & Information Providers.* Redmond, WA: Microsoft Press, c1988.

3. *Microsoft CD-ROM Yearbook.* Redmond, WA : Microsoft Press, c1989.

4. Bork, Alfred. "The 'History' of Technology and Education," MSS, 1989.

5. Winter, Robert. *Ludwig Van Beethoven Symphony no. 9: A Hypercard/CD Audio Program by Robert Winter.* Santa Monica, CA : Voyager, c1989.

BIBLIOGRAPHY

Barker, Philip, ed. *Multi-Media Computer-Assisted Learning*. New York : Nichols Publishing, c1989.

Barrett, Edward, ed. *The Society of Text: Hypertext, Hypermedia, and the Social Construction of Information*. Cambridge MA : MIT Press, 1989.

Basch, Reva. "Books Online: Visions, Plans, and Perspectives for Electronic Text." *Online*. 15(4):13-23, July 1991.

Best, David P. "Information Management in the 1990s." *The Law Librarian*. 21(1):12-14, April 1990.

Bork, Alfred. "The 'History' of Technology and Education," MSS, 1989.

Brown, Celestia S. "A Day in the Life of a CD-ROM Librarian." *CD-ROM Librarian*. 6(4):10-13, April 1991.

Brunner, Theodore F. "The Thesaurus Linguae Graecae: Classics and the Computer." *Library Hi Tech*. 9(1):61-67, 1991.

Cisler, Steve. "Sound Advice: New Uses for Audio on the Macintosh." *Online*. 15(2):84-86, March 1991.

Clausen, Helge. "The Future Information Professional: Old Wine in New Bottles? Part One." *Libri*. 40(4):265-277, December 1990.

Crawford, David. "Computers and Music Studies Today." *Library Hi Tech*. 9(1):35-43, 1991.

Forsman, Rich. "Incorporating Organization Values into the Strategic Planning Process." *Journal of Academic Librarianship*. 16(3):150-153, July 1990.

Garret, John R. "Text to Screen Revisited: Copyright in the Electronic Age." *Online*. 15(2):22-24, March 1991.

Hallman, Clark N. "Technology: Trigger for Change in Reference Librarianship." *Journal of Academic Librarianship*. 16(4):204-208, September 1990.

Hoadley, Irene, and Sherrie Schmidt. "Beyond Tomorrow: The Scholar, Libraries and the Dissemination of Information.' *Journal of Library Administration*. 14(2):103-113, 1991.

Interactive Multimedia: Visions of Multimedia for Developers, Educators & Information Providers. Redmond, WA: Microsoft Press, c1988.

Intner, Sheila, and Jane Anne Hannigan. *The Library Microcomputer Environment: Management Issues*. Phoenix, AZ : Oryx Press, 1988.

Jacob, M.E.L. *Strategic Planning: A How-to-do-it Manual for Librarians*. New York : Neal-Schuman, 1990.

Johnston, Jerome. *Electronic Learning: From Audiotape to Videodisc*. Hillsdale, NJ: Lawrence Erlbaum, 1987.

Kountz, John. "High Density Data Storage, the Sony Data DiscMan Electronic Book, and the Unfolding Multimedia Revolution." *Library Hi Tech*. 9(1):77-90, 1991.

Mack, Julia, and Seth Finn. "Film and Video Acquisition at the Library of Congress: MBRS Policies and Academic Values." *Collection Management*. 14(1/2):25-42, 1991.

Microsoft CD-ROM Yearbook. Redmond, WA: Microsoft Press, c1989.

Nicholls, Paul T. *CD-ROM Collection Builder's Toolkit: The Complete Handbook of Tools for Evaluating CD-ROMs.* Weston, CT : Pemberton Press, 1990.

Pankake, Marcia. "Humanities Research in the 90s: What Scholars Need, What Librarians Can Do." *Library Hi Tech.* 9(1):9-15, 1991.

Sadlier, C.D. "Evolutions in Information Technology." *Bulletin of the American Society for Information Science.* 17(4): 20-21, April/May, 1991.

Sullivan, Maureen. "A New Leadership Paradigm: Empowering Library Staff and Improving Performance." *Journal of Library Administration.* 14(2):73-86, 1991.

Teague, S. John. *Microform, Video and Electronic Media Librarianship.* London: Butterworths, 1985.

Wiberly, Stephen E., Jr. "Habits of Humanists: Scholarly Behavior and New Information Technologies." *Library Hi Tech.* 9(1):17-21, 1991.

Open vs. Closed Stacks for Academic Library Periodical Collections

Gretchen Roberts
Geraldine Wright

SUMMARY. Two prevalent systems of organizing bound and current periodical collections in academic libraries are the open stack and the closed stack methods. This paper examines, by means of a survey, which method is used by selected two-year colleges in New York State. The initial purpose of the survey was to determine whether open or closed stacks were a significant factor in the loss of periodicals. The survey was sent to 31 libraries; 27 libraries responded, all apparently satisfied with their current system. The response showed that when theft was a problem, libraries with open stacks noted a greater loss of periodicals.

A dramatic increase in enrollment at Onondaga Community College, Syracuse, N.Y., in the spring of 1991, together with the addition of a second CD-ROM index, resulted in a large increase in the use of periodicals. Since OCC's library has closed stacks for periodicals, this meant greater demands on those who retrieve them. Some of the staff thought that open stacks might ease the problem; others felt that open stacks might result in greater theft of periodicals.

A survey (Figure 1) was conducted in order to answer this question and a few others (including questions about use studies, theft prevention and circulation of periodicals). Questionnaires (Figure 2) were sent to 31 New York State two-year college libraries with periodical subscriptions of 300-700 titles (according to the 1990-91 edition of the *American Library Directory*). Twenty-six libraries (84%) responded. In addition, OCC's li-

Gretchen Roberts is Assistant Professor and Periodicals Librarian and Geraldine Wright is Adjunct Professor and Reference Librarian, both at Onondaga Community College, Rt. #173, Syracuse, NY 13215.

brary was included in the survey. Therefore, the results of the survey are based on 27 two-year college libraries. Many of the topics covered here were similar to those included in a 1977 survey of four-year college libraries. That survey was based on 147 moderate-sized libraries (Wright 234).

The first question on the survey asked for the actual number of periodical subscriptions. The answers ranged from 300 to 705 subscriptions with a mean of 472 and median of 465.

The responses to the question "Approximately how many titles do you bind?" were more varied than had been expected. While 9 (33%) of the polled libraries do not bind any titles, 16 libraries (59%) indicated a wide range in the number of titles bound, from 4 to over 600. Two libraries (8%) did not complete the question.

On the question of shelving arrangement, nine libraries (33%) shelve current issues of periodicals with bound volumes; 11 libraries (41%) do not shelve current and bound volumes together; 3 libraries (11%) said they shelve some of the bound and current issues together; 3 libraries (11%) indicated the question did not apply; and 1 library did not respond.

At Onondaga Community College, periodicals circulate for 3 days to faculty and staff only; however, the periodicals must be returned to the library, if requested by another patron. Current issues of popular titles are not allowed to circulate. Among the libraries polled, 4 libraries (15%) circulate their periodical collections; 10 libraries (37%) do not; and 13 libraries (48%) allow only faculty and staff to borrow issues.

When asked whether they had open or closed stacks, 14 libraries (52%) indicated open; 8 libraries (30%) indicated closed; 4 libraries (15%) indicated a combination; 1 library (3%) did not respond to the question. Examples of a combination (of open and closed stacks) were simply: "Open, except periodicals that are popular are kept on reserve." Or, a more complicated answer was: "Any titles that we eventually bind are in closed stacks. Once they are bound, they go into open stacks. Any titles that we eventually receive on microfilm are kept in the open stacks and are interfiled alphabetically with the bound issues."

Libraries were asked whether or not a tattle-tape, or similar system, was used to prevent theft. Of the 27 libraries, 18 libraries (67%) responded that they used a deterrent device. Of these 18, 10 libraries (56%) said the system was used only on certain high-risk titles.

A follow-up question was: "Do you lose many periodicals by theft?" Of the 27 libraries, 11 libraries (41%) answered "yes"; 13 libraries (48%) answered "no"; and 3 libraries (11%) indicated that mutilation was more of a problem than theft. Of the 11 libraries noting significant loss by theft, 8 libraries (73%) had open stacks and 3 libraries (27%) had closed stacks.

FIGURE 1

SURVEY OF THE PERIODICAL COLLECTIONS
at
Two-Year College Libraries in New York State *

QUESTION	YES	NO	OTHER	NOT AVAILABLE
Do you shelve current titles with bound volumes?	33%	41%	11% (some)	15%
Do you circulate periodicals?	15%	37%	48% (faculty/staff)	-
Are periodical stacks open ?	52%	30% (closed)	15% (combination)	3%
Are "tattle-tapes" used to control theft?	67%	30%	-	3%
Is theft of periodicals a problem?	41%	48%	11% (damaged)	-
If theft is a problem, are stacks open?	73%	27% (closed)	-	-
Do you conduct use studies?	56%	41%	-	3%

* Number of periodical titles in the libraries surveyed: 300 to 705 (472 - average)

FIGURE 2

DATE_____

NAME OF LIBRARY_____

ADDRESS_____

_____

_____

NAME OF PERSON COMPLETING QUESTIONNAIRE_____

1. Number of Periodical Subscriptions*_____

2. Number of Bound Volumes_____

3. Approximately how many Titles do you bind?_____

4. Do you shelve current issues with bound volumes?_____

5. Do you circulate any periodicals?_____
    If Yes, which ones?_____

    _____

    _____

6. Do you have closed or open stacks?_____

7. If open, do you use tattle-tape or a similar deterrent?_____

    _____

8. Do you lose many periodicals by theft?_____

    If Yes, approximately how many?_____

9. Are you able to do use studies?_____

    If Yes, how?_____

10. If cutbacks need to be made, how do you decide which subscriptions
    to cancel?_____

    _____

11. Would you like a copy of the survey results?_____

*   If you have had large cutbacks in the last 2 years, please
    give us the number of periodical subscriptions before the
    cutback, and the number of subscriptions after the cutback.

"Are you able to do use studies?" was another question on the survey. Of the 27 responses, 15 libraries (56%) answered "yes"; 11 libraries (41%) answered "no"; and 1 library (3%) did not answer this question. Three main methods for doing use studies were reported: 5 libraries kept track of the number of items reshelved; 5 libraries used sign-out cards; 3 libraries cited "in-house" surveys, which could actually mean either of the previous two methods cited. One library with closed stacks reported, "We count each periodical as it is requested and retrieved; an automated system keeps track of the periodicals' circulation."

The responses seem to indicate that use studies are a little easier to conduct when a library has closed stacks. However, many of the libraries with open stacks also conduct use studies. One response regarding use studies from such a library was: "Twice in the past 5 years, each time, for approximately two months each semester, the staff recorded the number of times any item was reshelved. Students were urged not to reshelve their own periodicals." Obviously, conditioning students not to reshelve periodicals is important in achieving an accurate use study.

During these difficult financial times, many library collections are affected by budget constraints. The escalating costs of periodical subscriptions make it difficult to trim collections in libraries whose budgets may not have increased in several years: "Academic and medical libraries may pay from 9 to 12% more for serials subscriptions in 1992. The cost of an academic subscription list has increased by an average of 14.6% each year over the last five years ("Moderate Subscription" 1)." With this financial concern in mind, librarians were asked what standards they use when cancelling subscriptions. Almost every response indicated that low patron use (determined either by actual statistics or by estimated, informal methods) was a primary consideration for cancelling a title. Whether or not a title was indexed and how faculty responded to surveys received equal attention as secondary considerations. Curriculum support ranked third as a major factor for deleting titles. The actual cost of the subscription was definitely a concern but ranked lower in affecting deletion of a title.

CONCLUSION

This survey provided a glimpse into the arrangement of periodical collections in New York State two-year college libraries. The major purpose of the survey was to determine if there was a correlation between the loss of periodicals and the organization of periodicals in open vs. closed stacks. Such a correlation was not proven as dramatically as we thought it would be. However, results did show that when theft was a problem, libraries with open stacks noted a higher loss of issues (see Figure 1).

Two-thirds of the libraries used tattle-tape or a similar method to prevent theft. Forty-one percent of the libraries indicated a problem with theft; of these libraries, 73% kept open stacks. As might be expected, regardless of open or closed stack situations, libraries noted that vandalism (usually in the form of missing or torn pages) was a recurrent problem.

The survey did not ask libraries with open stacks to indicate whether incorrect shelving by students was a frequent occurrence. Our own experience with closed stacks indicates that the retrieval and reshelving of periodicals by library staff, while time-consuming, is effective in ensuring the availability of titles requested by patrons. This system also provides frequent staff interaction with students, affording librarians the opportunity to assist students in focusing and refining their searches.

This study gave us insight into the organization of periodicals at two-year college libraries in New York State. A broader perspective would be gained from a larger survey including two-year college libraries in other states. Such a study would provide a more thorough assessment of open versus closed stacks.

REFERENCES

"Moderate Subscription Price Increases Predicted for 1992," *At Your Service* (EBSCO Subscription Services) p.1 (May 1991).
Wright, Geraldine. "Current Trends in Periodical Collections," *College and Research Libraries* 38:234-40 (May 1977).

Is the Sky Falling?
or
Using the Policies
and Procedures Manual
as an Evaluation Tool

Jo Ann O. McCreight

SUMMARY. At a time of budget freezes and income cuts libraries need methods for responding systematically and fairly while insisting on the library's right to make the decisions. Reviewing and updating the procedures manual is a worthwhile project for evaluating library services, redesigning procedures, enhancing staff teamwork and creating a benchmark to guide decisions.

A phone call from another faculty member whose office was in the Administration Building brought the news. A simple request for the addition of a book to the collection was prefaced, "I know you can't buy this now because of today's freeze, but when we can spend again could you . . . ." A year before I would not have understood the drift of her remark. That would have been before experiencing two spending freezes brought about by the budget problems of the state government and the late arrival of expected state funds on our campus. Last year had been a time of great frustration because we were not prepared to have fate block what was for us a major turn around in focusing our efforts to prepare for an automation project.

Jo Ann O. McCreight is Head Librarian at Fulton-Montgomery Community College, Johnstown, NY 12095.

DEALING WITH FUNDING CUTS

This fall, having survived the first full year of uncertain steps on the road to automation, we were ready for this new freeze. We had set our goals and could keep going because we had developed alternative plans for the safe, predictable, regular library year. If we couldn't move ahead at high speed, we could at least try a fast stroll toward our goals.

All levels of organizations may panic at first when informed that cuts, zero increases, freezes, etc., are coming. The thought that your library must show what it is doing that justifies "all that money" or "you must demonstrate your level of accountability" really upsets many people who work in libraries. We in Libraries tend to think we have already found all the right and proper ways to do things and that there can be no questioning of what we are doing. We are right and proper in what we do, just like "apple pie and motherhood!" Sorry, fellow Librarians, we are in deep trouble with regard to available funding. Don't panic. There are many ways we can keep going.

PRIORITIES

Whether we are facing a short term reduction or one expected to last several budget years, the first priority is to define the problem faced by the library. Will staff be reduced? Will hours be cut? Will purchases be stopped? How much freedom will the Library staff have to make the cuts or will the cuts be mandated by outside forces? Once the limits are defined, then analyze the goals and objectives for the Library and the college, and, as the students would say, "Go for it!" Anticipate circumstances, explore and justify cost patterns, review programs and policies, involve staff and communicate the Library's rationale.

We stand a better chance of retaining some control over our funding and therefore our level of services if we are able to communicate to those controlling the purse strings that libraries have difficulty with percentage cut backs or random outsider selection of line items to be cut out of a budget. We know that you cannot buy only 80% of a book or 8 months of a subscription but have you convinced your penny pinchers of this? Do you have procedures in place for dealing with cutbacks? Do you have written objectives for collections and services? For example, if you have not developed a procedure for cutting titles in the periodicals holdings similar to what you use to justify purchase of a new title, then you should get busy and develop it. An evaluation of the need for those services that have a high price tag should be made to determine just how important they are. Libraries are noted for adding new services as they become available but are also known as institutions which never want to weed out old services or titles. A purchase decision which was wise five years ago may not pass an evaluation if considered this year as a new purchase.

POLICIES AND PROCEDURES MANUALS

Some of you will feel that you already have a set of policies and procedures in place and do not need to be concerned about looking at or reconsidering them. This may be a dangerous position because in reality, procedures are constantly changing. Where the work force is stable and no new persons need to be trained, it is likely that the procedures manual may long have been gathering dust because "we all know how to do our work." That may be true within one department. Often forgotten is the relationship between the various parts of the library. Actions taken by one section often cause counter reactions in another department. One example of this is the increase in Inter Library Loan requests which follows several years of cutbacks in spending on new books and periodicals.

The concept of establishing mission statements, goals to direct services rendered and manuals listing how these may be accomplished has long been suggested as the best way to run an organization. Libraries tend to have more of a problem than many organizations in keeping their policies and procedures realistic and up-to-date because of the very nature of the library organization and distribution of power. Taking a good look at a library's policy and procedure manual is an excellent opportunity to re-evaluate a library, just what it is trying to do for its users, and how well the procedures are enabling those goals. In the rapidly growing technical world the drive is to keep adding all the wonderful new ways of getting information for our users. Almost all of these new services cost a great deal more than the services they replace. If money is short many painful decisions will have to be made. Deciding where to pull back so that as many as possible staff members agree is very important. It is counterproductive to have departments angry at each other because cuts were made in ways not acceptable to all.

A rule of thumb for policies and procedures updates is that a major update is needed every three to five years with a yearly review within each department. The larger the library the more separation there is between the various areas of responsibility. In a small library where every librarian and clerk handles a variety of activities there is by necessity more sharing of information. The larger libraries often do not do much sharing outside of their area of responsibility. This is where it gets dangerous. When the financial crunch can be foreseen it makes sense to take the time to involve the staff in a review of the policies and procedures manual. It is a very effective way to evaluate the library procedures, services and opportunities for change. It involves the librarians in analyzing not only their own jobs but also the relationships, synergies and gaps in the library whole.

THE REVIEW PROCESS

If your procedure manual is lost, strayed or stolen, how do you go about getting a working model? If an outdated manual exists for your institution, that would be a good place to start. After all, if it's outdated, fewer staff members will feel protective about it and productive deliberation will result. If no one wants to own up to having an old manual, then beg or borrow one from a similar library as a starting point. Have the various departments or areas of responsibility within the library compare what they are really doing and what the manual says they are doing. The manual really should reflect what the library is doing at this time. Discussing procedures within one department with representatives of the other departments will help develop methods that relate well to other functions of the library. Recommendations can be made for all areas to be changed. When those changes are ready to be implemented the new policies can be reviewed by the group and incorporated into the manual. (This is the encyclopedia method of updating.)

It may be that an outside the library person must be brought in to help coordinate the effort as neutral chairpersons of such a group are almost mandated. Emotions and power games can not be allowed to dictate policy. Too much is at stake. The end goal of providing the best service we can, given what we have with which to work, remains true.

A schedule needs to be established for the review with an agenda for each meeting. The chair person may need to consult with the department heads to make sure the evaluation/redesign/rewriting is proceeding properly, and to remind them that the immediate goal is accurate description of what is really happening. It is important to have the librarians as a group meet to discuss the sections of the manual. Depending on the library, the group would include line staff, including head clerks, as well as department heads. The pattern of a procedure in one area may help clarify procedures in another, and relationships between procedures will be more clearly articulated.

In the author's experience this group review of the manual is a comprehensive and positive way to introduce new staff members to the overall functioning of the library, its traditions and the logic behind the procedures. For the older staff members it is valuable to have to explain why things are the way they are to ears unfamiliar with the folklore of the library. As the librarians become better versed in the pressures and priorities of each of the departments, they function better as a team and are thus better prepared to deal with the exigencies of budget cuts. Surprisingly, the policies of an updated manual can also come into play when money suddenly becomes available if it can be spent immediately.

The policies and procedures manual should be a public document. Every department in the library needs a copy. Administrators should hear about it, as should accreditation groups. It should include documents such as the ALA statement on the freedom to read that the staff may need to refer to as library policy. Many articles and guidelines are available to what the manual should include.

Once a policy and procedures manual is in place, a point of reference will have been established. Decisions about spending, services offered, etc., may be made following a logical evaluation. It will hurt to know that we could do more, but we must continue. Libraries have made it through tough times before. History shows us that we are needed most when funds are shortest, so all of us must do all that we can to keep supplying the services that our users need.

Accountability
in Book Acquisition and Weeding

Harold Ettelt

There are two kinds of librarian accountability, that to our superiors, and the more important (usually) accountability to ourselves as professionals entrusted with an important task. Regarding either, we cannot account for our performance without data on what and how we are doing. One area where this is obviously critical is in the acquisition and deacquisition of books. A large portion of our budgets and staff are used up here, and a large measure of our effectiveness as librarians is determined here.

At C-GCC we use a fairly simple manual survey each year that samples about 10% of the circulating collection. The raw data is largely gathered by student aides and then analyzed by a professional. For each book the call number, acquisition year, and use record since 1977 is noted (1977 is the year we started recording use in our books). The entire survey takes a maximum of 200 person-hours in our 45,000 book library. It is well worth it. In larger libraries it would take more hours, but then larger libraries generally have larger staffs so that as a percent of total available staff time they might be in even better shape to do it. In a pinch, a library could do half the collection each year. The details of how a given library should do the survey will be as varied as the libraries themselves, but the sheer usefulness of such a survey is universal. Libraries in the act of computerizing might want to build in the capability.

Here is just a sample of what you will be able to answer about your library, to yourself, to your boss. I give the answers for my library as of last year.

1. "What percent of our books ever get used?" (or are you wasting money?)

> Eighty-three percent of the entire collection has been used since 1977, as have 91% of the books purchased since 1977, and 82% of

Harold Ettelt is Head Librarian, Columbia Green Community College, P.O. Box 1000, Hudson, NY 12534.

257

the books acquired in 1990 were already used by June 1991. This library does *not* waste book funds, boss.

2. "What percent get used in one year?"

Twenty-five percent of the entire collection, but it is never the same 25%. The 80/20 rule does not hold here, boss. I checked.

3. "Which subject areas get used and how much?" (or are you buying blind?)

In Psychology (BF), 96% of the books were ever used, 59% were used in the last 2-1/2 years, and average circulations per book over 2-1/2 years is 1.36. For Substance Abuse the corresponding figures are 100%, 95%, and 3.61 and for English Literature it is 74%, 38% and .74 So we *know* where to buy books. We've got the whole collection on a big graph on the wall of my office, boss.

4. "Why do we have to keep buying so many new books. Can't we cut back?"

A use graph of books acquired since 1969 shows that for classes P-PT there is a use curve over the last 1-1/2 years that starts at 20% for the 1969 books and rises to 36% for the 1984 books, then swoops up steeply to 74% for books acquired in 1990. And that's for the relatively time-immune part of the collection. For fiction and Q-Z the rise is much steeper. New books get used *lots* more, and that's pretty much the point of having a library, isn't it?

5. "How likely are we to be wrong in weeding?" (or why do we need a bigger library?)

If we don't get a bigger library we will have to start throwing out books as fast as they come in. That's simple arithmetic. If we have to do that, we'll start with the oldest unused books, simply because it would be insane to throw out books we just got or that are being used. My studies show that in this library after five years of non-use a book stands a 10% chance of being used the next year and that does not decrease in any subsequent years. So if we weeded a hundred books, say after 8 years of non-use, we'd be wrong on 20-X of them by two years later and that "wrongness" would increase by 10 each year. And if you think we can somehow use our judgement to predict which unused ones *won't* be used later, remember it was our judgement that bought those books in the first place. We just ain't that smart.

On the other hand, a brand new book has a 46% chance of being used in the year we get it and a previously used old book has at least a 20% chance of being used the following year, so if we absolutely *have* to weed, the old unused ones is where we start. Not buying new books so we don't have to weed old ones is a dumb choice if we want people to use this library.

Of course there are other questions such a survey can answer, so you can *know* what is going on in your library, but that's a start. I've published some of this stuff from past years and a list follows if you want to see it, but please remember that it pertains to *my* library and may not be true of yours. You have to do your own legwork.

REFERENCES

"What price weeding?" *Community and Junior College Libraries*, Vol. 3, no. 3, Spring 1985, pages 69-77.
"What price weeding II" ED 272-214
"What our book use study shows us," ED 274-376
"When can you weed an unused book?" ED 297-762
"Does the 80/20 rule apply to books?" ED 298-963
"New books and those previously used, lead the band, by a lot," *Unabashed Librarian*, No. 75, June 1990, pages 15-16.

VII. BIBLIOGRAPHY

This is an idiosyncratic bibliography prepared by the editors as work on this issue progressed. When we began our search, "assessment" in *Books in Print* referred to real estate and "accountability" to the criminal justice system. Many people were involved in trying to improve librarians' grasp of statistics (note Jo Bell Whitlatch's column on research and statistics in the quarterly *RASD Update*). Sharon Baker had joined Wilfrid Lancaster in a second edition of *Measurement and Evaluation of Library Services*. We talked knowledgeably about 80/20 rules and obtrusive measures, but the practice of accountability–justifying the existence of libraries, of *our* library–was not yet a coherent professional method combining evaluation, planning and public relations with the skills, collections and services managed by the reference librarian grounded in a well-constructed theory of why: libraries. This bibliography contains only references we found helpful in and of themselves and *also* as examples of a type of publication one might look for more of.

ACRL Standards for Two Year College Learning Resources Programs see Joint Committee of the Association for Educational Communications and Technology and ACRL . . . .

"About non-resident fees, or, why do I have to pay for library service?" *Unabashed Librarian* 71 (1989): 31-2.

"The Acquisitions Budget," *Acquisition Librarian* 2. Binghamton, N.Y., The Haworth Press, Inc., 1989.

Adelman, Clifford, ed. *Performance and Judgment: Essays on Principles and Practice in the Assessment of College Student Learning*. Washington, U.S. Dept. of Education, 1988.

American Association of Law Libraries. "Standards for Appellate Court and County Law Libraries," *Law Library Journal* 81 (Spring 1989): S1-16.

American Library Association. Reference and Adult Services Division. BRASS Committee on Business Reference in Academic Libraries. *The Academic Library and Business School Accreditation.* Chicago, ALA, July 1991.

Angiletta, Tony. "Review of *Measuring Academic Library Performance* by Nancy Van House," *College & Research Libraries* 52:4 (July 1991): 387-8.

Argyris, Chris. "Teaching smart people how to learn," *Harvard Business Review* 69 (May-June 1991): 99-109.

Association of College and Research Libraries. "Standards for university libraries: evaluation of performance," *College & Research Libraries News* 50:8 (Sept. 1989): 679-91.

_____. College Library Standards Committee. "Standards for College Libraries, 1986," *College & Research Libraries News* 47 (March 1986): 189-200.

Baker, Sharon and F. Wilfrid Lancaster. *The Measurement and Evaluation of Library Services.* 2d ed. Arlington, Va. Information Resources Press, 1991.

Bickford, D. L. *An Assessment of the Marketing of Public Library Reference Service to the Business Community.* MSLS thesis, University of North Carolina at Chapel Hill, 1989.

Blagden, John. *Do We Really Need Libraries?* New York, K.G. Saur, 1980.

Bone, Larry Earl, ed. "Community analysis and libraries," *Library Trends* 24:3 (Jan. 1976). Extensive bibliography pp. 429-643.

Britten, W.A. "A use statistic for collection management: the 80/20 rule revisited," *Library Acquisitions* 14:2 (1990): 183-9.

Burlingame, Dwight, ed. *Library Development: A Future Imperative.* Binghamton, N.Y., The Haworth Press, Inc., 1990.

Chen, Ching-chih, ed. *Quantitative Measurements and Dynamic Library Services.* Phoenix, Oryx Press, 1978.

Clapp, Werner W. and Robert T. Jordan. "Quantitative criteria for adequacy of academic library collections," *College & Research Libraries* 50 (March 1989): 154-63. reprint

Clayton, Peter. "Nominal group technique and library management," *Library Administration and Management,* 4 (Winter 1989): 24-26.

Cohen, Donna K. "A recent history of the library criterion in the Southern Association of Colleges and Schools," *The Southeastern Librarian* 39 (Spring 1989): 9-12.

Commission on Colleges of the Southern Association of Colleges and Schools. *Resource Manual on Institutional Effectiveness.* Atlanta, The Commission, 1989. 2d ed.

Cooper, Robin and Robert S. Kaplan. "Profit priorities from activity-based costing," *Harvard Business Review* 69 (May-June 1991): 130-135.

"DC libraries are #2 favored city service; there's positive perception but scant use and declining budget," *Library Journal* 115 (Nov. 1, 1990):20-1.

Elzy, Cheryl and others. "Evaluating reference service in a large academic library," *College & Research Libraries* 52:5 (Sept. 1991):454-64.

Ergeldinger, E. A. " 'Use' as a criterion for the weeding of reference collections," *The Reference Librarian* 29 (1990): 119-28. Bibliography.

Fontaine, E. "The role of public relations in fund raising," *Journal of Library Administration* 12:4 (1990): 15-38.

Ford, G. "Approaches to performance measurement: some observations on principles and practice," *British Journal of Academic Librarianship* 4:2 (1989): 74-87.

Friedlander, Jack and Peter R. MacDougall. "Responding to mandates for institutional effectiveness," *New Directions for Community Colleges* 72 (Winter 1990).

Frick, E. "Survey or standards? Teaching user services as a policy issue," *The Reference Librarian* 25-26 (1989): 507-19.

Frommeyer, Ron. "Point of view: (OLA) Academic and Special Libraries Division," *Ohio Libraries* 1 (May-June 1988):4.

Getz, M. "Analysis and library management," *Academic Libraries* (1990) bibliographic essay.

Goodell, John S. *Libraries and Work Sampling.* Littleton, Co. Libraries Unlimited, 1975.

Greer, Arlene and Lee Weston, Mary Alm. "Assessment of learning outcomes: a measure of progress in library literacy," *College & Research Libraries* 52:6 (Nov. 1991): 549-557.

Hafner, Arthur. *Descriptive Statistical Techniques for Librarians.* Chicago, American Library Association, 1989.

Hamilton, David P. "Trivia Pursuit," *Washington Monthly* (March 1991): 36-42.

Henty, M. "Priorities in library use: a survey," *Australian Academic & Research Libraries* 20 (June 1989): 85-99.

Hernon, Peter. *Statistics for Library Decision Making: A Handbook.* Norwood, N.J. Ablex, 1989. Extensive bibliography.

_____. and Charles R. McClure. *Unobtrusive Testing and Library Reference Services.* Norwood, N.J. Ablex, 1987.

_____. reviewed by Norman Stevens in *Wilson Library Bulletin* 62 (Oct. 1987): 75-6.

Holleman, Margaret, ed. "The role of the Learning Resources Center in instruction," *New Directions for Community Colleges* 71 (Fall 1990).

Ihrig, Alice B. *Decision Making for Public Libraries.* Hamden, Ct. Shoe String Press, 1989.

Information Power: Guidelines for School Library Media Programs. Washington, Association for Educational Communications and Technology with the American Association of School Librarians, 1988.

Joint Committee of the Association for Educational Communications and Technology and the Association of College and Research Libraries. "Standards for community, junior and technical college learning resources programs," *College & Research Libraries News* 51 (Sept. 1990): 757-67.

Joint Committee on Standards for Educational Evaluation. *Standards for Evaluations of Educational Programs, Projects and Materials.* New York, McGraw-Hill, 1981.

Kania, Antoinette M. "Academic library standards and performance measures," *College & Research Libraries* 49 (Jan. 1988): 16-23.

_____. "Self-study methods for the library and the LRC," *New Directions for Community Colleges* 7 (Fall 1990): 81-90.

Kent, Allen and others. *Use of Library Materials: the University of Pittsburgh Study.* New York, Marcel Dekker, 1979.

Labdon, P.R. "The disappearing borrower: a review article," *Journal of Librarianship* 22 (April 1990): 107-13.

Lindsey, Jonathan A., ed. *Performance Evaluation: A Management Basic for Librarians.* Phoenix, Oryx Press, 1986.

Lougee, W.P. and others. "The Humanistic Scholars Project: a study of attitudes and behavior concerning collection storage and technology," *College & Research Libraries* 51 (May 1990): 231-40.

Lushington, Nolan and James M. Kusack. *The Design and Evaluation of Public Library Buildings.* Hamden, Ct. Library Professional Publications, 1991.

Lutzker, M. "Bibliographic instruction and accreditation in higher education," *College & Research Libraries News* 51 (Jan. 1990): 14-19.

Magrill, R.M. and J.B. Corbin. *Acquisitions Management and Collection Development in Libraries.* 2d ed. Chicago, American Library Association, 1989. bibliography

Martin, Lowell. "User studies and library planning," *Library Trends* 24:3 (Jan. 1976): 483-496.

Munn, R.F. "The bottomless pit, or, the academic library as viewed from the administration building," *College & Research Libraries* 50 (Nov. 1989): 635-7. Reprint.

Newhouse, R. C. "A library essential: needs assessment," *Library Review* 39:2 (1990): 33-6.

Niemeyer, K.K. "The role of the school library media program in performance based accreditation of Indiana schools: a presentation to the Indiana State Board of Education," *Indiana Media Journal* 11 (Fall 1988): 9-12.

Pace, C. Robert. "Assessing the undergraduate experience," *Assessment Update* 2:3 (Fall 1990): 1+.

Parrish, Marilyn. "Academic community analysis: discovering research needs of graduate students at Bowling Green State University," *College & Research Libraries News* 50 (Sept. 1989): 644-646.

Pascarella, Ernest T. and Patrick T. Terenzini. *How College Affects Students*. San Francisco, Jossey-Bass, 1991.

Potter, W.G. "Insurmountable opportunities: advanced technology and the academic library," *Academic Libraries,* 1990: 165-91. Bibliographic essay.

Potthoff, J.K. and D.S. Montanelli. "Use of library facilities: behavioral research as a tool for library space planning," *Journal of Library Administration* 12:1 (1990): 47-61.

Resnick, Lauren B. "Literacy in school and out," *Daedalus* 119:2 (Spring 1990): 169-185.

Robbins, Jane. "Research in information services practices," *Library and Information Science Research* 12 (April-June 1990): 127-8.

St.Clair, G. "Communicating with external constituencies about numbers," *Library Administration and Management* 3 (Fall 1989): 205-8.

Schlomann, B.F. "Multifaceted assessment of facility needs in an academic library," *Journal of Library Administration* 12:1 (1990): 9-21.

Schuman, Patricia Glass and John Berry. "Tough times bring tough questions," *Library Journal* (Nov. 1, 1991): 52-55.

Shaughnessy, J. "Assessing library effectiveness," *Journal of Library Administration* 12:1 (1990): 1-8.

Slater, Margaret, ed. *Research Methods in Library and Information Studies*. London, Library Association, 1990.

Smith, Lisa L. "Evaluating the reference interview: a theoretical discussion of the desirability and achievability of evaluation," *RQ* 31 (Fall 1991): 75-81.

Special Libraries Association. Geography and Map Division. Committee on Standards. *Standards for University Map Collections*. Chicago, the Association, 1987.

Spiller, D.J. and M. Baker. "Library service to residents of public housing developments: a study and commentary," *Public Libraries* 28 (Nov. Dec. 1989): 358-61. Bibliography.

Stevens, Norman D. "Evaluating reference books in theory and practice," *The Reference Librarian* 15 (Fall 1986): 9-19.

_____. review of *The Role of the Academic Reference Librarian* by Jo Bell Whitlatch in *Wilson Library Bulletin* 65 (Sept. 1990): 108-109.

"Survey reveals rising library use; more people are visiting libraries but not necessarily to get books," *Library Journal* 115 (Nov. 1, 1990): 22.

Tiefel, Virginia. "Output or performance measures: the making of a manual *(Measuring Academic Library Performance),*" *College & Research Libraries News* 50:6 (June 1989): 475-8.

Van House, Nancy and Beth Weil, Charles McClure. *Measuring Academic Library Performance.* Chicago, American Library Association, 1990.

White, Philip M. "College library formulas applied," *College & Research Libraries News* 47 (March 1986): 202-6.

Whitlatch, Jo Bell, ed. *Evaluation of Reference and Adult Services Manual* (work in progress). Chicago, American Library Association, 1992?

_____. "Research and statistics column," *RASD Update,* quarterly column.

_____. "Unobtrusive studies and the quality of academic library reference services," *Collage & Research Libraries* 50:3 (March 1989): 181-194.

Widdows, Richard and others. "The focus group interview: a method for assessing users' evaluation of library service," *College & Research Libraries* 52:4 (July 1991): 352-9.

Williams, D.E. "Accreditation and the process of change in academic libraries," *Advances in Library Administration and Organization* 7 (1988):161-207. Bibliography.

Williams, P. "How should the public library respond to public demand," *Library Journal* 115 (Oct. 15, 1990): 54-6.

Wittkopf, Barbara and Patricia Cruse. "Using the ACRL performance manual; the LSU Libraries experience," *College & Research Libraries News* 52:9 (Oct. 1991): 570-2.

Worley, Karen Aileen. *The Measurement and Evaluation of Reference Service in Academic Libraries: a Survey.* MSLS thesis, University of North Carolina at Chapel Hill, 1989.

Young, Harold Chester. *Planning, Programming, Budgeting Systems in Academic Libraries.* Detroit, Gale, 1976.

Zweizig, D. and E.J. Rodger. *Output Measures for Public Libraries.* Chicago, American Library Association, 1982.

The People's Palace (New York Public Library). Videotape. New York, Peter Kuphardt, producer, 1991. 55 min.